CAMBRIDGE COMMENTARIES
WRITINGS OF THE JEWISH AND CHRIS
200 BC TO AD 200
VOLUME 2

The Qumran Community

CAMBRIDGE COMMENTARIES ON
WRITINGS OF THE JEWISH AND CHRISTIAN WORLD
200 BC TO AD 200

General Editors:

P. R. ACKROYD

A. R. C. LEANEY

J. W. PACKER

THE QUMRAN COMMUNITY

MICHAEL A. KNIBB
Professor of Old Testament Studies
King's College London

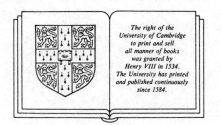

The right of the
University of Cambridge
to print and sell
all manner of books
was granted by
Henry VIII in 1534.
The University has printed
and published continuously
since 1584.

CAMBRIDGE UNIVERSITY PRESS

Cambridge
London   New York   New Rochelle
Melbourne   Sydney

Published by the Press Syndicate of the University of Cambridge
The Pitt Building, Trumpington Street, Cambridge CB2 1RP
32 East 57th Street, New York, NY 10022, USA
10 Stamford Road, Oakleigh, Melbourne 3166, Australia

First published 1987

Printed in Great Britain by
the University Press, Cambridge

British Library cataloguing in publication data

The Qumran community. – (Cambridge
commentaries on writings of the Jewish
and Christian world 200 BC to AD 200; v. 2)
1. Dead Sea scrolls – Commentaries
I. Knibb, Michael A.
221.4′4   BM487

Library of Congress cataloguing in publication data

Knibb, Michael A. (Michael Anthony), 1938–
The Qumran community.
(Cambridge commentaries on writings of the Jewish and
Christian world 200 BC to AD 200; v. 2)
'Provides a new translation of substantial extracts
from the Qumran writings together with an exegetical
commentary' –
Includes index.
1. Dead Sea scrolls – Criticism, interpretation, etc.
2. Qumran community. I. Dead Sea scrolls. English.
Selections. 1987. II. Title. III. Series: Cambridge
commentaries on writings of the Jewish and Christian
world 200 B.C. to A.D. 200; v. 2.
BM487.K6   1987   296.1′55   86-24450

ISBN 0 521 24247 9 hard covers
ISBN 0 521 28552 6 paperback

Contents

General Editors' Preface

The three general editors of the Cambridge Bible Commentary series have all, in their teaching, experienced a lack of readily usable texts of the literature which is often called pseudepigrapha but which is more accurately defined as extra-biblical or para-biblical literature. The aim of this new series is to help fill this gap.

The welcome accorded to the Cambridge Bible Commentary has encouraged the editors to follow the same pattern here, except that carefully chosen extracts from the texts, rather than complete books, have normally been provided for comment. The introductory material leads naturally into the text, which itself leads into alternating sections of commentary.

Within the severe limits imposed by the size and scope of the series, each contributor will attempt to provide for the student and general reader the results of modern scholarship, but has been asked to assume no specialised theological or linguistic knowledge.

The volumes already planned cover the writings of the Jewish and Christian World from about 200 BC to AD 200 and are being edited as follows:

A seventh volume by one of the general editors, A. R. C. Leaney, *The Jewish and Christian World 200 BC to AD 200*, examines the wider historical and literary background to the period and includes tables of dates, relevant lists and maps. Although this companion volume will preface and augment the series, it may also be read as complete in itself and be used as a work of general reference.

P.R.A.   A.R.C.L.   J.W.P.

Abbreviations

JOSEPHUS

War · *The Jewish War*
Ant. · *Antiquities of the Jews*

PHILO

Omn Prob Lib · Quod Omnis Probus Liber sit
Spec Leg · De Specialibus Legibus
Vit Cont · De Vita Contemplativa

PSEUDEPIGRAPHA

1 En. · 1 (Ethiopic) Enoch
Jub. · Jubilees
Pss. Sol. · Psalms of Solomon
Testaments of the Twelve Patriarchs

    T. Asher · Testament of Asher
    T. Benj. · Testament of Benjamin
    T. Dan · Testament of Dan
    T. Jud. · Testament of Judah
    T. Levi · Testament of Levi
    T. Reub. · Testament of Reuben
    T. Sim. · Testament of Simeon
    T. Zeb. · Testament of Zebulum

QUMRAN DOCUMENTS

See the list of Qumran writings with accompanying abbreviations on pp. 2–3.

RABBINIC WRITINGS

Mishnah

    Ab. · Abot
    Ber. · Berakot
    Meg. · Megillah
    Sanh. · Sanhedrin
    Šeb. · Šebiit
    Taʿan · Taʿanit

Babylonian Talmud
   b.Pes.   Pesaḥim

Note on brackets used in the texts
( ) The words so enclosed are not in the Hebrew or Aramaic texts,
     but have been supplied for the sense.
[ ] The words or letters so enclosed have been supplied to restore gaps
     in the manuscript.
⟨ ⟩ The use of these brackets indicates that insertions or corrections
     have been made in the text.

Note on the bibliographies
Books and articles in the bibliographies have been listed in the
following order: (1) editions of the text; (2) translations and commentaries; (3) other studies.

Chronological Table

175–164 BC	Antiochus IV Epiphanes
167	Desecration of the temple and proscription of Jewish religion. Jewish revolt led by the family of Mattathias
166	Judas assumes leadership of the nationalist forces
164	Rededication of the temple
161–159	Alcimus high priest
160	Death of Judas
160–152	Jonathan leader of the nationalist forces
152–143	Jonathan high priest
143	Jonathan captured by Trypho
143–134	Simon high priest and ethnarch
142	Murder of Jonathan
140	Legitimation of Simon's position by the Jewish people
134–104	John Hyrcanus I high priest and ethnarch
104–103	Aristobulus I high priest and king
103–76	Alexander Jannaeus high priest and king
76–67	Alexandra queen; Hyrcanus II high priest
67	Hyrcanus II king and high priest. Deposed by his brother Aristobulus II
67–63	Aristobulus II king and high priest
63	Intervention of Pompey
63–40	Hyrcanus II high priest
40–38	Parthian invasion
40–37	Antigonus king and high priest
37–4	Herod the Great
4 BC–AD 6	Archelaus ethnarch of Judaea and Samaria
AD 6–41	Judaea ruled by Roman prefects/procurators
41–44	Herod Agrippa I king
44–66	Judaea ruled by Roman procurators
66–74	Jewish Revolt
70	Fall of Jerusalem
74	Fall of Masada
132–135	Second Jewish Revolt

Introduction

This volume is intended to provide a representative selection of extracts from the Qumran sectarian literature under the three categories of legislative writings, poetic and liturgical writings, and exegetical writings. It has been thought more helpful to give substantial extracts from a limited number of works than to attempt to take account of everything.

The Qumran scrolls form only part of the Dead Sea scrolls, which – on the broad understanding given to this term – include the discoveries made at other sites in the vicinity of the Dead Sea, such as Murraba'at, Masada, or Naḥal Ḥever; but these latter discoveries are not our concern. The scrolls from Qumran themselves are by no means restricted to sectarian writings. It is important to bear in mind that manuscripts of the books of the Old Testament form a major part of the manuscripts found at Qumran. These biblical manuscripts, which include copies of every book in the Old Testament except Esther, are important for the history of the text of the Old Testament. Reference should also be made here to the manuscripts of books in the Apocrypha (Ecclesiasticus, Tobit, and a small Greek fragment of the Letter of Jeremiah). Another group of scrolls consists of manuscripts of apocryphal and pseudepigraphical works, such as Jubilees or the Ethiopic Book of Enoch, that were known before the discovery of the scrolls. These are works which were accepted by the Qumran community and in some cases may have been regarded as having a canonical status, but they are not sectarian writings in the narrow sense of the term. These manuscripts are again important for the history of the text of the works in question. The remainder of the scrolls consist of works that (apart from the Damascus Document) were unknown before the discoveries at Qumran, and many of these are to be regarded as sectarian in character, that is to say as writings which reflect closely the beliefs and practices of the community based at Qumran in which they were produced. It is these sectarian writings that are our primary concern.

The decision to give substantial extracts from only a limited number of writings has meant that some important works have been excluded. Thus the poetic and liturgical writings from Qumran are represented

here only by three columns from the Hymns, and in the category of
legislative writings the War Scroll and the Temple Scroll have been
left out. So far as the Temple Scroll is concerned, it is perhaps worth
pointing out that it is by no means clear that it is a sectarian writing;
there is perhaps more to be said for the view that it is a work,
embodying older traditions, that was taken over by the Qumran
community. In contrast two works that are probably not sectarian, the
Genesis Apocryphon and the Prayer of Nabonidus, have been included
because of their interest as exegetical writings.

The following is a list of the Qumran writings referred to in this
volume:

CD	Cairo Damascus Document
1QapGen	Genesis Apocryphon
1QDM	Words of Moses
1QH	Hymns (Hodayot)
1QM	War Scroll
1QpHab	Commentary on Habakkuk
1QpMic	Commentary on Micah
1QpPs	Commentary on Psalms
1QpZeph	Commentary on Zephaniah
1QS	Community Rule
1QSa	Rule of the Congregation
1QSb	Words of Blessing
4QD$^{a-g(h)}$	Manuscripts of the Damascus Document
4QFlor	Florilegium
4QPBless	Patriarchal Blessings
4QpHos^a ⎫ 4QpHos^b ⎭	Commentaries on Hosea
4QpIsa^a 4QpIsa^b 4QpIsa^c 4QpIsa^d 4QpIsa^e	Commentaries on Isaiah
4QpNah	Commentary on Nahum
4QpPs^a ⎫ 4QpPs^b ⎭	Commentaries on Psalms
4QpZeph	Commentary on Zephaniah
4QPrNab	Prayer of Nabonidus
4QPsDan ar^{a-c}	Apocalyptic work in which Daniel speaks
4QPsDan A^a	'Son of God' text

4QPssJosh	Psalms of Joshua
4QS^{a-j}	Manuscripts of the Community Rule
4QTestim	Testimonia
5QD	Manuscript of the Damascus Document
5QJN ar	The New Jerusalem
5QS	Manuscript of the Community Rule
6QD	Manuscript of the Damascus Document
11QMelch	Melchizedek Document
11QPs^a	Psalms Scroll
11QPs^a DavComp	David's Compositions
11QTemple	Temple Scroll
11QtgJob	Targum of Job

Eleven of the above writings are presented in this volume: the Damascus Document, the Community Rule, the Rule of the Congregation, the Hymns, the Genesis Apocryphon, the Prayer of Nabonidus, the Commentary on Nahum, the Commentary on Habakkuk, the Commentary on Psalms (4QpPs^a), Florilegium, and Testimonia. For information about the other writings listed above, and about other Qumran writings not mentioned here, see in the first instance J. A. Fitzmyer, *The Dead Sea Scrolls: Major Publications and Tools for Study* (Society of Biblical Literature, Sources for Biblical Study, 8), revised edition, Missoula, Montana, 1977) and G. Vermes (with the collaboration of P. Vermes), *The Dead Sea Scrolls: Qumran in Perspective*, revised edition, London, 1982.

The writings included in this volume have been presented as a group because of their common origin, but in terms of their literary form and their content they could well have been placed in other volumes in this series, particularly volume 3, *Early Rabbinic Writings*, or volume 4, *Outside the Old Testament*. Thus, for example, the Hymns deserve to be read alongside the Psalms of Solomon, and the Genesis Apocryphon alongside Jubilees (see *Outside the Old Testament*, pp. 159–77, 111–44). Every effort has been made throughout this volume to indicate parallels of both form and content with other writings.

The story of the discovery of the Dead Sea scrolls has been told many times and is not repeated here. But something needs to be said about the results of the excavation of the site of Qumran and about the history of the community which occupied the site in order to provide a framework for the writings presented in this volume.

The earliest occupation of Khirbet Qumran ('the ruin of Qumran') belongs in the Israelite period and is perhaps to be associated with the building activities of Jehoshaphat (2 Chron. 17:12) or Uzziah (2 Chron. 26:10). The occupation of the site in this period did not last beyond the end of the monarchical period, and the presence of ashes suggest that the settlement suffered a violent destruction, perhaps at the hands of the Babylonians during the course of one of their invasions. Thereafter the site remained unoccupied for several centuries.

It is the next period of the occupation of the site, from the second half of the second century BC to AD 68, that is our real concern. During this period the buildings at Qumran served as the centre for a quasi-monastic community whose members lived in the surrounding caves or in huts or tents. The beliefs and practices of the members of this community are reflected in the Qumran sectarian writings. It is assumed here, in common with the views of many scholars, that this community formed part of the wider movement of Essenes, whose members – according to the accounts in Philo and Josephus – were to be found living in the towns and villages of Palestine, and that Qumran is the site of the settlement of the Essenes on the shore of the Dead Sea to which the Roman author Pliny refers in his Natural History (v.15(73)).

The occupation of the site by the Essenes divides clearly into three phases. The first of these (phase Ia) was on a very modest scale. The remains of the Israelite buildings were reused and some additions made. The buildings would have served for only a small number of people, perhaps a few dozen. It is impossible to say exactly when this phase of occupation began, but its end can be dated reasonably precisely to about 100 BC. (This date, like most of those to do with the history of the occupation of the site, is based on the evidence of the coins that were found there.) In view of this the start of phase Ia is to be placed in the second half of the second century, perhaps not long after 150 BC (see below for further discussion of this point).

At the end of the second century BC or the very beginning of the first century the community buildings were considerably enlarged. This expansion, which marks the start of phase Ib, points to a sudden and dramatic increase in the membership of the community. It is not known where these new members came from. It is often assumed that they were Pharisees who were seeking to escape from the hostility of John Hyrcanus (134–104 BC), a hostility apparently caused by their opposition to his tenure of the office of high priest (cp. Josephus, *Ant.* XIII. 10.5–6 (288–98)). However, it is also possible that the new members were Essenes from other parts of the land; the Essenes are equally likely to have opposed the tenure by John Hyrcanus of the office of high priest and may have been caught up in the quarrel with him. Whoever the new members were, phase Ib, which lasted some seventy years, formed the most flourishing stage in the life of the community.

The end of phase Ib was marked by a fire and an earthquake and was followed by a period during which the site was completely or largely abandoned. It has often been assumed that the fire and the earthquake were connected, and that the former was caused by the latter. But it is also possible that the two occurred independently of one another, and that the fire was the result of a deliberate attempt to destroy the settlement. In this case it has been suggested that the settlement was burned during the course of the struggle for the throne between the Hasmonaean Antigonus and Herod the Great (40–37 BC); Antigonus had the support of the Parthians, who had invaded Syria and Palestine at that time, whereas Herod was supported by the Romans. On this view the fire preceded the earthquake and was the cause of the abandonment of the site. The earthquake itself has been associated with a major earthquake which, according to Josephus (*War* I.19.3(370); *Ant.* XV.5.2(121–2)), occurred in 31 BC and can be dated with some confidence to that year.

Following the fire and the earthquake the site was abandoned for several decades. It is not known why this was so, or where the members of the community went – perhaps to other centres of the Essene movement. It has been argued that the abandonment of the site was total, but some have thought it likely that a limited number of Essenes did remain in occupation of the site during the interval. Whatever the truth of these matters, it is clear that the site was reoccupied shortly after the end of the reign of Herod the Great, more precisely in the period 4 BC – 1 BC/AD; this marks the beginning of phase II of occupation, which lasted until AD 68. The community that reoccupied the site was the same as the one that had occupied it previously. The buildings of phase Ib were reused, but with some modifications and with some rooms no longer used.

The end of phase II can be dated fairly precisely to AD 68. The buildings suffered a violent destruction at that time as a result of military action, and this suggests that the members of the community, or some of them, had become involved in the revolt against the Romans which culminated in the fall of Jerusalem (AD 70) and the fall of Masada (AD 74). The destruction of Qumran is not mentioned in Josephus, but we do know that Roman troops were in the area at that time, and there is no doubt that it was they who were responsible for the destruction. It was at this time (AD 68) that the Qumran manuscripts were hidden in Cave 4, the cave in which by far the largest hoard of manuscripts were found and which seems clearly to have been intended as a safe hiding-place for the manuscripts. Perhaps those who hid the manuscripts hoped to recover them fairly quickly. The year AD 68 provides a clear date before which all the manuscripts found at Qumran must have been copied.

The occupation of the site of Qumran by the Essenes came to an end in AD 68. For a few years after this the Romans occupied part of the site as a military post, but this occupation (phase III) appears to have come to an end in 74, at the time when Masada was taken and the Jewish revolt was brought to a final end. Subsequently the site was briefly occupied by insurgents during the second Jewish revolt of AD 132–135. These two periods of occupation lie outside our concern.

The above provides the bare bones of the history of the occupation of Qumran by the Essenes. (No attempt has been made to describe the remains of buildings, pottery, and so on that were found in the course of the excavation of the site, or to describe the picture, that can be built up on the basis of these remains, of the day-to-day life of the community that lived there, for these matters lie outside the concerns of this book.) Much more deserves to be said by way of elaboration or justification of the various points that have been made, but in practice, although the excavation of Khirbet Qumran provided very clear and reliable evidence for the various phases of the occupation of the site by the Essenes, the results of the excavations cannot take us very much further in reconstructing the history of the community that occupied the site than has been given in the sketch above. To get any further we need to turn to the scrolls themselves, but unfortunately the evidence they provide is limited in extent and not easy to interpret. Such evidence as there is relates primarily to the first phase of the community's existence, phase Ia.

The majority of the Qumran sectarian manuscripts do not contain information about the history of the community, but statements of a historical kind are to be found in the Damascus Document, the biblical commentaries, and – less clearly – the Hymns. The information given in these writings is not straightforward, but is cast in language that is indirect and opaque, rather like the language used in Dan. 11. Nicknames ('the teacher of righteousness', 'the wicked priest', 'the liar') are used instead of real names, and in the case of the commentaries the language used is often strongly influenced by the language of the biblical text that is commented on rather than by the actual character of the event that is described. With this in mind, it is possible to consider what light the texts cast on the earliest phase of the community's history.

We have seen that the archaeological evidence indicates that the first phase of the occupation of Qumran falls in the second half of the second century BC and came to an end at about 100 BC. We are pointed to the same period (the second half of the second century BC) by the dates of two important manuscripts. The Cave 1 manuscript of the Community Rule, which was intended to govern the life of those living at Qumran, dates from 100–75 BC. But since that document represents the final stage of a composite work that was put together over a period of time and presupposes the evolution of the structures governing the community, it is clear that the origins of the community's occupation of the site have to be pushed back into the second century BC. Similar conclusions follow from the evidence of the Damascus Document, the oldest manuscript of which dates back to the first half of the first century BC. This writing presupposes the settlement at Qumran, but it too has a complex literary pre-history and points us back to the second century BC for the origins of the settlement at Qumran.

It is the Damascus Document which, in an important passage (1.1–12), tells us something of the origins of the Qumran community and of the events which preceded its establishment. According to this passage, three hundred and ninety years after the start of the exile God brought into existence a reform movement ('a root of planting'), but this movement was confused and unsure of itself until, after twenty years, God 'raised up for them a teacher of righteousness to lead them in the way of his heart'. The Damascus Document also refers to an opponent of the teacher of righteousness called 'the scoffer', 'the liar', or 'the preacher of lies'; this individual was the leader of a group which broke away from the group led by the teacher of righteousness. These same two individuals, the teacher and the liar, are also mentioned in the biblical commentaries. In these there is also reference to a further opponent of the teacher of righteousness called 'the wicked priest'.

The significance of the three hundred and ninety years of Damascus Document 1.1–12 will be discussed below, but here it is sufficient to notice that although the figure cannot be relied on as exact, it carries us down into the second century BC. The emergence of the reform movement (the 'root of planting') mentioned in the Damascus Document has often been associated with the emergence of the Hasidim, who played a leading role in the resistance to the measures imposed by Antiochus Epiphanes. The Hasidim are, however, only mentioned three times in our sources (1 Macc. 2:42; 7:13; 2 Macc.

14:6), and we know far less about them than is often assumed. It is
perhaps more important to observe that there are significant links
between the Damascus Document and Jubilees. The latter book very
probably dates from about 170 BC; it represents the viewpoint of a
group of conservative Jews who were concerned about the increasing
threat which hellenisation posed to the Jewish faith. It is plausible to
connect the 'root of planting' with the group that lies behind the book
of Jubilees and to find here the beginnings of the Essene movement.
The Damascus Document gives the impression that the emergence of
this movement was marked by the occurrence of some specific event,
but we do not know what this was, and the text does not go into any
details. In any case it is unlikely that the emergence of the movement
occurred suddenly; it represented rather the culmination of a gradually
developing attitude towards the religious and political circumstances
of the time.

What has been said so far presupposes that the emergence of the
Essenes is to be associated with the activities of Jews living in Palestine.
As an alternative view it has been argued that the origins of the Essene
movement are to be traced to the exiles who went from Judah to
Babylon in the sixth century BC, although it is not clear exactly when
the movement came into existence. On this view some members
of the movement returned from Babylon to Palestine shortly after 165
BC, where they attempted to win support for their views. Such a view
of the origins of the Essene movement is not impossible, but there is
insufficient evidence to make it appear convincing, at least at present,
and it is assumed here that the origins of the Essene movement belong
in Palestine.

The Damascus Document indicates that for the first twenty years
of its existence the 'root of planting' remained in an uncertain and
confused state until God 'raised up for them a teacher of righteousness
to lead them in the way of his heart'. It is unfortunately not clear when
exactly the twenty-year period began, or whether the twenty years
provide an exact figure or have primarily a symbolic value. But if it
is right to link the emergence of the 'root of planting' with the group
that lies behind the book of Jubilees, the composition of which is very
probably to be dated at about 170 BC, the twenty years would carry
us down to about 150 BC. The teacher of righteousness is associated
with Qumran, and although it is nowhere stated in the scrolls, it is
plausible to link the appearance of the teacher of righteousness with
the move of part of the Essene movement to Qumran, a move reflected
in the scrolls in the oldest layer of material in the Community Rule,

i.e. columns VIII–IX. Thus from what has been said so far, the appearance of the teacher of righteousness and the start of the settlement at Qumran are to be placed at about 150 BC. Support in general terms for this view can be found in the biblical commentaries in the information they provide about the identity of one of the opponents of the teacher of righteousness, namely the wicked priest.

The wicked priest is mentioned in the Commentary on Habakkuk and the Commentary on Psalms. From what is said about him it is clear that he was a high priest, and he can only have been one of the Hasmonaean high priests of the second half of the second century BC. Many scholars have in fact identified the wicked priest with either Jonathan (high priest from 152 to 143) or Simon (high priest from 143 to 134), and it seems fairly clear that he is to be identified with one or other of these figures. It is difficult to decide with certainty between the two on the basis of the evidence of the biblical commentaries because much of what is said in them about the wicked priest is cast in language that is by its very nature susceptible of more than one interpretation. However, on balance the view that Jonathan was the wicked priest seems to make best sense of the evidence, and it is this view that is followed in this book. It is easy to see why the Essenes would have regarded Jonathan's tenure of the office of high priest with hostility. Jonathan belonged to a priestly, not a high-priestly family. Furthermore, he was appointed high priest not by Jews, but by Alexander Balas, the Seleucid king (1 Macc. 10:18–21). In the eyes of pious Jews Jonathan must have been regarded as an illegitimate holder of office. From the scrolls it is clear that the Essenes who settled at Qumran viewed the religious situation in Jerusalem with considerable disquiet: the law was not being observed properly, the proper religious calendar was not being followed, the temple cult itself had been defiled. It is argued that in these circumstances it was in response to Jonathan's assumption of the office of high priest that part of the Essene movement, under the leadership of the teacher of righteousness, withdrew into the wilderness to settle at Qumran. This must have happened sometime after 152 BC, but when exactly between 152 and 143 is not known.

The evidence provided by the Damascus Document and the biblical commentaries about the origins of the Essene movement and the settlement at Qumran fits in with the archaeological evidence about the first phase of Essene occupation of Khirbet Qumran (phase Ia), but with one element of uncertainty. We have seen that although the end of phase Ia can be dated on archaeological grounds to about 100 BC, the beginning of this phase cannot be dated precisely – it belongs somewhere in the second half of the second century BC. Phase Ia must have lasted some time, and it is highly unlikely that the beginning of this phase belongs in the time of either Aristobulus I (104–103 BC) or John Hyrcanus (134–104 BC), not least because the things said in the biblical commentaries do not fit the identification of either as the wicked priest. We are thus pushed back to the time of Simon or Jonathan for the beginning of phase Ia, but it is impossible to say on the basis of the archaeological evidence in which of their periods of office this phase began. The archaeological evidence is compatible with the view that phase Ia began in the time of Jonathan, i.e. with the view that he is the wicked priest, and that the appearance of the teacher of righteousness and the withdrawal of part of the Essene movement to Qumran belong in the period 152–143 BC, but it does not demand such an interpretation.

There is evidence in the scrolls to suggest that at one stage the teacher of righteousness functioned as high priest in Jerusalem, and some scholars have thought that the teacher held office as high priest between the death of Alcimus in 159 BC (1 Macc. 9:56) and the appointment of Jonathan in 152 (1 Macc. 10:18–21). Nothing is said in 1 Maccabees as to whether there was a high priest in this period, while Josephus states that 'the city continued for seven years without a high priest' (*Ant.* XX.10.3(237)). But the evidence of Josephus is unreliable in this matter (he elsewhere says that Judas was high priest (*Ant.* XII.10.6 (414)), and it is historically unlikely that there was no high priest – if only because without one the ritual of the day of atonement could not be celebrated. The view that the teacher of righteousness was the high priest, and that he was ousted from office by Jonathan in 152 is attractive and has a good deal to be said for it. It would fit in with the view of the origins of the Qumran community outlined above and would explain the hostility between the teacher of righteousness and the wicked priest. The actual name of the teacher is unknown and is likely to remain so.

As we noted earlier, the teacher of righteousness was opposed not only by the wicked priest, but also by a figure called 'the scoffer', 'the liar', 'the preacher of lies'. This figure appears as the leader of a group which broke away at an early stage from the group associated with the teacher. It is not known who this person was, nor is it entirely clear what became of the group associated with him. It has been argued that this group ultimately became the Pharisees, and this view, although not certain, seems likely. But it has also been suggested that this group consisted of those Essenes who did not accept the authority of the teacher and did not withdraw with him to Qumran.

Suggestions for further reading

The best source of bibliographical information concerning all the Dead Sea scrolls is J. A. Fitzmyer, *The Dead Sea Scrolls: Major Publications and Tools for Study* (Society of Biblical Literature, Sources for Biblical Study, 8), revised edition, Missoula, Montana, 1977. P. R. Davies, *Qumran* (Cities of the Biblical World), Guildford, 1982, provides a good account of the archaeology of the Qumran site and of the history of the community which occupied it; for greater detail see R. de Vaux, *Archaeology and the Dead Sea Scrolls* (The Schweich Lectures of the British Academy, 1959), revised English edition, London, 1973. The volume by P. R. Davies provides an excellent first book to read on Qumran.

For the history of the period see E. Schürer, G. Vermes and F. Millar, *The History of the Jewish People in the Age of Jesus Christ (175 B.C.–A.D. 135)*, volume 1, Edinburgh, 1973; and for the Essenes see volume 2 of the same work (Edinburgh, 1979), pp. 555–90. The best and most up-to-date handbook on the Qumran scrolls is G. Vermes (with the collaboration of P. Vermes), *The Dead Sea Scrolls: Qumran in Perspective*, revised edition, London, 1982. However, two older handbooks, although now out of date in a number of respects, are still worth consulting: see J. T. Milik, *Ten Years of Discovery in the Wilderness of Judaea* (Studies in Biblical Theology, 26), London, 1959; and F. M. Cross, Jr, *The Ancient Library of Qumran and Modern Biblical Studies*, London, 1958; Garden City, New York, 1961; revised edition, Grand Rapids, 1980. For an introduction to the Qumran sectarian writings see E. Schürer, G. Vermes, F. Millar and M. Goodman, *The History of the Jewish People in the Age of Jesus Christ (175 B.C.–A.D. 135)*, volume 3, part 1, Edinburgh, 1986, pp. 380–469.

The texts of the writings included in this volume can be most conveniently found in E. Lohse (ed.), *Die Texte aus Qumran Hebräisch und Deutsch*, 2nd edition, Munich, 1971; and B. Jongeling, C. J. Labuschagne and A. S. van Woude (eds.), *Aramaic Texts from Qumran with Translations and Annotations* (Semitic Study Series, New Series, 4), Leiden, 1976.

The most useful English translation of the Qumran sectarian writings is G. Vermes, *The Dead Sea Scrolls in English*, 2nd edition, Penguin, Harmondsworth, 1975. However, this translation does not give line-numbers, and so it is difficult to find individual passages. A translation which does give line-numbers is A. Dupont-Sommer, *The Essene Writings from Qumran*, Oxford, 1961. For the Temple Scroll see

J. Maier, *The Temple Scroll: An Introduction, Translation and Commentary* (Journal for the Study of the Old Testament Supplement Series, 34), Sheffield, 1985.

The theology of the Qumran writings is discussed in H. Ringgren, *The Faith of Qumran: Theology of the Dead Sea Scrolls*, Philadelphia, 1963.

For the apocryphal and pseudepigraphical writings referred to in this volume see H. F. D. Sparks (ed.), *The Apocryphal Old Testament*, Oxford, 1984. The works of Philo and Josephus can most conveniently be consulted in the Loeb editions of their writings. For the Mishnah see H. Danby, *The Mishnah*, Oxford, 1933; and for references to the Babylonian Talmud see the translation edited by I. Epstein (35 volumes, London, 1935–52). Extracts from many of the writings mentioned in this volume, but not necessarily the actual passages referred to, may be found in other volumes in this series.

The Damascus Document

Several writings of a legislative character were discovered amongst the Qumran scrolls, one of which is the work known as the Damascus Document (CD = the Cairo manuscripts of the Damascus Document (see below)) or, as it is sometimes called, the Damascus Rule. It is given this title because it refers several times to a new covenant which was made 'in the land of Damascus' (VI.19; VIII.21; XIX.34; XX.12), and because Damascus is mentioned in some other important passages (VI.5; VII.15, 19); the significance of the references to Damascus will need to be discussed later. In fact this writing was known long before the discovery of the Qumran scrolls. At the end of the nineteenth century two mediaeval manuscripts of this work were found – along with a vast hoard of other manuscripts – in the store room (*Genizah*) of a synagogue in Cairo, and these were published in 1910 under the title 'Fragments of a Zadokite Work'. The use of this title reflects the fact that the group that lies behind the document claimed in some sense to be 'the sons of Zadok' (cp. III.20*b*–IV.4*a*), and until recently this work was still sometimes called 'the Zadokite Fragments' or 'the Zadokite Document'. When this writing was first discovered it was difficult for scholars to place it properly in its historical context, and many suggestions were made about it. But the discovery of fragments of nine, or possibly ten, manuscripts of this document in Caves 4, 5, and 6 at Qumran (4, 5, and 6QD) showed that it was an Essene work.

The two Cairo manuscripts of the Damascus Document are both incomplete. Manuscript A, dating from the tenth century, has sixteen columns, and its contents fall very clearly into two parts: an exhortation (columns I–VIII) and a collection of laws (columns IX–XVI). Only two columns of manuscript B, dating from the twelfth century, have survived, and these were numbered XIX and XX by the original editor; column XIX overlaps with columns VII and VIII of manuscript A, but presents a somewhat different version of the text, while column XX contains the end of the exhortation. Translations of both texts are given in parallel columns below (see pp. 50–69) where the two manuscripts overlap. The fragments of the Damascus Document from Caves 5 and 6 are quite small, and their contents differ little from the text known from Cairo manuscript A, apart from one fragment which has no parallel. But the fragments from Cave 4, as yet unpublished, attest a longer and different version of this work. In the Cave 4 manuscripts additional material stood at the beginning of the exhortation, and at the beginning and the end of the collection of laws; the material at the end contains a liturgy for the feast of the renewal of the covenant. In addition the Cave 4 manuscripts indicate that columns xv–xvi of Cairo manuscript A precede columns ix–xiv. The translation of the Damascus Document in this book, like other translations of this work, has been made from the Cairo manuscripts, but it should be understood that a somewhat different picture of this writing will emerge when the fragments from Cave 4 are eventually published.

The Damascus Document is addressed in ii.2 to all 'who are entering the covenant', and there are frequent references to entry into the covenant (cp. e.g. vi.11*b*; viii.1). We have already noted that the Cave 4 manuscripts of this work include at the end a liturgy for the feast of the renewal of the covenant. These facts suggest that in its final form this work was intended for use at this annual ceremony (cp. Community Rule (1QS) i.16–iii.12). We are perhaps to envisage a solemn recitation of the laws that were peculiar to the Essene movement preceded by an exhortation addressed to those about to join the movement as well as to existing members. But, as we shall see also in the case of the Community Rule, the Damascus Document is composite. It acquired its present form by a process of accretion and revision, a point underlined by the existence of different versions of this work in Cairo manuscripts A and B. The individual sections of which this work is composed may in some cases have had purposes different from the one to which they were put in the document as a whole; they reflect differing circumstances and differing stages of growth in the life of the movement which lies behind it.

The Damascus Document has much in common with the Community Rule. There is admittedly nothing comparable to the exhortation (CD i–viii; xix–xx) in the Community Rule. But this aside, there are many similarities between the two writings as regards the language used, the theological ideas, and the legislation which they contain, as well as some differences (for example there is nothing comparable to the teaching on the two spirits (1QS iii.13–iv.26) in the Damascus Document). The fact that there should be two similar collections of legislative material seems at first sight surprising. It has often been explained on the assumption that whereas the Community Rule – or at least the bulk of it – was intended specifically for the group which lived at Qumran, the Damascus Document was intended for the members of the wider Essene movement who lived amongst their fellow Jews in the towns and villages of Palestine. Here we should note that Josephus (*War* II.8.4 (124)) reports that the Essenes occupied more than one town, and Philo speaks of them living 'in many cities of Judaea and in many villages' (Apologia pro Iudaeis, as quoted in Eusebius, Praeparatio Evangelica VIII.11.1); elsewhere Philo says that 'they live in villages and avoid the cities' (Omn Prob Lib 76). Such a view of the Damascus Document seems to be right and is the one followed here. Recently it has been argued that the origins of the Essenes are to be traced back to before the second century BC to Jews living in Babylon, and that the laws in the Damascus Document (CD IX–XVI) belong to the period in Babylon and reflect the circumstances of the life of the Essenes there rather than in Palestine. Thus, for example, one scholar has argued that the Essenes only came to Palestine after 165 BC, and that a major section of the exhortation, namely CD II.14–VI.1, is a kind of Missionary Document, composed shortly after the return to Palestine and intended to explain the origins of the Essenes and to win support for the movement. Views of this kind are not impossible, but there is insufficient evidence at present to make them appear convincing. It is assumed here both that the origins of the Essenes belong in Palestine, and that the legislation of the Damascus Document was intended for those members of the Essene movement who lived in the towns and villages of Palestine.

The Qumran manuscripts of the Damascus Document date back to the first half of the first century BC, but the work may well be older than this. Some of the sources used in its composition probably date from the second century BC.

Only the exhortation (CD I–VIII; XIX–XX) has been translated here. Of the collection of laws (CD IX–XVI) it must suffice to say here that there are many similarities with the legal sections of the Community Rule, which is translated below. The collection of laws may well be older than the exhortation, and may antedate the settlement at Qumran; the exhortation was probably composed as an introduction to the collection of laws.

BIBLIOGRAPHY

C. Rabin, *The Zadokite Documents*, 2nd edition, Oxford, 1958.
P. R. Davies, *The Damascus Covenant: An Interpretation of the 'Damascus Document'* (Journal for the Study of the Old Testament Supplement Series, 25), Sheffield, 1983.

J. Murphy-O'Connor, 'An Essene Missionary Document? CD II,14–VI,1',
    Revue Biblique 77 (1970), 201–29.
    'A Literary Analysis of Damascus Document VI,2–VIII,3', *Revue Biblique*
    78 (1971), 210–32.
    'The Critique of the Princes of Judah (CD VIII,3–19)', *Revue Biblique* 79
    (1972), 200–16.
    'A Literary Analysis of Damascus Document XIX,33–XX,34', *Revue Biblique*
    79 (1972), 544–64.
    'The Essenes and their History', *Revue Biblique* 81 (1974), 215–44.
    'The Essenes in Palestine', *Biblical Archaeologist* 40 (1977), 100–24.
M. A. Knibb, 'Exile in the Damascus Document', *Journal for the Study of the
    Old Testament* 25 (1983), 99–117.
J. Murphy-O'Connor, 'The Original Text of CD 7:9–8:2 = 19:5–14',
    Harvard Theological Review 64 (1971), 379–86.
G. J. Brooke, 'The Amos–Numbers Midrash (CD 7, 13b–8, 1a) and Messianic
    Expectation', *Zeitschrift für die alttestamentliche Wissenschaft* 92 (1980),
    397–404.

The Exhortation

The exhortation (CD I–VIII; XIX–XX) has something of the character
of a sermon and is addressed in II.2, as we have noted, to all 'who are
entering the covenant'. Its contents are somewhat mixed and include
an account of the origins of the movement which lies behind the
document, attacks on rival groups, theological teaching, reflections on
the lessons of history, criticisms of the religious and civil authorities
of the day, a summary of the duties of members of the movement,
and warnings against apostasy. In some sections we find references to
a figure called the teacher of righteousness who, according to this
document, played a decisive part in the history of the Essene
movement, and to a rival figure called 'the scoffer' and 'the liar'; these
individuals are only mentioned elsewhere in the scrolls in the biblical
commentaries.

The exhortation has a discursive and repetitive character, in part
caused by the fact that it is composite. The structure is not entirely clear,
and various different analyses have been made. However, the following
major sections appear to be discernible: historical introduction, I.1–II.1;
theological introduction, II.2–13; reflections on the lessons of history,
II.14–VI.11a; duties of the members and a warning against disobedience,
VI.11b–VIII.2a; XIX.1–14; a further warning, VIII.2b–21a; XIX.15–33a;
the exclusion of apostates, VIII.21b; XIX.33b–XX.22a; a final warning
and promise, XX.22b–34. The nucleus of the work consists of
II.14–VI.11a, and the exhortation as a whole has been built up around

this. The latest material is probably represented by xix.33*b*–xx.22*a*; this section, together with associated material (1.13–18*a*; iv.19*c*–20*a*; viii.12*c*–13) belongs to a secondary stage in the composition of the exhortation, and reflects a situation in which there was a real risk of the wholesale defection of members to a rival movement under the leadership of 'the scoffer'.

We have noted that the Damascus Document was intended for those members of the Essene movement who lived in the towns and villages of Palestine. However, the exhortation – whatever may be true of the collection of laws – was written from a Qumran perspective. It presupposes the appearance of the teacher of righteousness and the settlement at Qumran. It is possible that material which was originally written before the settlement at Qumran has been included in the exhortation, particularly in the case of 11.14–vi.11*a*. But even this section, as it has come down to us, presupposes the appearance of the teacher and has been written from a Qumran perspective, and it is not clear that it is possible to get behind this.

THE ORIGINS OF THE ESSENE MOVEMENT

1.1 And now, listen all you who know what is right
and consider the deeds [2] of God,
for he has a dispute with all flesh
and will execute judgement on all who despise him.
[3] For when they were unfaithful in that they forsook him,
he hid his face from Israel and his sanctuary
[4] and gave them to the sword.
But when he remembered the covenant with the men of
    former times,
he left a remnant [5] to Israel
and did not give them to destruction.
And in the time of wrath, three hundred [6] and ninety years
    after he had given them into the hand of Nebuchadnezzar,
    king of Babylon,[7] he visited them
and caused a root of planting to spring from Israel and Aaron,
to possess [8] his land,
and to grow fat on the good things of his ground.
And they considered their iniquity

and knew that [9] they were guilty men;
but they were like blind men
and like men who grope for the way [10] for twenty years.
And God considered their deeds,
for they sought him with a whole heart;
[11] and he raised up for them a teacher of righteousness
to lead them in the way of his heart.
And he made known [12] to the last generations
what he had done to the last generation, to the congregation
    of traitors.

[13] They are those who turn aside from the way. This is the time about which it was written, 'Like a stubborn heifer, [14] thus was Israel stubborn', when the scoffer appeared who dripped over Israel [15] waters of lies, and led them astray in a trackless waste, bringing down the everlasting heights, turning aside [16] from the paths of righteousness, and pulling up the boundary stone which the men of former times had set up in their inheritance, to [17] cause the curses of his covenant to cling to them, delivering them up to the avenging sword [18] of the covenant. For they sought smooth things and chose illusions, they watched [19] for openings and chose the fair neck, they declared the wicked righteous and the righteous wicked, [20] they transgressed the covenant and broke the statute, they banded together against the life of the righteous man, and their soul loathed all those who walked [21] perfectly, they persecuted them with the sword and exulted in the strife of the people. And the anger of God was kindled [11.1] against their congregation, ravaging all their multitude, and their deeds were impure before him.

The section which opens the Damascus Document in the form known to us from Cairo manuscript A (I.I–II.I) describes the origins of the Essene movement (I.I–12) and the rejection of Israel (I.18b–II.I). The intervening material (I.13–18a) is almost certainly secondary; it has the effect of making the whole of I.13–II.I into an attack on a specific rival group. Lines I–12 of column I appear to be cast in a rhythmic form.

I.I–2. An introduction consisting of a call for attention; it may be compared with II.2–3a, which introduces II.2–13, and II.14–16a, which introduces II.14–VI.11a. Such calls for attention occur frequently in the prophetic and wisdom literature, cp. e.g. Mic. 1:2; Prov. 4:1. *listen all you who know what is right*: a quotation, with one minor change, of Isa. 51:7. *for he has a dispute with all flesh and will execute judgement on all who despise him*: based on Jer. 25:31, but cp. also Hos. 4:1. These words announce the theme of judgement: in the immediate context there is a reference to the judgement upon Israel at the time of the exile, but the underlying concern is with the judgement of the wicked in the author's own day.

3–12. The origins of the movement are linked here, as in other passages in the Damascus Document (III.9b–17a; v.20–vi.5), with the events of the exile.

3–5a. The survival of a remnant at the time of the exile from which God later caused 'a root of planting' to emerge. *when they were unfaithful in that they forsook him*: based on Lev. 26:40, although this is more obvious in the Hebrew. *he hid his face from Israel and his sanctuary and gave them to the sword*: an allusion to the events of 587 BC. The passage draws on the language of Ezek. 39:23. The Old Testament does not speak of God hiding his face from his sanctuary, but see Lam. 2:7; Ezek. 8:6; 10:18–19; 11:22–3 for the thought of God abandoning the temple at the time of the exile. *remembered the covenant with the men of former times*: quoted from Lev. 26:45, an indication that the covenant referred to is the one made with Moses. In vi.2b–5 the emergence of the Essene movement itself is attributed to God's remembrance of the covenant with the men of former times. *a remnant*: at the time of the fall of Jerusalem the exiles were regarded as the remnant preserved by God from destruction (cp. for instance Jer. 24:4–7; Ezek. 11:14–20, although the actual word 'remnant' is not used in these passages), while in the post-exilic period the community in Jerusalem could be described as 'the remnant' (cp. for instance Hag. 1:12–14; 2:2 (NEB 'rest'); Zech. 8:6, 11–12 (NEB 'survivors')). The theme of the remnant is important in a number of post-exilic passages, including Isa. 10:20–3, and the concept was later applied to the early Christian community (cp. Rom. 9:27–9; 11:5). The Essene movement likewise appropriated this concept to itself and in other passages in the scrolls calls itself 'the remnant'; see 1QM XIII.8; 1QH VI.8.

5b–8a. The origins of the Essene movement. The beginnings of the movement are attributed to the intervention of God three hundred and ninety years after the people went into exile in the time of Nebuchadnezzar, i.e., presumably, three hundred and ninety years after 587 BC. This dating brings us down to the early second century BC, and on other grounds it seems likely that the beginnings of what

became the Essene movement are to be traced back to roughly this
period. But the dating is certainly not the result of mathematical
calculation, and the three hundred and ninety years cannot be relied
on as providing any sort of precise chronological information. The
figure has been taken from Ezek. 4:5, and the author apparently drew
on a tradition according to which the number of the years of Israel's
punishment correspond to the number of the years of her iniquity. This
idea, in the form days of punishment corresponding to years of iniquity,
is already present in the Massoretic text of Ezek. 4:5, but it has been
overlaid, particularly in the Septuagint, by other layers of interpretation; the three hundred and ninety years are a round figure for the
period during which Solomon's temple remained in existence. The
author of the Damascus Document drew on this tradition and was in
effect saying that the events to which he was referring marked the end
of the period of Israel's punishment, i.e. the end of the exile. Underlying
this passage, as well as the other passages in the Damascus Document
dealing with the origins of the Essene movement (III.9b–17a;
v.20–VI.5), is a distinct theological pattern that is known to us from
other literature of the period. According to this pattern Israel remained
in a state of exile long after the return in the last decades of the sixth
century until the exile was brought to an end in the events of a much
later period; see for example Dan. 9:24–7; 1 En. 93:9–10 (discussed
below). The intention of the author was thus not so much to provide
an exact date, as to make a theological point linking the beginnings
of the movement with the ending of Israel's state of exile. One further
comment needs to be made here. Some scholars have thought that the
words 'three hundred and ninety years...Nebuchadnezzar, king of
Babylon' are secondary because they fall outside the rhythmic structure
discernible in I.1–12. On this view the passage originally ran:

> And in the time of wrath he visited them
> and caused a root of planting to spring from Israel and Aaron.

This view may be right, but if so, the inserted words must be regarded
as an early reworking of the passage which was intended to provide
a fuller picture of the origins of the community. The theological pattern
would remain the same without the words in question because the exilic
context is already given in lines 3–4a; the only difference would be
that there would be no indication at all of the date of the origins of
the Essene movement.

  5b. *the time of wrath*: the expression occurs elsewhere in the scrolls only in 1QH III.28, where it refers to the eschatological judgement; here it means the period in which the author was living which would be brought to an end by the judgement.

7a. *he visited them*: in the Old Testament God sometimes 'visits' his people to punish them (see for example Jer. 6:15, NEB 'on the day of my reckoning'), and sometimes to bless them (e.g. Jer. 29:10, NEB 'I will take up your cause'); here the word has a positive meaning.

7b–8a. *and caused a root of planting to spring...to possess his land*: based on Isa. 60:21, but with the order of the words changed and 'root' substituted for 'shoot'; the translation 'a root of a plant' would also be possible. The reality underlying the symbolic language is the appearance of a reform movement amongst the Jews in Palestine which marked the beginning of the Essene movement. The language used by the author gives the impression that the emergence of this movement was associated with some specific event, but we do not know what this was, and the text does not go into any details. Plant imagery is also used in 1 En. 93:9–10 to describe the emergence of a reform movement at the end of the post-exilic period: 'And after this in the seventh week an apostate generation will arise, and many (will be) its deeds, but all its deeds (will be) apostasy. And at its end the chosen righteous from the eternal plant of righteousness will be chosen, to whom will be given sevenfold teaching concerning his whole creation.' In this passage the history of the Jewish people is schematised in a series of 'weeks', and the seventh week consists of the exilic and post-exilic periods. No reference is made to the return from exile in the sixth century, but the whole period is condemned as one of apostasy. The end of this period of apostasy is marked by the appearance of a reform group ('the chosen righteous from the eternal plant of righteousness') – exactly the same theological pattern as in the Damascus Document. For the use of plant imagery see also 1QS VIII.5a; 1QH VIII.4–11, part of a psalm which makes use of the imagery of trees and planting to refer to the community; Jub. 16:26; 21:24; Isa. 61:3. *from Israel and Aaron*: i.e from the laity and the priests, cp. VI.2b–3a; 1QS V.6; VIII.5b–6a.

8b–10a. The beginnings of the movement were marked both by recognition of guilt and by uncertainty as to what God demanded of them. *like blind men and like men who grope for the way*: cp. Isa. 59:10. *for twenty years*: these words, like the passage 'three hundred and ninety years...Nebuchadnezzar, king of Babylon', fall outside the rhythmic structure and have been regarded by some scholars as secondary. It is also not clear whether the twenty years are to be taken literally, or whether, as in the case of the three hundred and ninety years, they have primarily a symbolic value, and for this reason it is misleading to attempt to use the information given here to reconstruct an exact chronology of the early history of the Essene movement.

10b–12. The teacher of righteousness. According to this passage a decisive step in the history of the Essene movement occurred when the teacher of righteousness emerged as the leader. This individual is mentioned elsewhere in xx.1, 28, 32, but otherwise only in the biblical commentaries (frequently in 1QpHab; 1QpMic 8–10 6; 4QpPs^b 1 4; 2 2; and in 4QpPs^a 1–10 III.15, 19; IV.27). His identity is unknown, but it is very likely that his period of activity is to be placed during the period of office of either the Maccabean leader Jonathan (160–143 BC) or his brother Simon (143–134 BC) because there are good grounds for thinking that one or other of these individuals was the enemy of the teacher of righteousness known as the wicked priest (see above, pp. 6–10). It may well be, as has sometimes been suggested, that it was in reaction to the assumption by Jonathan of the office of high priest in 152 BC (cp. 1 Macc. 10:18–21) that the teacher of righteousness emerged as the leader of the Essenes. This passage states that before the appearance of the teacher the movement had been somewhat unsure of itself, and the teacher is to be regarded as the founder, or rather refounder, of the Essene movement. Although nowhere stated in the scrolls, it seems probable that the teacher was responsible for the withdrawal of the Qumran community into the wilderness of Qumran (see above, pp. 8–9), a move reflected in the oldest layer of the Community Rule (columns VIII–IX). *And God considered their deeds*: cp. lines 1b–2a, 8. *And he made known*: or 'and to make known'; the former translation presupposes that God is the subject, the latter, the teacher of righteousness. Both translations are possible, but there is little real difference in meaning because it is to be assumed that God's revelation will have been given through the teacher. In 1QpHab VII.1–5 it is the teacher who interprets the secret revelation contained in Old Testament prophecy about the fate of the last generation. *to the last generations*: the generations contemporary with the author. *what he had done*: the Hebrew is sometimes emended to 'what he would do', or this meaning is assumed for the Hebrew. But the passage apparently referred, at least originally, to God's actions in the past, his rejection of pre-exilic Israel because of her sin; this theme is further developed in 1.18b–II.1. *to the last generation*: this phrase is intrusive and is probably a gloss which serves to identify 'the congregation of traitors' with the author's own generation. *to the congregation of traitors*: this probably referred originally to pre-exilic Israel, whose unfaithfulness and rejection by God is described in lines 3–4*a*. But the word 'traitors' is used in 1QpHab II.1, 3, 5 (and perhaps in 1QH II.10*a*) to refer to apostates, and the insertion of lines 13–18*a* will no doubt have led to 'the congregation of traitors' being understood as a reference to apostates, namely the group described in lines 13–18*a*.

I.13–II.I. The remainder of the introduction consists formally of a description of 'the congregation of traitors', but it is apparent that the passage is not a unity. There are in fact two parallel passages (I.13–18*a*; I.18*b*–II.1), which both describe the sins of a group and both end with the theme of judgement. Furthermore, there is a harsh break, more obvious in the Hebrew, between the two halves of line 18. It is the second passage (I.18*b*–II.1) that apparently forms the original continuation of line 12. It explains why God rejected pre-exilic Israel, but implicit in I.1–12 + I.18*b*–II.1 is the claim that the Israel of the author's day remained rejected, and that God's dealings were now with the Essene movement; for this theme see IV.12*b*–V.15*a*. The inserted passage (I.13–18*a*) is concerned not with the nation as a whole, but with a specific group associated with 'the scoffer', which had apparently broken away from the movement. The effect of the insertion is to make the whole of I.13–II.1 refer to this rival group.

13–16*a*. *They are those who turn aside from the way*: or 'who turned aside'; there is perhaps an allusion to such passages as Exod. 32:8; Deut. 9:16. The fact that this charge is made suggests that the members of the rival group had once belonged to the Essene movement. 'The way' means the way of obedience to the law within the movement; for the use here of the expression almost in a technical sense to denote Essene belief and practice cp. II.16; 1QS IX.17*b*–18*a*; and the similar usage in Acts 9:2 (NEB, 'the new way'); 22:4 (NEB, 'this movement'). '*Like a stubborn heifer, thus was Israel stubborn*': Hos. 4:16, but with the addition of the word 'thus'; in the Hebrew there is a play on the words 'turn aside' and 'be stubborn'. The author applies this text to the rival group he is attacking. *when the scoffer appeared who dripped over Israel waters of lies*: the leader of the rival group is called 'the scoffer'. It is difficult not to identify this figure with the individual referred to as 'the liar' (xx.15; 1QpHab II.1*b*–2*a*, 'the traitors with the liar'; v.11; 4QpPs^a 1–10 1.26; IV.14) or as 'the preacher of lies' (CD VIII.13 = XIX.25*b*–26*a*; 1QpHab x.9; cp. CD IV.19*b*–20*a*). It is likewise difficult not to identify his followers with the group elsewhere called 'the scoffers' (CD xx.11; 4QpIsa^b II.6, 10). *who dripped over Israel waters of lies*: the charge levelled here against 'the scoffer' (i.e. 'the liar') is that of spreading false teaching by which is meant a non-Essene interpretation of the law. It is this which the various expressions in the following lines have in mind. *dripped*: the Hebrew word can mean 'drip' or 'preach' and is the same word that occurs in the title 'the preacher of lies' (see references above); in the Old Testament it occurs in this sense in Ezek. 21:2; Amos 7:16; Mic. 2:6, 11. *and led them astray in a trackless waste*: quoted from Job 12:24 or Ps. 107:40; cp. 1QpHab x.9, 'The interpretation of the passage concerns the preacher of lies who led astray many'; 4QpPs^a 1–10 1.26*b*–27*a*, 'Its [interpretation] concerns the liar who led many astray with false words.' The followers of 'the scoffer' wander 'in a trackless waste' because they do not possess the proper interpretation of the law. *bringing down the everlasting heights*: or 'the everlasting pride'. The meaning of the phrase, which is perhaps based on Hab. 3:6, is not entirely clear, but the context suggests that it is perhaps a figurative expression for treating the law with contempt. *and pulling up the boundary stone...inheritance*: the 'boundary stone' is the law; the passage is based on Deut. 19:14, which is quoted with reference to changing the law in Philo, Spec Leg IV.149; cp. CD v.20; XIX.15*b*–16*a*; XX.25.

16*b*–18*a*. The actions of the followers of 'the scoffer' will inevitably, in the view of the author, bring God's judgement upon them. *the curses of his covenant*: the covenant of God, either the Mosaic covenant, or the covenant made with the movement (cp. III.13); for the expression cp. 1QS II.15*b*–16*a*; Deut. 29:19–21, and see also Deut. 27:15–26; 28:15–19. *delivering them up...the covenant*: based on Lev. 26:25 (more obvious in the Hebrew than the NEB), perhaps conflated with Ps. 78:62.

18*b*–21*a*. This passage apparently forms the original continuation of line 12 and consists of six pairs of statements. It describes the sins of pre-exilic Israel but implicitly also those of the Israel of the author's own day. Much of the description is made up of expressions drawn from the Old Testament. *they sought smooth things and chose illusions*: based on Isa. 30:10*b*. In other Qumran documents (1QH II.15*b*, 32; 4QpIsa^c 23 II.10; particularly 4QpNah) the expression 'the seekers after smooth things' is used to refer to a distinct group, and from the Commentary on Nahum it is clear that this group is to be identified with the Pharisees. Although the present passage refers in the first instance to pre-exilic Israel, it was no doubt also read as referring to 'the seekers after smooth things' of the author's own day. *they watched for openings*: i.e. for loopholes in the law. *and chose the fair neck*: apparently an allusion to Hos. 10:11, but the meaning is not clear. Possibly 'the fair neck' was understood as a symbol of Israel's unwillingness to obey the law. *they declared the wicked righteous and the righteous wicked*: based on Prov. 17:15; contrast IV.7 and Deut. 25:1. *they transgressed the covenant and broke the statute*: apparently an adaptation of Isa. 24:5*b*. *they banded together against the life of the righteous man*: a quotation from Ps. 94:21; this makes it unlikely that any specific incident is in mind. *and their soul loathed all those who walked perfectly*: possibly inspired by the language of Ps. 15:2 and Amos 5:10.

I.21*b*–II.1. God's judgement on 'the congregation of traitors'. The passage refers in the first instance to the events of 587 BC, for which cp. I.3–4*a*; but see the comment below. *And the anger of God was kindled against their congregation*: this, or a closely similar, statement occurs several times as a kind of refrain throughout the exhortation. It is sometimes used, as here, with reference to the past (II.21; III.8*b*–9*a*; V.16). But it is also used in VIII.13 = XIX.26 (cp. VIII.18*b* = XIX.31*b*–32*a*) with reference to the judgement of a group of apostates, apparently the same group as that described in I.13–18*a*. Thus it is likely that the present passage, which refers primarily to the past, was also given a contemporary reference. The usage in the remaining passage, XX. 15*b*–16*a*, probably part of a secondary section, is slightly different. *and their deeds were impure before him*: cp. 1QS V.19*b*–20*a*.

ESSENE TEACHING ABOUT GOD

II.2 And now, listen to me all you who are entering the covenant, and I will open your ears concerning the ways ³ of the wicked. God loves knowledge; wisdom and understanding he has established before him, ⁴ discernment and knowledge serve him. Patience and abundant forgiveness are with him ⁵ to make expiation for those who turn from transgression; but strength, and might, and great fury with flames of fire ⁶ at ⟨the hand⟩ of all the destroying angels against those who rebel against the way and loathe the statute, without remnant ⁷ or survivor for them. For God did not choose them in ancient times; before they were created he knew ⁸ their deeds, and he loathed the generations on account of the blood and hid his face from the land, ⁹ from ⟨Israel⟩, until they were consumed. He knew the years of existence and the number and exact statement of the times of all ¹⁰ the things that have happened throughout the ages and the things that will happen for ever, what will come about in the times of all the years of eternity. ¹¹ And in all of them he raised up for himself renowned men, in order to leave survivors for the land and to fill ^{12} the face of the world with their descendants. And he taught them through those anointed with his holy spirit and those who ^{13} see the truth. And with exactness he established their names, but those whom he hated he led astray.

Teaching about God, particularly his treatment of the righteous and the wicked, forms the content of the second introduction to the Damascus Document in the form known to us from Cairo Manuscript A. The teaching has a strongly dualistic and deterministic character and as such is reminiscent of the teaching on the two spirits in 1QS III.13–IV.26.

II.2–3a. Call for attention, cp. 1.1–2; II.14–16a. *all you who are entering the covenant*: as suggested above (see p. 14), it is plausible to think that the Damascus Document in its final form was intended for use at the annual ceremony of the renewal of the covenant.

3b–4a. God's knowledge. *wisdom and understanding...discernment and knowledge*: these four divine attributes are spoken of here almost as if they were independent entities, much in the way that wisdom is personified in Prov. 8 and Ecclus. 24:1–22. The theme of God's knowledge is taken further in lines 7b–10.

4b–7a. God's treatment of the righteous and the wicked. What is said here may be compared with the statements about God's 'visitation' of those dominated respectively by the spirit of truth and the spirit of injustice, 1QS IV.6b–8, 11b–14. *to make expiation for*: in the Damascus Document it is God who makes expiation for the iniquities of those who repent (III.18; IV.6, 9b–10a; XX.34); cp. 1QS II.8 and contrast such passages as 1QS V.6. *those who turn from transgression*: i.e. the members of the movement; the phrase is taken from Isa. 59:20, as is more obvious in XX.17b where the fuller phrase 'those who turned from the transgression of Jacob' occurs; cp. also 1QH II.9a and the references to 'the converts (literally 'those who (re)turn') of Israel' in CD IV.2; VI.5; VIII.16 = XIX.29. *at ⟨the hand⟩ of all the destroying angels*: cp. 1QS IV.12. *against those who rebel against the way*: in contrast to I.13–18a no specific opponents are in mind here, the reference being rather to all those who do not accept the movement's teaching; for the technical use of 'the way' see 1.13 and the comment on 1.13–16a. *and loathe the statute*: the law, as interpreted by the Essenes. *without remnant or survivor for them*: cp. 1QS IV.14 and the comment there. The lack of a remnant for the wicked stands in contrast to the survival of a righteous remnant, 1.4b–5a; II.11; III.12b–13a.

7b–10. The fate of the rebels is attributed to the fact that they were not chosen by God because he knew in advance what their deeds would be. The strongly deterministic character of these lines is reminiscent of 1QS III.15b–17a. *For God did not choose them*: contrast 1QS IV.22b. *created*: literally 'founded, established'. *he knew their deeds*: cp. 1QS IV.25c. *on account of the blood*: perhaps the sense is 'on account of the bloodshed', but the text is obscure. *and hid his face from the land, from ⟨Israel⟩*: cp. 1.3; Ezek. 39:23. The author is speaking in general terms of God's attitude towards the wicked, but almost imperceptibly in lines 8b–9a there is a shift to the thought of God's punishment of Israel at the time of the exile.

11–13. The preservation of a faithful remnant throughout the ages. There are links here backwards to 1.4b–5a, and forwards to III.12b–13a, as well as to what is said about Abraham, Isaac and Jacob in III.2–4a. Although the author is speaking in general terms about the preservation by God of a remnant throughout history, the underlying thought is that the Essene movement formed the remnant in what was for the author the end of the exile (lines 8b–9a) and the climax of history. *renowned men*: literally 'those called by name', a term based on two different expressions used at the end of Num. 16:2 (literally 'called to the assembly, men of name'); cp. IV.4. The actual phraseology of Num. 16:2 is used in 1QSa II.2; 1QM II.6–7. *to fill the face of the world with their descendants*: cp. the promise of descendants in Isa. 54:1–3, a prophecy of restoration from the exilic period. *those anointed with his holy spirit and those who see the truth*: the prophets, cp. Ps. 105:15; 1 Kings 19:16; 1QS VIII.16. *And with exactness he established their names*: perhaps an allusion forward to IV.4b–5a, 'Here is an exact list of their names'; it appears that originally a list of the members of the movement was included in the Damascus Document after IV.6a. *but those whom he hated he led astray*: for the thought cp. 1QS III.25–IV.1.

AN ADDRESS TO MEMBERS OF THE MOVEMENT

The core of the exhortation consists of a section which begins in II.14 and apparently ends at VI.11a; the statement in VI.11b, 'None of those brought into the covenant...', seems to mark a new beginning. This section may well have had an independent existence before its incorporation into the Damascus Document. Its purpose is to explain how the Essene movement came into being, to justify its right to exist, and to expose the moral laxity of contemporary society. As such this section or document was perhaps originally intended for the instruction

of those on the verge of joining the movement or of members who
had just joined. But it can also be seen that the character of this material
rendered it suitable for use in its present context, namely as part of a
larger document intended for use at the annual ceremony of the renewal
of the covenant. For convenience the material is divided here into four
parts: II.14–III.12a; III.12b–IV.12a; IV.12b–V.15a; V.15b–VI.11a.

THE LESSONS OF THE PAST

II.14 And now, my sons, listen to me, and I will open your eyes that
you may see and understand the deeds 15 of God, that you may choose
that in which he delights and reject that which he hates, that you may
walk perfectly 16 in all his ways and not follow after the thoughts of
the guilty inclination and lustful eyes. For many 17 have gone astray
through them, and mighty warriors have stumbled through them from
former times until now. When they walked in the stubbornness 18 of
their hearts the watchers of heaven fell; they were caught through it
because they did not keep the commandments of God. 19 And their
sons, whose height was like the height of cedars and whose bodies were
like mountains, they fell. 20 All flesh on dry land perished; they became
as though they had never been because they did 21 their own will and
did not keep the commandments of their maker, so that his anger was
kindled against them. III.1 Through it the sons of Noah and their
families went astray, and through it they were cut off. 2 Abraham did
not walk in it, and he was counted as a friend because he kept the
commandments of God and did not choose 3 the will of his own spirit.
And he handed (them) on to Isaac and Jacob, and they kept (them)
and were recorded as friends 4 of God and party to the covenant for
ever. The sons of Jacob went astray through them and were punished
in accordance with 5 their error. And their sons in Egypt walked in
the stubbornness of their hearts, plotting against 6 the commandments
of God and each man doing what was right in his own eyes. They
ate the blood, and their males were cut off 7 in the wilderness. ⟨And
he said⟩ to them at Qadesh: 'Go up and take possession of ⟨the land.'
But they chose the will⟩ of their own spirit; they did not obey 8 the
voice of their maker ⟨and did not keep⟩ the commandments of their

teacher, but murmured in their tents. And the anger of God was kindled against [9] their congregation. Through it their sons perished, and through it their kings were cut off; through it their warriors [10] perished, and through it their land was made desolate. Through it the first ones who entered the covenant incurred guilt and were delivered up [11] to the sword, because they forsook the covenant of God, and chose their own will, and followed after the stubbornness [12] of their hearts, each man doing his own will.

The author begins by urging his listeners to put into practice the lessons to be drawn from an understanding of 'the deeds of God', and not to 'follow after the thoughts of the guilty inclination and lustful eyes' (II.14–16a). This exhortation serves as an introduction to, and is reinforced by, a summary of some of the main events of Israel's past in which it is shown that by following the guilty inclination God's people had repeatedly brought punishment upon themselves. The purpose of the summary governed the choice of the events and persons mentioned in that almost all are negative in character. The summary extends from the antediluvian period to the time of the exile, which is presented as the consequence of Israel's guilt (II.16b–III.12a). Recitals of Israel's history occur frequently in the Old Testament and are used for a variety of purposes (see the commentary on 2 Esdras in the Cambridge Bible Commentary, p. 114); here comparison may be drawn with such passages as Ezek. 20:1–31 and Ps. 106.

II.14–16a. A call for attention, similar to those in I.1–2; II.2–3a, but developed at somewhat greater length as a statement of the purpose of the following section. *my sons*: the use of this mode of address is typical of wisdom instruction: cp. e.g. Prov. 4:1; Ecclus. 2:1. *see and understand the deeds of God*: from what follows it is clear that the author is thinking particularly of God's dealings with his people, and the lessons to be drawn from them; cp. I.1–2a. *that you may choose*: the sense is 'and may in consequence choose'. The language and thought of lines 15–16 reveal marked similarities with 1QS 1.3b–4a, 6, part of the introduction (I.1–15) of the Community Rule. *and not follow after the thoughts of the guilty inclination and lustful eyes*: reminiscent of Num. 15:39; cp. Ezek. 6:9. For the concept of the 'guilty inclination' see the comment on 1QS v.4b–5.

II.16b–III.12a. The exhortation of lines 14–16a is supported by a series of examples drawn from Israel's history.

16b–17a. Transition from the words of exhortation (lines 14–16a) to the series of examples. *through them*: the thoughts of the guilty inclination and lustful eyes. *have stumbled*: used here figuratively of divine punishment, the consequence of 'going astray'; such a figurative use occurs frequently in the Old Testament, cp. e.g. Ps. 9:3 (NEB, 'fall headlong').

17*b*–18. The watchers. The story of the watchers, a term used for angels, appears in its most developed form – in two intertwined traditions – in I En. 6–16 (see the volume in this series *Outside the Old Testament*, pp. 29–43). According to one of these traditions, which is based on Gen. 6:1–4, the watchers came down from heaven because of their lust for the daughters of men; the offspring of the marriage of the watchers and the women were giants. It is this tradition to which reference is made in lines 17*b*–19. *When they walked in the stubbornness of their hearts*: this expression is characteristic of the language of the Deuteronomistic layers of Jeremiah: cp. for instance 11:8 or, slightly different, 9:14. *The watchers*: for this term see Dan. 4:13, 17, 23; I En. 10:7, 9; 12:2. *fell...were caught*: figurative expressions, like 'have stumbled' in line 17, for the punishment which was the consequence of the sin of the watchers (cp. I En. 10:4–8, 11–14); for the former expression cp. Jer. 6:15, for the latter cp. Eccles. 9:12. *through it*: used interchangeably with 'through them' to refer back to 'the thoughts of the guilty inclination and lustful eyes' (line 16).

19. The sons of the watchers. *whose height was like the height of cedars*: an adaptation of Amos 2:9; according to I En. 7:2 the height of the giant sons of the watchers was three thousand cubits. *they fell*: for the punishment of the sons of the watchers cp. I En. 10:9–10.

20–1. The flood generation. *All flesh on dry land perished*: an allusion to Gen. 7:22. *they became as though they had never been*: quoted from Obad. 16. *so that his anger was kindled against them*: see the comment on I.21*b*–II.1.

III.1. The sons of Noah. The author no doubt had in mind not only the story of Ham (Gen. 9:20–7), and possibly the story of the Tower of Babel (Gen. 11:1–9), but also extra-biblical traditions about the sins of the sons of Noah of the kind mentioned in Jub. 7:27; 10:1–2; 11:2–7. *were cut off*: i.e. were killed, cp. Lev. 17:14: Isa. 29:20–1 (NEB, 'shall be exterminated').

2–4*a*. Abraham, Isaac, and Jacob. These are the only exceptions in what is otherwise a series of negative examples. *a friend*: an allusion to Isa. 41:8, a passage also referred to in Jub. 19:9 and James 2:23. *because he kept the commandments of God*: there is a deliberate contrast with the repeated accusation 'they did not keep the commandments', cp. II.18, 21; III.5*b*–6*a*, 8; these words also point forward to what is said in III.12b–13 about those with whom God established his covenant. *And he handed (them) on*: the verb in the Hebrew is *māsar*, the technical term for the transmission of the law used in Mishnah Ab. 1.1 *party to the covenant for ever*: the covenant with Isaac is mentioned in Gen. 17:19, 21, and there is an implicit allusion to a covenant with Jacob in Gen. 35:11–12; see also Exod. 2:24. But the underlying thought is of the covenant made with the members of the Essene movement.

4b–5a. *The sons of Jacob.* The Old Testament mentions a number of incidents in which 'the sons of Jacob went astray': the slaughter of the Shechemites (Gen. 34:25–31, cp. 49:5–7), Reuben's sin with Bilhah (Gen. 35:22, cp. 49:3–4), the sale of Joseph (Gen. 37), Judah's sin with Tamar (Gen. 38:12–26). These incidents were taken up in writings from the intertestamental period, namely in Jubilees and in the Testaments of the Twelve Patriarchs (for these works see in this series *Outside the Old Testament*, pp. 111–44, 71–91). In the Testaments in particular the sins of the sons of Jacob, and the punishments which they suffered in consequence, form an important theme; cp. e.g. T. Reub. 1:6–10; T. Sim. 2:6–14; T. Jud. 11–13.

5b–7a. *The generations in Egypt and in the wilderness. their sons in Egypt*: for the tradition that the period in Egypt was a time of sin see Ezek. 20:5–9; 23:3; Josh. 24:14. The period in Egypt is not so presented in the book of Exodus apart from the brief references in 5:20–1; 6:9, 12. *each man doing what was right in his own eyes*: for the language cp. Judg. 17:6; 21:25; Deut. 12:8. *They ate the blood*: for the prohibition on eating blood see e.g. Gen. 9:4–5; Lev. 17:10–14. No such incident is said in the Old Testament to have occurred during the period in Egypt and in the wilderness, but Jub. 6:18–19 states that the sons of Noah ate blood (verse 18) and implicitly accuses the generation of the time of Moses of doing so (verse 19). It is curious that this should be singled out for mention, and not some incident such as those recorded in Exod. 15:22–16:36 or 32:1–35; but it is clear from numerous references that eating meat from which the blood had not been drained was a matter of considerable concern to Jews at the time at which the Damascus Document was composed (cp. e.g. Jub. 6:7, 11–13; 1 En. 98:11; Acts 15:20, 29).

7b–9a. *The unsuccessful attempt to enter the land from Kadesh. Go up and take possession of the ⟨the land*: quoted from Deut. 9:23a (more obvious in the Hebrew than in the NEB); for the tradition of the unsuccessful entry see Num. 13–14. *But they chose the will⟩*: the text is defective; the restoration is based on the formulaic expressions of lines 2b–3a, 11. *they did not obey the voice of their maker*: an allusion to Deut. 9:23b combined with Ps. 106:25b. *⟨and did not keep⟩ the commandments* *of their teacher*: some words appear to have been omitted by mistake; the restoration is based on the formula used in ii.18, 21. The 'teacher' is either God – as the parallelism with 'their maker' would suggest – or Moses. *but murmured in their tents*: quoted from Ps. 106:25a, cp. Deut. 1:27. *And the anger of God was kindled against their congregation*: see the comment on i.21b–ii.1.

9b–12a. A summary of the remainder of Israel's history down to the exile. It might seem strange that the author should pass over the period of the settlement, the Judges and the monarchy so quickly, but he no doubt felt that he had already made his point. We find a similar curtailment in the historical retrospect in 2 Esdras 3, which likewise culminates in the exile; see 2 Esdras 3:23–7. See also Neh. 9 where the period down to the settlement is treated in detail, but the period after the settlement only in summary fashion. *their land was made desolate*: the desolation of the land at the time of the exile; the word translated 'was made desolate' is from a Hebrew root (*šāmam*) that is used with reference to the exile in such passages as Lev. 26:31–5; 2 Chron. 36:21. The following words explain why the disaster of 587 and the exile occurred. *the first ones who entered the covenant*: the covenant is the Mosaic covenant; cp. i.4, 'the covenant with the men of former times' or, as it could also be translated, 'the covenant with the first ones'. In the present passage the reference in the first instance is to the generation that experienced the exile, but the phrase includes within its scope all the pre-exilic generations inasmuch as all were members of the covenant made at Sinai. *because they forsook the covenant of God*: cp. i.3. *and followed after the stubbornness of their hearts*: adapted from Num. 15:39 (NEB, 'and not go your own wanton ways'); cp. ii.16.

THE ESTABLISHMENT OF THE COVENANT

iii.12 But with those who held fast to the commandments of God, 13 who were left over from them, God established his covenant with Israel for ever, revealing 14 to them the hidden things in which all Israel had gone astray: his holy sabbaths and his glorious feasts, 15 his righteous testimonies and his true ways, and the desires of his will which a man must do 16 that he may live through them. (These) he laid open before them, and they dug a well of abundant waters; 17 those who reject them shall not live. They had defiled themselves through human transgression and through impure ways, 18 and they had said: 'This is ours.' But God in his wonderful mysteries made expiation for their iniquity and pardoned their transgression. [19] He built for them a sure house in Israel, the like of which has not appeared in Israel from former times until [20] now. Those who hold fast to it are (destined) for eternal life, and all the glory of Adam shall belong to them. This was in accordance with what [21] God had established for them through Ezekiel the prophet: 'The priests and the Levites and the sons [IV.1] of Zadok who remained in charge of my sanctuary when the children of Israel went astray [2] from me, they shall offer me fat and blood.' The priests are the converts of Israel [3] who went out from the land of Judah, and ⟨the Levites are⟩ those who joined them, and the sons of Zadok are the chosen ones [4] of Israel, the renowned men who shall appear at the end of days. Here is an exact list [5] of their names according to their genealogy, the time when they lived, the number of their afflictions, and the years [6] of their sojourn and an exact list of their deeds...⟨the fir⟩st holy ⟨ones⟩ for whom God made expiation, [7] who declared the righteous righteous and the wicked wicked, and all those who entered after them [8] to act according to the exact interpretation of the law in which the first were instructed until the completion [9] of the time ⟨according to the number⟩ of those years. In accordance with the covenant which God established with the first to make expiation [10] for their iniquities, so God will make expiation for them. But when the time is completed according to the number of those years, [11] there will be no more joining the house of Judah, but each man shall stand on [12] his watch-tower; the wall is built, the boundary far extended.

The next event mentioned after the exile is the founding of the Essene movement, here expressed as the (re-)establishment of the covenant. This theme occupies the whole of III.12b–IV.12a.

III.12b–16a. As in column I, the exile (III.9b–12a) and the founding of the Essene movement are linked directly together. The founding of the movement is presented as the climax of history and as the event which brought Israel's state of exile to an end; for this theological pattern see the comments on I.5b–8a. *But with those who held fast to the commandments of God, who were left over from them*: the initial members of the movement are presented as a faithful remnant which survived the exile; cp. I.3–5a; II.11–13, and the comments on these passages. But we are given no precise information here about the identity of this remnant, nor are we told when or where the covenant with it was made. Further, no reference is made in this passage to the role of the teacher; contrast I.II; VI.7b–8a. *God established his covenant with Israel for ever*: the founding of the movement is interpreted as the (re-) establishment of God's covenant with Israel (cp. 1QS VIII.10), the implication being that the movement now represents the true Israel. The covenant concept is of fundamental importance in the scrolls, and in the movement which lies behind them. *revealing to them the hidden things in which all Israel had gone astray*: the founding of the movement was accompanied, if not rather inspired, by a revelation from God about the meaning of the law. 'The hidden things' means Essene interpretation of the law, the secrets of the law revealed by study; cp. the use of the expression in 1QS V.11, 'the hidden things in which they have guiltily gone astray', and the related passage in 1QS VIII.11b–12a, 'nothing which was hidden from Israel, but found by the man who studies'. In effect the author is claiming divine authority for Essene interpretation of the Old Testament. *his holy sabbaths and his glorious feasts*: the content of the revelation is defined in a series of phrases which stand in apposition to 'the hidden things in which all Israel had gone astray'. The first two items relate to the calendar which, as is apparent from several references in the scrolls, was a matter of some importance to the Essene movement. The so-called *mišmarot* texts from Cave 4 and the work known as David's Compositions (11QPs^a DavComp) show that the movement followed a 364-day solar calendar that is also known from Jubilees and 1 En. 72–82. According to this calendar the year consisted of exactly fifty-two weeks or four quarters of ninety-one days; each quarter consisted of three months of thirty days plus one additional day. The year began on a Wednesday, and the feast-days (e.g. Passover, the day of atonement) automatically fell on the same day of the week every year. This solar calendar is also presupposed in some of the later writings in the Old Testament (Ezekiel, the Priestly material in the Pentateuch, Chronicles–Ezra–Nehemiah), but it is a matter of dispute whether – and, if so, for how long – this calendar was actually used for cultic purposes within the Jewish community. It does appear, however, that the Essene movement was concerned to maintain observance of this ancient priestly calendar, and that this was an important distinguishing mark from those outside. The latter followed a lunisolar calendar, and in this they are held to have 'gone astray'. But it remains uncertain how far disputes over the calendar played a part in the emergence of the Essene movement. *which a man must do that he may live through them*: based on Lev. 18:5; Ezek. 20:11, 13, 21.

16b–17a. (*These*) *he laid open before them, and they dug a well of abundant waters*: the 'well' is a symbolic expression for the law, cp. VI.3b–5; the link between the divine revelation and the interpretation of the law is thus made clear. *those who reject them shall not live*: a warning to the listeners not to reject the life-giving waters of Essene interpretation of the law; those who do so will forfeit eternal life (contrast lines 15b–16a and 20).

17b–18a. The author steps back in time for a moment to describe the situation of the members of the movement prior to the establishment of the covenant, and then proceeds to describe the effects of the establishment of the covenant: forgiveness (18b) and the building of 'a sure house' (19–20a). *and they had said: 'This is ours'*: an apparent allusion to Ezek. 11:15 (more obvious in the Hebrew than the English), here used to characterise the self-seeking attitude of the members of the movement before God established his covenant with them.

18b. Forgiveness of sin is seen as the first effect of the establishment of the covenant. *God...made expiation for their iniquity*: see the comment on II.5.

19–20a. *He built for them a sure house in Israel*: 'house' has a figurative meaning, and the passage is based on the words of 1 Sam. 2:35 referring to the replacement of the priestly dynasty of Eli by that of Zadok, 'I will build him a sure house' (NEB, 'I will establish his family'). As we shall see below (pp. 105–6), the Essenes claimed in some sense to be the legitimate successors of Zadok. The author of the Damascus Document is claiming that when God established his covenant (line 13), he brought into being in Israel a new movement or group which possessed a privileged status such as was promised in 1 Sam. 2:35. *Those who hold fast to it are (destined) for eternal life*: in contrast to those outside the movement, those who reject Essene interpretation of the law (cp. line 17a). For an indication of what the author understood by 'eternal life' see 1QS IV.6b–8; the concept is not developed or explained in the Damascus Document itself, but cp. VII.4b–6a = XIX.1–2a; XX.33b–34. *and all the glory of Adam shall belong to them*: i.e. they will be restored to the state which Adam enjoyed before the fall; for similar statements cp. 1QS IV.23a; 1QH XVII.15. In Jewish and Christian writings Adam tends to become a more and more glorious figure, even though his responsibility for man's sin is also emphasised (cp. e.g. 2 Esdras 3:21; 4:30; 7:[118]; Rom. 5:12–14). An early example of this tendency is to be found in the Hebrew version of Ecclus. 49:16 (where the word for 'glory' is different from that in the scrolls):

Shem, Seth and Enosh are honoured,
   but the glory of Adam is above that of every living being.

Typical also is the view of the Life of Adam and Eve, 12–17, where
the angels are instructed to worship Adam, who had been created in
the image of God.

   III.20*b*–IV.4*a*. The author claims divine authority for the existence
of the movement by presenting the building of the sure house as the
fulfilment of the promise given in Ezek. 44:15. *The priests and the*
Levites and the sons of Zadok: the Massoretic text of Ezek. 44:15 refers
to only one group (NEB, 'the levitical priests of the family of Zadok');
it is not clear whether the author of the Damascus Document made
use of an existing textual variant, or whether he deliberately altered
the text known to him in order to accommodate it to his interpretation.
they shall offer me fat and blood: the last part of the quotation has been
telescoped, and a different verb is used from that in the Massoretic text.
The priests are the converts of Israel: the three groups described in the
interpretation of Ezek. 44:15 are most probably the initial members
of the movement, those who joined at a later stage, and all those who
belonged to the movement 'at the end of days', the time in which the
author believed himself to be living. *the converts of Israel who went out*
from the land of Judah: probably best understood as referring to those
who left Jerusalem and its immediate environs to settle at Qumran. But
the meaning of this description of the initial members of the movement
is discussed more fully in connection with VI.5, 'the converts of Israel
who went out from the land of Judah and sojourned in the land of
Damascus'. *and ⟨the Levites are⟩ those who joined them*: the restoration
is based on the assumption that some words were left out of the Hebrew
by mistake. The explanation is based on word-play with the Hebrew
verb *lāwāh*, 'to join', as in Gen. 29:34; Num. 18:2, 4. The clear
distinction made in lines 6*b*–12*a* between the first members and 'all
those who entered after them' supports the view that the second group
are those who joined the movement after its foundation. *and the sons*
of Zadok are the chosen ones of Israel: the third group are 'the sons of
Zadok' of the Ezekiel text, here explained as referring to the members
of the movement in general; for the significance of the expression
elsewhere in the scrolls see the comment on 1QS V.2*b*–3*a*. *the renowned*
men: see on II.11. *who shall appear at the end of days*: see the comment
above.

   IV.4*b*–6*a*. Here is an exact list of their names...and an exact list of their
deeds: but no list follows. It is to be assumed that at some stage in the

transmission of the text the list was omitted because it was no longer of interest. The occurrence of a list in the Damascus Document may be compared with the occurrence of lists in such passages as Ezra 2, whose purpose was to establish who were the true members of the community. But the list in the Damascus Document was apparently not quite the same because it is said to have included details of the lives of those recorded in it. *and the years of their sojourn*: the same Hebrew word is used as in VI.5, and the reference is apparently the same as in VI.5, namely to sojourn 'in the land of Damascus'.

6b–12a. The author now deals with the position of those who joined the movement after its foundation; they are said to have the same obligations as the first members (lines 7b–9a) and will receive the same divine forgiveness (lines 9b–10a). But there is a warning: the opportunity of joining the movement will come to an end 'when the time is completed' (lines 10b–12a). Implicitly these lines form an invitation to those addressed to join the movement before it is too late.

6b–7a. ⟨*the fir*⟩*st holy* ⟨*ones*⟩: the text is corrupt, the loss perhaps occurring as a consequence of the omission of the list. The exact restoration of the text is uncertain, but there was clearly a reference to the founders of the movement. *for whom God made expiation*: cp. III. 18b. *who declared the righteous righteous and the wicked wicked*: an allusion, based on Deut. 25:1, to the participation of members in the giving of legal decisions; cp. 1QS v.6b–7a; vi.22b–23, and contrast CD I.19b.

7b–9a. *and all those who entered after them to act*: or perhaps 'shall act'; the exact translation is uncertain because of the lacuna in line 6. *according to the exact interpretation of the law*: the law as understood and interpreted by the movement. The same phrase (together with 'to act') occurs in VI.14. *in which the first were instructed*: 'the first' are the founders of the movement; cp. 1QS IX.10b–11, which in a similar fashion speaks of the original legislation remaining in force 'until the coming of the prophet and the messiahs of Aaron and Israel'. *until the completion of the time*: the period until the end of the existing age, described in the related passage in VI.14 as 'the time of wickedness' (see the comment on that passage). The language used indicates that the author believed that the length of this period had been predetermined, a point reiterated in lines 10b–12a. ⟨*according to the number*⟩ *of those years*: the restoration is based on the wording of line 10.

9b–10a. *the covenant which God established with the first*: the covenant made with the founders of the movement, III.12b–13. *to make expiation for their iniquities*: cp. III.18b; IV.6b–7a. *so God will make expiation for them*: those who join after the founders receive the same forgiveness; implicitly those addressed are being invited to take the opportunity of receiving this forgiveness by joining the movement and thus of securing eternal life for themselves (cp. III.16b–20a).

10b–12a. *But when the time is completed according to the number of those years, there will be no more joining the house of Judah*: 'house of Judah' is a symbolic name for the movement (cp. 1QpHab VIII.1; 4QpPsᵃ 1–10 II.14; 4QpNah 3–4 III.4). When the pre-determined length of the existing age was complete, there would be no further opportunity of joining the movement; those addressed were in effect being urged to take the opportunity before it was too late. This message is reinforced by allusions to two biblical passages. *but each man shall stand on his watch-tower*: apparently an allusion to Hab. 2:1:

> I will stand at my post,
> I will take up my position on the watch-tower,
> I will watch to learn what he will say through (or 'to') me,
> and what I shall reply when I am challenged.

In the Damascus Document each man is to stand on his watch-tower in order, so it would appear, to receive God's decision at the judgement as to his fate. The point of the passage is that 'when the time is completed', it will be too late to do anything to affect the decision. *the wall is built, the boundary far extended*: based on Micah 7:11, a prophecy of the expansion of the Jewish community in the post-exilic period, but here applied to the Essene movement. The author is claiming that the prophecy has now been fulfilled, the expansion was complete. The point being made is that the opportunity for joining the movement was fast running out because the predetermined length of the existing age was (all but) over. *the boundary*: the Hebrew word (*ḥōq*) could also be translated 'the statute', possibly an intentional allusion to the role of the law in the movement.

BELIAL LET LOOSE AGAINST ISRAEL

IV.12 During all those years Belial will be let loose 13 against Israel, as God said through Isaiah the prophet, the son 14 of Amoz: 'Terror, and the pit, and the snare (are) upon you, O inhabitant of the land.' Its interpretation: 15 (these are) the three nets of Belial, about which Levi the son of Jacob said 16 that he catches Israel in them and makes them appear to them as three kinds 17 of righteousness. The first is fornication, the second wealth, the third [18] making the sanctuary unclean. He who escapes from one will be caught in another, and he who saves himself from that will be caught [19] in the third.

The builders of the wall who went after 'Ṣaw' – 'Ṣaw' is a preacher [20] of whom he said: 'They shall surely preach' – they will be caught twice in fornication: by taking [21] two wives during their lifetime, whereas the principle of creation is 'male and female he created them'. [V.1] And those who went into the ark, 'two by two they went into the ark'. And concerning the prince it is written: [2] 'He shall not acquire many wives.' As for David, he had not read the sealed book of the law which [3] was in the ark, for it was not opened in Israel from the day that Eleazar and Joshua and the elders died [4] because they worshipped Ashtoreth. It was hidden [5] ⟨and⟩ was ⟨not⟩ revealed until the coming of Zadok. And the deeds of David were cancelled, except the murder of Uriah, [6] and God allowed them to him.

Also they make the sanctuary unclean inasmuch as they do not [7] keep separate in accordance with the law, but lie with a woman who sees the blood of her discharge.

And each man takes [8] his brother's daughter or his sister's daughter (as wife), whereas Moses said: 'You shall not approach [9] your mother's sister; she is a blood-relation of your mother.' The law of incest was written for men, [10] but it applies also to women. If a brother's daughter has intercourse with her father's brother, [11] she (also) is a blood-relation.

Also they have made their holy spirit unclean, and with a blaspheming tongue [12] they have opened their mouth against the statutes of the covenant of God, saying: 'They are not right.' They speak abominable things [13] about them. All of them are kindlers of fire and lighters of firebrands; their webs are spiders' webs, [14] and their eggs are vipers' eggs. He who approaches them [15] shall not escape punishment; the more he does so, the more guilty he will become, unless he is pressed.

In the section or source running from II.14 to VI.11*a* the author has so far shown how Israel had brought punishment on herself, and how the Essene movement had come into being to take her place; God's covenant with Israel was now established with this movement, and those addressed were implicitly invited to join while there was still time (cp. IV.9*b*–12*a*). But the author was faced with the problem of the continuing existence of non-Essene Judaism, and his purpose in IV.12*b*–v.15*a* is to show that non-Essene Judaism was in fact under the control of Belial. He attempts to do this by demonstrating that practices which were regarded as orthodox in Jewish society of the day were devices by which Belial exercised his control over Israel; the examples used for this have primarily to do with sexual sins. The passage divides into two parts: the first consists of a midrashic interpretation of Isa. 24:17 which was intended to show that Belial had been 'let loose against Israel' (IV.12*b*–19*a*); the second consists of a commentary which applies the midrash to conditions in contemporary society (IV.19*b*–v.15*a*). Because the commentary does not exactly match the midrash it seems likely that the midrash was taken over by the author from another source as a traditional piece of interpretation. It also seems likely that the commentary has been secondarily expanded, in IV.19*c*–20*a* and in v.6*b*–7. For the meaning of the term 'midrash' see below, pp. 184–5.

IV.12*b*–19*a*. *During all those years*: a link back to lines 9*a* and 10. The author is referring to the existing age, the age preceding the judgement. *Belial will be let loose against Israel*: 'Belial' is the name used most frequently in the scrolls for the leader of the spiritual forces of wickedness; elsewhere he is called 'the angel of enmity' (CD XVI.5; 1QM XIII.11) and 'the prince of the kingdom of wickedness' (1QM XVII.5*b*–6*a*), while in the passage on the two spirits in the Community Rule (1QS III.13–IV.26) he is referred to as 'the spirit of injustice' (III.18*b*–19*a*) and as 'the angel of darkness' (III.20*b*–21*a*). The word 'Belial' occurs in the Old Testament, but its meaning is disputed. In the past it was often thought to mean 'worthlessness', but more recent suggestions have included 'confusion' and 'swallower' (referring to Sheol as swallower, and hence becoming a name for that realm and its ruler). It remains uncertain whether 'Belial' is used as a name in the Old Testament; but it is clearly used in the scrolls as the name of the leader of the forces of wickedness, and a variant form 'Beliar' occurs frequently in other writings of the period (cp. e.g. Jub. 1:20; T. Reub. 2:2; 2 Cor. 6:15 (NEB, 'Belial')). It was a common view of the time that the present age was under the control of Belial, but here it is 'Israel', i.e. non-Essene Judaism, that is specifically said to be dominated by him. *as God said through Isaiah…'Terror, and the pit, and the snare (are) upon you, O inhabitant of the land'*: the argument is supported by the quotation of Isa. 24:17 and the midrashic interpretation which is attached to it. *Its interpretation*: the Hebrew word (*pēšer*) is the same as that used in the biblical commentaries (e.g. 1QpHab) to introduce the pieces of interpretation; for the usage here cp. 1QpHab x.3. *(these are) the three nets of Belial…that he catches Israel in them and makes them appear to them as three kinds of righteousness*: the Isaianic passage is interpreted to refer to sins prevalent in contemporary society which were regarded by non-Essene Judaism as orthodox behaviour ('righteousness'); for the author they were in reality the means by which Belial exercised his control over Israel. *about which Levi the son of Jacob said*: no such words are found in the Testament of Levi, but we should no doubt see here an allusion to a tradition of the kind contained in the Testaments of the Twelve Patriarchs or the book of Jubilees. *The first is fornication, the second wealth, the third making the sanctuary unclean*: the three elements in the Isaiah passage, initially interpreted as 'the three nets of Belial', are now identified as specific sins. The first of these (fornication) is taken up at length in the following commentary (iv.19*b*–v.15*a*), and reference is also made there to the third (making the sanctuary unclean: see v.6*b*–7*a*) – but in such a way as to suggest that this was done at a secondary stage. No mention at all is made of the second (wealth; but cp. vi.15*b*–17*a*). It is this discrepancy which suggests that the midrash on Isa. 24:17 was either taken over from an existing source, or that at the very least the author was using a traditional piece of interpretation. *He who escapes…will be caught in the third*: in language obviously inspired by Isa. 24:18 the author emphasises the inescapable hold which these sins have on society. *escapes from*: literally 'climbs out of', the word used in Isa. 24:18.

iv.19*b*–v.15*a*. In a kind of commentary the author applies the midrash on Isa. 24:17 to conditions in contemporary society. He accuses those whom he attacks of four things: (1) they practise polygamy (iv.20*b*–v.6*a*); (2) they make the sanctuary unclean (v.6*b*–7*a*); (3) they marry their nieces (v.7*b*–11*a*); (4) they make their holy spirit unclean (v.11*b*–15*a*). The structure of this material is not entirely straightforward, but it seems most probable that the first and third of these accusations are presented as examples of 'fornication', the first of the nets of Belial. There is clear evidence that polygamy and marriage of a niece were practised by Jews at the time at which the Damascus Document was written, and the attack here is directed not at a particular group, but at Jewish society in general; polygamy and niece-marriage are presented as examples of the way in which non-Essene Judaism was under the control of Belial. In both cases the

practices are shown to be wrong because they are contrary to the
provisions of the Old Testament. The second accusation (making
the sanctuary unclean, the third of the nets of Belial) breaks the
connection between the two examples of fornication; it is also much
shorter than these and makes no reference to the Old Testament. For
these reasons it is possible that this accusation was inserted at a second
stage, or that it has been misplaced from after v.11a. The last accusation
is much more general in character; it ends with the warning: 'he who
approaches them shall not escape punishment'.

19b–20a. *The builders of the wall who went after 'Ṣaw'*: the application
of the midrash to contemporary society begins abruptly. Two biblical
passages are used to characterise those whom the author attacks. The
first is Ezek. 13:10: 'because they (the false prophets) have misled my
people, saying, "Peace", when there is no peace; and because, when
the people build a wall, these prophets daub it with whitewash' (RSV).
In Ezekiel a distinction is drawn between the people, who build the
wall, and the prophets, who mislead them, and the use of the expression
'the builders of the wall' in the Damascus Document serves to
characterise those attacked as a group that has been misled. It is used
here as a term for non-Essene Judaism; it cannot be regarded as the
title of a specific rival group within Judaism because the two main
accusations made against 'the builders of the wall' (polygamy and
niece-marriage) apply to Jewish society in general. The Ezekiel passage
is also drawn upon in VIII.12 = XIX.24b–25a and VIII.18 = XIX.31,
which indicates that the interpretation was traditional. The second
passage that is used is Hos. 5:11b, 'because he (Ephraim) was
determined to go after vanity' (NEB, 'doggedly pursuing what is
worthless'). The Hebrew word ṣaw ('vanity') has been left untranslated because of the way it has been used to introduce a reference to
a specific figure. '*Ṣaw' is a preacher of whom he said: 'They shall surely
preach'*: these words are most probably a secondary insertion: they have
the effect of making charges levelled against non-Essene Judaism in
general refer to a specific group under the leadership of an individual
called 'the preacher'. This figure is elsewhere called 'the preacher of
lies', 'the liar', 'the scoffer'; see above, pp. 23–4, and cp. 1.14b–15a;
VIII.13 = XIX.25b–26a. The biblical background to the use of the title
'the preacher of lies' is to be found in Mic. 2:6, 11; part of Mic. 2:6
is quoted in the present passage, but not in the form known from the
Massoretic text.

IV.20b–v.6a. *they will be caught twice in fornication: by taking two wives during their lifetime*: the first example of 'fornication' is apparently polygamy, although the accusation is drawn more widely than this. The possessive pronoun in 'during their lifetime' is masculine, and the phrase is most naturally taken as referring to the husbands, not the wives; from this it appears that what is attacked here is the whole idea of a man having a second wife during his lifetime, whether through polygamy, or through a second marriage after the divorce or death of a first wife. But from what follows (the quotation of Deut. 17:17 and the reference to David) it seems clear that polygamy is primarily in mind. *whereas the principle of creation is 'male and female he created them'*: Three passages (Gen. 1:27; 7:9; Deut. 17:17) are quoted to show that having more than one wife is contrary to the provisions of the law. *As for David, he had not read the sealed book of the law*: the fact that David, remembered as the ideal king, should have had several wives (2 Sam. 3:2–5; 5:13–16) was clearly an embarrassment for the author, and he offers an excuse for him. *which was in the ark*: cp. Exod. 25:16, 21; 40:20; Deut. 10:2, 5; see also Deut. 31:26. *for it was not opened in Israel from the day that Eleazar and Joshua and the elders died*: for the tradition that Israel's apostasy only began after the death of Joshua and the elders see Josh. 24:29–31; Judges 2:7–10. The death of Eleazar is mentioned in close proximity to the first of these passages in Josh. 24:33; he was perhaps mentioned here because of his importance as the supposed ancestor of Zadok (see below, p. 106). *because they worshipped Ashtoreth*: cp. Judg. 2:13. *until the coming of Zadok*: Zadok is mentioned for the first time in 2 Sam. 8:17, i.e. after David is said to have married several wives. *And the deeds of David were cancelled, except the murder of Uriah, and God allowed them to him*: the translation is uncertain.

v.6b–7a. *Also they make the sanctuary unclean*: most naturally taken as referring to the temple-priests, although this does not mean that the other accusations are directed specifically at priests; cp. 1QpHab XII.7b–9a. *they do not keep separate...but lie with a woman who sees the blood of her discharge*: an allusion to Lev. 15:19, cp. 15:31. Underlying this accusation are disputes about the interpretation of the laws relating to the ritual uncleanness of a woman after menstruation. A similar accusation is made in Ps. Sol. 8:13.

> They trampled the altar of the Lord, *coming straight* from all
>   *kinds of* uncleanness,
> And with menstrual blood they defiled the sacrifices,
>   as *though they were* common flesh.

7b–11a. And each man takes his brother's daughter or his sister's daughter (as wife): the structure of the material is not entirely straightforward, but niece-marriage is probably best taken as a second example of 'fornication' (IV.20), the Hebrew word (*zenūt*) here meaning marriage within the prohibited degrees of kinship (cp. Lev. 18:6–18). *whereas Moses said: 'You shall not approach your mother's sister; she is a blood-relation of your mother'*: Lev. 18:13, but in a form slightly different from the Massoretic text. *The law of incest was written for men, but it applies also to women*: the law expressly forbids a man to marry his aunt, and by analogy a woman may not marry her uncle. Niece-marriage is thus shown to be contrary to the law. *has intercourse with*: literally 'uncovers the nakedness of'.

11b–15a. Also they have made their holy spirit unclean: cp. VII.3b–4a and the Hebrew (not the Greek) Testament of Naphtali 10:9, 'Blessed is the man who does not defile the holy spirit of God which has been put and breathed into him.' 'Holy spirit' is used here to refer to the force within a man which enables him to make moral decisions. *and with a blaspheming tongue they have opened their mouth against the statutes of the covenant of God, saying: 'They are not right'*: defiling the holy spirit is linked here with the rejection of 'the statutes of the covenant of God', i.e. the law as interpreted by the Essene movement (cp. xx.11b–12). These words suggest that, at least at the time to which this material refers, there was some public knowledge of Essene beliefs and perhaps an open attempt to win converts; but see the comment on 1QS VIII.11b–12a. An accusation similar to the one in the Damascus Document occurs in 1QH IV.16b–18a, and for the expression 'a blaspheming tongue' cp. 1QS IV.11. *All of them are kindlers of fire...their eggs are vipers' eggs*: phrases drawn from Isa. 50:11 and Isa. 59:5 are used to characterise the attitude of those who reject Essene teaching; the latter passage is also used in 1QH II.27b–28a. *He who approaches them shall not escape punishment; the more he does so, the more guilty he will become, unless he is pressed*: those for whom this material was written were apparently under some pressure not to join the movement; these words form a warning of the inevitability of punishment for those who remained associated with non-Essene Judaism. For the author salvation was only to be found within the Essene movement (cp. III.16b–20a).

GOD'S REMEMBRANCE OF THE COVENANT

v.15 For already in former times God visited [16] their deeds, and his anger was kindled against their actions. For they are a people without understanding; [17] they are a nation that lacks counsel, inasmuch as there is no understanding in them. For in former times Moses and Aaron arose [18] by the hand of the prince of lights, and Belial raised up Jannes and [19] his brother by his schemes when Israel was saved for the first time.

[20]And in the time of the desolation of the land movers of the boundary arose and led Israel astray, [21] and the land was made desolate because they preached rebellion against the commandments of God (given) through Moses and [VI.1] through the holy anointed ones; and they prophesied lies to turn Israel away from following [2] God. But God remembered the covenant with the men of former times, and he raised up from Aaron men of understanding, and from Israel [3] men of wisdom, and made them hear (his voice). And they dug the well: the well which the princes dug, which the nobles of the people laid open [4] with the sceptre. The well is the law, and those who dug it are [5] the converts of Israel who went out from the land of Judah and sojourned in the land of Damascus. [6] God called all of them princes because they sought him, and their ⟨re⟩nown was not disputed [7] by the mouth of anyone. And the sceptre is the interpreter of the law of whom [8] Isaiah said: 'He produces a tool for his work.' And the nobles of the people are [9] those who come to lay open the well with the staffs with which the ruler decreed [10] that they should walk during all the time of wickedness, and without which they will find nothing, until there appears [11] the one who shall teach righteousness at the end of days.

In iv.12b–v.15a the author attempted to show that non-Essene Judaism was under the control of Belial, and warned that those who associated with non-Essene Judaism would not escape punishment. The warning is now reinforced by a reminder that God had already punished Israel in the past as a nation that lacked understanding (v.15b–17a). This point is further developed in v.20–vi.2a (v.17b–19 appear to be secondary); false prophets had led Israel astray, and in consequence 'the land was made desolate'. The author refers here to the desolation of the land at the time of the exile, and this reference provides the opportunity for him to describe once more the events which in his view had brought Israel's state of exile to an end, namely, the emergence of the Essene

movement (vi.2b–11a); this passage, which is similar to iii.12b–iv.4a,
brings the section or source that began in ii.14 to a conclusion by
reminding those addressed of the group with which God now had his
dealings.

v.15b–17a. *For already in former times God visited their deeds*: God's
visitation is here clearly in order to punish his people; contrast i.7a and
see the comment on that passage. In the light of line 21 it would appear
that the author particularly had in mind the punishment of Israel at
the time of the exile. *their deeds...their actions*: the possessive 'their'
refers back ultimately to 'the builders of the wall' (iv.19), but the
author is thinking of Israel's guilty actions in the past. *and his anger was
kindled*: see the comment on i.21b–ii.1. *For they are a people without
understanding...there is no understanding in them*: Isa. 27:11 and Deut.
32:28 are used to characterise Israel in the past and to explain why
God's anger was kindled against her.

17b–19. This passage is probably secondary. It breaks the thread of
the argument inasmuch as it does not obviously explain what is said
in lines 15b–17a in the way that v.20–vi.2a does. Furthermore, it is
characterised by a dualism – the contrast between the activities of the
prince of lights and of Belial (cp. 1QS iii.13–iv.26) – which is alien to
the context. *Moses and Aaron arose by the hand of the prince of lights*: cp.
1QS iii.20. *and Belial raised up Jannes and his brother*: Jannes and Jambres
were the names given in later tradition to the Egyptian magicians,
unnamed in the Old Testament (see Exod. 7:11), who opposed Moses
and Aaron; they are mentioned in 2 Tim. 3:8 as typifying opposition
to the truth. A considerable body of legends grew up about them.
According to one Jewish strand of tradition Jannes and Jambres
professed conversion and accompanied Israel in the exodus; but their
conversion was insincere, and they incited the people to make the golden
calf. It is, however, not clear how far this wider tradition is in mind
here because the passage merely draws a contrast between Moses and
Aaron, who acted under the inspiration of the prince of lights, and
Jannes and Jambres, who acted under the inspiration of Belial. This
passage was perhaps inserted here (see above) as a comment on Israel's
past because Jannes and his brother were seen to typify opposition to
the true representatives of God, and this theme is an important element
in the context. The effect of the insertion of this passage is to make
a link back to the reference to Belial in iv.12b–13a. *when Israel was saved
for the first time*: the deliverance at the time of the exodus.

v.20–vi.2a. The argument of v.15b–17a is developed further: Israel was led astray by false prophets, and this was the cause of the desolation of the land at the time of the exile. This passage is comparable to III. 9b–12a. *the time of the desolation of the land*: the period culminating in the exile. *movers of the boundary arose*: an allusion to Hos. 5:10, also used in XIX.15b–16a = VIII.3; cp. Deut. 19:14; 27:17. Here the 'movers of the boundary' are the false prophets. *and led Israel astray*: possibly an allusion to Jer. 23:13, part of a passage (Jer. 23:9–40) dealing with the false prophets. *and the land was made desolate*: cp. Ezek. 19:7 (NEB, 'the land...was aghast'); the Hebrew root (*šāman*) is the same as that used in III.10 with reference to the exilic period. (The word translated 'desolation' in v.20 is from a different Hebrew root.) *because they preached rebellion against the commandments of God*: cp. Deut. 13:5 and the repeated accusation in II.16b–III.12a, 'they did not keep the commandments'. *(given) through Moses and through the holy anointed ones*: the 'anointed ones' are the prophets (cp. II.12 and 1QS 1.2b–3a). As frequently in the Old Testament, the exile is presented as the consequence of Israel's failure to heed the word of God given by his prophets; cp. e.g. 2 Kings 17:13–14; 2 Chron. 36:15–16. *and they prophesied lies*: cp. Jer. 14:14; 23:25.

VI.2b–11a. As in earlier passages (1.3–8a; III.9b–17a) the reference to the exile is followed immediately by a passage relating the origins of the Essene movement and specifically here the settlement at Qumran; for the theological pattern see the comment on 1.5b–8a. The present passage is in fact similar to III.12b–IV.4a. Its core consists of a midrashic interpretation of Num. 21:18, which is based on the symbolism of the well as the law, and as such it is known as the Well midrash. The passage has something of a self-contained character about it and may have been taken over by the author from an already existing source. Its function, as the conclusion of II.14–VI.11a, was to remind those addressed of the group with which God now had his dealings.

2b–3a. But God remembered the covenant with the men of former times: the covenant is the Mosaic covenant, and the founding of the movement is presented as the fulfilment of Lev.26:45, on which this passage is based; in 1.4 the preservation of a remnant at the time of the exile is attributed to God's remembrance of the covenant. *and he raised up from Aaron...from Israel*: from the priests and the laity; see on 1.7b–8a. *men of understanding...men of wisdom*: in contrast to Israel of the past which lacked understanding, cp. v.16b–17a. The Hebrew word for 'to understand' (*bīn*) is used in 1.1 and II.14, where those to whom the Damascus Document is addressed are urged to 'consider'

or 'understand' the deeds of God. *and made them hear (his voice)*: the
founding of the movement was linked to a revelation from God; cp.
iii.13*b*–14*a*.

3*b*–4*a*. *And they dug the well*: cp. iii.16, 'and they dug a well of
abundant waters'; as in the earlier passage (iii.12*b*–iv.4*a*) the revelation
from God consists of a particular (i.e. Essene) interpretation of the
meaning of the law. *the well which the princes dug...with the sceptre*: the
symbolism of the well as the law is given scriptural authority by the
quotation of Num. 21:18. There then follows in lines 4*b*–11*a* a
midrashic interpretation of each of the elements in this passage.

4*b*–5. *those who dug it are the converts of Israel*: the expression translated
'the converts of Israel' (literally 'those who (re)turn of Israel') is
ambiguous. In addition to the present passage it occurs in iv.2 (part
of a passage which we have seen is similar to the present one) and
viii.16 = xix.29 ('the converts of Israel who turn aside from the way
of the people'); a related expression, 'those who turn from transgression', is used in ii.5 and xx.17. The fact that in the last four passages
the '(re)turning' clearly has a religious significance suggests that in the
present passage and in iv.2 'those who (re)turn of Israel' should be
understood as 'the converts of Israel'. But some scholars have translated
the expression as 'the returnees of Israel' and have taken it to refer to
Jews who had returned – in the literal sense – from Babylon to
Palestine. The Hebrew expression, differently interpreted, could also
mean 'the captivity of Israel'. *who went out from the land of Judah and
sojourned in the land of Damascus*: the meaning of these words is also
surrounded with uncertainty. 'The land of Damascus' is mentioned,
in addition to the present passage, in vi.19; viii.21 = xix.34; xx.12.
Apart from these passages we have no evidence to connect the Essenes
with the Damascus region, and it does not seem likely that 'the land
of Damascus' is to be understood literally. Instead it has often been
thought that the expression is a symbolic name for Qumran which was
based on a particular understanding of Amos 5:26–7; see the
interpretation of the Amos passage in vii.13*b*–21*a*, in which 'Damascus'
(line 19) clearly seems to signify Qumran. However, this view, which
is the one followed here, is not without difficulty. Because Qumran
lies in the territory of Judah, it seems contradictory to speak of going
out from the land of Judah to sojourn in the land of Damascus if the
latter is a symbolic name for Qumran. But it seems that 'the land of
Judah' is used here (and in iv.3) in an imprecise way to refer to
Jerusalem and its immediate environs. Alternatively it has been
suggested that 'the land of Judah' is a symbolic designation of the

prince-priest class of Jerusalem and its adherents; on this view there is no contradiction of the kind mentioned above because the passage refers to the separation of those who settled at Qumran ('the land of Damascus') from the prince-priest class in Jerusalem ('the land of Judah'). A quite different suggestion has also been made, namely that 'Damascus' is a symbolic name for Babylon. On this view the origins of the Essene movement are to be traced to the exiles who went out from the land of Judah to sojourn in Babylon, although it is not clear when exactly the movement would have come into existence. The passage may then be understood to refer to the exiles amongst whom the movement arose, not as 'the converts of Israel', but as 'the returnees of Israel' (thus indicating that the members of the movement had now returned from Babylon to Palestine), or as 'the captivity of Israel' (see above). Such an understanding of this passage, and of the origins of the Essene movement, is not impossible, but there is insufficient evidence at the moment to make it appear convincing (see further above, pp. 8, 15).

6–7a. *because they sought him*: cp. 1.10.

7b–8a. *And the sceptre is the interpreter of the law*: the explanation is based on the fact that the Hebrew word *meḥōqēq*, translated here as 'sceptre', means both 'ruler', the one who prescribes (Hebrew *ḥāqaq*) the laws, and 'sceptre', the staff carried by a ruler; for the former meaning see Deut. 33:21; Isa. 33:22 (NEB, 'the LORD our law-giver'), for the latter see Num. 21:18; Gen. 49:10 (NEB, 'nor the staff from his descendants'). The author is playing on the two meanings of the word, and he continues this word-play in line 9. The individual called here 'the interpreter of the law' is apparently the same as the one called 'the teacher of righteousness' in 1.11; cp. 1QpHab ii.8–10a; vii.1–5a, where the teacher is the one to whom God made known the true meaning of the words of the prophets. It is interesting to observe that whereas CD 1.3–12 and the present passage assign a decisive role in the history of the Essene movement to the 'teacher' or 'interpreter', no reference is made to him in iii.12b–iv.4a. The title 'the interpreter of the law' is used of a future, i.e. a messianic, figure in vii.18 and in 4QFlor 1–3 i.11. *of whom Isaiah said: 'He produces a tool for his work'*: part of Isa. 54:16 (NEB, 'and forge weapons each for its purpose'), quoted in a sense quite different from its original meaning. The quotation serves to indicate that the interpreter of the law was commissioned by God; cp. 1.11, '(God) raised up for them a teacher of righteousness'.

8b–11a. *And the nobles of the people are those who come to lay open the well*: those who joined the movement after it had come into being;

the distinction made here between the original members (lines 4*b*–5)
and those who joined later is comparable to the one made in IV.2*b*–4*a*.
with the staffs with which the ruler decreed that they should walk: a
continuation of the word-play of lines 7*b*–8*a*, based, like the earlier
passage, on the reference to 'the sceptre' in line 4. The word translated
here as 'staff' (or 'sceptre', *m*ᵉ*ḥōqᵉqāh*) is a variant form of
*m*ᵉ*ḥōqēq* = 'sceptre'. It is related in Hebrew to *m*ᵉ*ḥōqēq* = 'ruler', and
the verb 'to decree' (or 'to prescribe') is from the same Hebrew root
(*ḥāqaq*); see the comment on lines 7*b*–8*a*. But 'the staffs' (*m*ᵉ*ḥōqᵉqōth*)
also suggests in Hebrew the word for 'statutes' (*ḥuqqōth*). The point
being made by means of the word-play is that those who joined the
movement after it had come into being were under an obligation to
obey the law as it was defined by 'the interpreter'. The word-play
could be partly made apparent by the translation 'with the sceptres with
which "the sceptre" decreed that they should walk'. *during all the time
of wickedness*: the present age, which was believed to be under the
control of the forces of evil, and which would be brought to an end
by the intervention of God to establish his rule; other expressions used
to describe this age are 'the reign of Belial' (cp. e.g. 1QS 1.18*a*) and
'the kingdom of wickedness' (1QM XVII.5*b*–6*a*). *and without which they
will find nothing*: a final warning to those hesitating to join the
movement. *until there appears the one who shall teach righteousness at the
end of days*: the expression 'the one who shall teach righteousness' is
similar to, but not identical with, the one regularly translated 'the
teacher of righteousness'. Here, however, the reference is to a messianic
figure, perhaps to the figure elsewhere called 'the messiah of Aaron';
see the comment on 1QS IX.9*b*–11. The passage is based on Hos. 10.12,
NEB 'till he comes and gives you just measure of rain', but which could
be translated 'till he comes and teaches you righteousness'.

DUTIES AND A WARNING

The abruptness of the transition in line 11 suggests that a new section
begins at this point; it apparently ends at VIII.2*a*. The purpose of this
section is to provide both a summary of the duties of the members of
the movement (VI.11*b*–VII.9*a*; cp. XIX.1–5*a*) and a warning of the
consequences of disobedience (VII.9*b*–VIII.2*a*; cp. XIX. 5*b*–14).

A SUMMARY OF THE DUTIES OF MEMBERS

VI.11 None of those brought into the covenant 12 shall enter the sanctuary to kindle fire upon his altar in vain. They shall be those who close 13 the door, of whom God said: 'Would that one among you would close my door, that you might not kindle fire upon my altar 14 in vain!' But they shall be careful to act according to the exact interpretation of the law during the time of wickedness;

to separate themselves 15 from the sons of the pit;

to keep away from the unclean wealth of wickedness (acquired) by vowing or devoting 16 or from the wealth of the sanctuary; (this is) 'to rob the poor of his people, to make widows their spoil, 17 and they murder the fatherless';

to make a distinction between the unclean and the clean, and to teach the difference between 18 the holy and the common;

to keep the sabbath day according to its exact rules, and the feasts, 19 and the fast-day according to the finding of those who entered the new covenant in the land of Damascus;

20 to set aside the holy things according to the exact rules about them;

to love each man his brother 21 as himself;

to help the poor, the needy, and the proselyte;

to seek the well-being of one VII.1 another and not to act unfaithfully towards a blood-relation;

to keep from fornication 2 according to the rule;

to reprove one another according to the commandment and not to bear a grudge 3 from one day to the next;

to separate themselves from all kinds of uncleanness according to the rule about them, and for each man not to contaminate 4 his holy spirit according to the separation which God made for them.

All those who walk 5 by these (rules) in perfect holiness according to all the instructions ⟨of the covenant⟩ – the covenant of God

Manuscript A	Manuscript B
is an assurance for them 6 that they will live for a thousand generations.	XIX.1 is an assurance for them that they will live for thousands of generations, as it is written:

Manuscript A

Manuscript B

'(He) keeps covenant and
steadfast love [2] with those who
love ⟨him⟩ and keep his
commandments for a thousand
generations.'

And if they live in camps
according to the rule of the
land, and take [7] wives, and
beget children, they shall walk
in accordance with the law and
according to the rule [8] of the
instructions, according to the
rule of the law which says:
'between a man and his wife,
and between a father [9] and his
son'.

And if they live in camps
according to the rule [3] of the
land which existed from ancient
times, and take wives according
to the usage of the law, and
beget children, [4] they shall walk
in accordance with the law and
according to the rule of the
instructions, according to the
rule of the law [5] which says:
'between a man and his wife,
and between a father and his
son'.

This section begins with a prohibition on visiting the temple
(vi.11*b*–14*a*) and continues with a series of twelve injunctions –
according to the arrangement followed here – that summarise the
duties of the members of the movement (vi.14*b*–vii.4*a*); these duties
are set out in much greater detail in the collection of laws (columns
ix–xvi). There follows a promise to those who observe the injunctions
(vii.4*b*–6*a*; xix.1–2*a*), and this is balanced by the warning that begins
in vii.9*b* = xix.5*b*. The passage relating to married members
(vii.6*b*–9*a* = xix.2*b*–5*a*) may be out of place. The influence of the
so-called Holiness Code (Lev. 17–26) may be discerned in a number of
places in the series of injunctions.

vi.11*b*–14*a*. Despite some uncertainties about the translation, this
passage seems to constitute a clear prohibition on visiting the temple.
This is consonant with the view of v.6*b*–7 and 1QpHab xii.7*b*–9*a* that
the temple had been defiled. But it stands in sharp contrast with the
statements of the collection of laws, which envisage not only that the
members of the movement would send offerings to the temple, but
also that they themselves would offer sacrifices in the temple

(XI.17b–21a). This contradiction is perhaps to be explained by the assumption that the present passage and the collection of laws reflect different stages in the evolution of the beliefs and attitudes of the movement. See also the comment on 1QS IX.3–6. *to kindle fire upon his altar in vain*: based on Mal.1:10; the biblical passage is then quoted.

14b. The first injunction is quite general and serves as an introduction to the ones which follow. *to act according to the exact interpretation of the law*: the law as it was defined within the movement, cp. IV.8. In the injunctions which follow, the importance of observing the law exactly as it was defined by the movement – and hence not in accordance with practice outside – is several times emphasised: cp. VI.18, 'according to its exact rules', and similarly VI.20 – in both cases the same Hebrew word that is translated here 'the exact interpretation'; VI.19 'according to the finding of those who entered the new covenant in the land of Damascus'; VII.2, 3 'according to the rule'; VII.3 'according to the commandment'. *during the time of wickedness*: see the comment on VI.10.

14c–15a. *to separate themselves*: for the obligation to keep separate cp. 1QS V.10b–20a and see the comment on that passage. *from the sons of the pit*: i.e. of Sheol, conceived of as the abode of evil (cp. 1QH III.18, 26). But the translation 'the men of destruction' would also be possible. According to CD XIII.14–15a those who joined the movement were forbidden to trade with the sons of the pit except for cash.

15b–17a. *to keep away from the unclean wealth of wickedness (acquired) by vowing or devoting*: the practice whereby a man could avoid using his money to help others by declaring that he had dedicated it to the temple; cp. Mark 7:10–13 and XVI.14b–15, 'Let [no] man consecrate the food of his m[outh to Go]d, for it is as he said, "They hunt each other with a votive offering"' (Mic. 7:2). (In the passage quoted from Micah the author plays on the meaning of the word *ḥerem*, which can be both 'net', as in Micah itself, and 'votive-offering'.) *or from the wealth of the sanctuary*: misuse of money belonging to the temple, but the precise nature of the abuse is unclear. (*this is*) '*to rob the poor of his people…and they murder the fatherless*': Isa. 10:2 combined with Ps. 94:6 is quoted to show why the acquisition of money in the ways mentioned was illegitimate and hence forbidden to members of the movement.

17b–18a. *to make a distinction…between the holy and the common*: based on Ezek. 22:26 and Lev. 10:10. The same injunction is also given in XII.19b–20a.

18b–19. *to keep the sabbath day*: rules for the observance of the sabbath are given in some detail in X.14–XI.18. *and the feasts*: the religious festivals. *and the fast-day*: probably the day of atonement, the day on which Jews were to 'mortify' themselves (cp. Lev. 16:29, 31 and 1QpHab XI.6*b*–8*a*). *according to the finding of those who entered the new covenant in the land of Damascus*: i.e. in accordance with the calendar followed by the movement which, according to III.13*b*–14, was revealed by God to the members when the movement was founded. As we noted, observance of this calendar was an important distinguishing mark of the movement. *the new covenant*: an allusion to Jer. 31.31; cp. VIII.21*b* = XIX.33*b*–34*a*; XX.12. *the land of Damascus*: assumed here to be a symbolic name for Qumran; see the comment on VI.4*b*–5.

20*a*. *to set aside the holy things*: the verb 'to set aside' is used as a technical term for the offering of a cake made from the first kneading of dough in Num. 15:17–21, and for the offering of tithes in Num. 18:19, 25–32. Lines 11*b*–14*a* appear to forbid visiting the temple, but despite this the proper offerings were still to be made. Josephus reports that although the Essenes did not offer sacrifices, they did send offerings to the temple (*Ant.* XVIII.1.5(19)), and this practice is presupposed in CD XI.18*b*–21*a*; it is perhaps the sending of offerings that is envisaged here.

20*b*–21*a*. *to love each man his brother as himself*: based on Lev. 19:18; cp. Matt. 19:19.

21*b*. *to help the poor, the needy, and the proselyte*: based on Ezek. 16:49, to which allusion is also made in the more detailed law of XIV.14–16*a*.

VI.21*c*–VII.1*a*. *and not to act unfaithfully towards a blood-relation*: probably a reference to any kind of betrayal of family obligations.

VII.1*b*–2*a*. *to keep from fornication according to the rule*: in IV.19*b*–V.11*a* polygamy and niece-marriage were condemned as examples of 'fornication' (IV.17, 20; see above, p. 41). It appears that 'fornication' is likewise used here to refer to marriages of a kind which, although permitted in the Judaism of that time, were prohibited for members of the movement. (The text has 'from prostitutes'; the translation 'from fornication' follows a widely adopted minor correction.)

VII.2*b*–3*a*. *to reprove one another…and not to bear a grudge*: based on Lev. 19:17–18, to which reference is also made in the more detailed law of IX.2–8*a* and in 1QS V.25*b*–VI.1*ab*.

VII.3*b*–4*a*. *to separate themselves from all kinds of uncleanness*: the uncleanness caused by not observing the movement's dietary laws; these are set out in XII.11*b*–15*a*, cp. Lev. 11. *and for each man not to contaminate his holy spirit according to the separation which God made for* *them*: probably based on Lev. 20:25: cp. 11:43 and XII.11b; for the phrase 'to contaminate his holy spirit' see also v.11b.

VII.4b–6a; XIX.1–2a. (Manuscript B (see above, p. 13) begins abruptly in the middle of this section; translations of both texts are given in parallel.) A promise to those who observe the injunctions; a similar promise, forming the end of a section in columns IX–XVI, occurs at XIV.1b–2: 'All those who walk by these (rules) – the covenant of God is an assurance for them that they will be saved from all the snares of the pit, but the foolish will be punished'. *the covenant of God is an assurance for them*: possibly based on Ps. 89:28b. Manuscript B begins with 'is an assurance'. *that they will live for thousands of generations* (B): little is said in the Damascus Document about the future destiny of faithful members of the movement apart from the statement of the belief that they are destined for eternal life; see the comment on III.19–20a. On the basis of the wording of Deut. 7:9, which is quoted, this belief is here expressed as life for thousands of generations; Deut. 7:9 is also used in XX.21b–22a. In manuscript A some words have been omitted by mistake.

VII.6b–9a; XIX.2b–5a. This passage is intrusive in the context and may well be secondary; it breaks the connection between the promise which ends in VII.6a = XIX.2a and the warning which begins in VII.9b = XIX.5b. It deals with the position of the families of married members and indicates that those who become members of the movement through marriage or birth were also required to obey the Mosaic law and the movement's own regulations. The passage was perhaps inserted here by an editor for the sake of completeness. *And if they live in camps*: the use of the word 'camps' to refer to the towns and villages in which the Essenes lived (see above, pp. 14–15) recalls the circumstances of Israel in the wilderness; in the narratives about the wilderness period there are frequent references to the 'camp' (e.g. Exod. 16:13) or 'camps' (e.g. Num. 2:17) of the Israelites. The word, in both the singular and the plural, is used frequently in columns IX–XVI and in the War Scroll. *according to the rule of the land which existed from ancient times* (B): the meaning is something like 'as men do'. *and take wives according to the usage of the law* (B): cp. Gen. 2:24. *they shall walk*: i.e. the wives and children. *in acccordance with the law*: i.e. the Mosaic law. *and according to the rule of the instructions*: the movement's own regulations; cp. the reference to 'the instructions' in VII.5. (The word translated 'rule' is not the same as that translated 'rule' in the immediately preceding and following occurrences.) Some scholars emend the text to 'and according to the rule about binding obligations'

and link this passage to what is said about vows in XVI.6b–12. This
would fit the immediately following quotation of Num. 30:16, but
would give the passage a narrower application than is suggested here;
it is not clear that the emendation is correct. *according to the rule of the
law which says: 'between a man and his wife, and between a father and his
son'*: the quotation of Num. 30:16 implies a reference to all that is said
about the vows and oaths of women in Num. 30 and serves as a
reminder of the law governing vows made by wives and daughters.
However, the form of the quotation differs from that in the Massoretic
text, which has 'between a father and his daughter'. Unless this is just
a mistake, the form of the quotation in the Damascus Document may
have been deliberately adopted in order to include male children within
the terms of the law about vows.

A WARNING

Manuscript A	Manuscript B
VII.9 But all those who refuse will be paid the reward of the wicked when God visits the earth, 10 when the word comes to pass which is written in the words of Isaiah the son of Amoz, the prophet, 11 who said: 'There will come upon you and upon your people and upon your father's house days such as 12 have ⟨not⟩ come since the day that Ephraim broke away from Judah.' When the two houses of Israel separated, 13 it was Ephraim who broke away from Judah. All the apostates were delivered up to the sword, but those who held fast 14 escaped to the land of the north, as he said: 'I will exile	XIX.5 But all those who reject the commandments 6 and the statutes will be paid the reward of the wicked when God visits the earth, 7 when the word comes to pass which is written ⟨as he said⟩ through the prophet Zechariah: 'O sword, awake against 8 my shepherd

Manuscript A

the Sikkuth of your king [15] and
the Kiyyun of your images from
my tent to Damascus.' The
books of the law are the
booth [16] of the king, as he said:
'I will raise up the booth of
David which is fallen.' The
king [17] is the assembly. And the
bases of the images ⟨...⟩ are
the books of the prophets [18]
whose words Israel despised.
The star is the interpreter of the
law [19] who will come to
Damascus, as it is written: 'A
star shall come forth out of
Jacob, and a comet shall
rise [20] out of Israel.' The comet
is the prince of the whole
congregation, and when he
appears he shall beat down [21] all
the sons of Seth. These escaped
at the time of the first
visitation,[VIII.1] but the apostates
were delivered up to the sword.
Such shall be the case of all
those who enter his covenant
but [2] do not hold fast to these;
they will be visited for
destruction at the hand of Belial.

Manuscript B

and against the man who is my
companion', says God. 'Strike
the shepherd, and the flock will
be scattered, [9] and I will turn
my hand towards the little
ones.' Those who heed him are
the poor of the flock. [10] These
will escape at the time of the
visitation, but the remainder
will be handed over to the
sword when the messiah [11] of
Aaron and Israel comes, as it
was at the time of the first
visitation about which he
said [12] through Ezekiel: 'A
mark shall be put on the
foreheads of those who groan
and lament.' [13] But the
remainder were delivered up to
the avenging sword of the
covenant.

Such shall be the case of all who
enter [14] his covenant but do not
hold fast to these, the statutes;
they will be visited for
destruction at the hand of Belial.

This passage constitutes a warning of the punishment which awaited
those outside the movement who rejected its laws (cp. VII.9*b* = XIX.5*b*–
6*a*) and those inside who were not steadfast in observing them (cp.
VIII.1*b*–2*a* = XIX.13*b*–14). The warning counterbalances the promise
of VII.4*b*–6*a*, XIX.1–2*a*, but it has been developed at greater length, and

it includes in the B-text an assurance that faithful members would escape punishment (xix.10). This section, as part of a document that in its final form was probably intended for use at the annual ceremony of the renewal of the covenant, will have served the purpose of encouraging both those on the verge of joining the movement not to hesitate and those who were already members not to waver in their observance of its laws. The pattern of promise followed by warning is similar to the pattern of promise and warning in Lev. 26 at the end of the so-called Holiness Code (Lev. 17–26) and in Deut. 28 at the end of Deuteronomy.

There are significant differences between the A-text and the B in this section. Thus whereas in both texts a comparison is drawn between former and future punishment, in the A-text this is developed by the use of quotations from Isaiah, Amos and Numbers, but in the B-text by the use of quotations from Zechariah and Ezekiel. A number of scholars have argued that the original text is substantially represented by vii.9*b*–13*a* (A) plus xix.7*b*–14 (B), and this view is followed here. In the B-text the quotation from Isaiah and the comment thereon was lost by a simple mistake. In the A-text a midrash based on passages from Amos and Numbers was inserted at a secondary stage in place of the original text which made use of passages from Zechariah and Ezekiel.

vii.9*b*. *But all those who refuse*: it is not clear whether this or 'But all those who reject the commandments and the statutes' (B) forms the original text ('refuse' and 'reject' represent the same word in Hebrew); in either case a contrast is intended with 'All those who walk by these (rules) in perfect holiness according to all the instructions ⟨of the covenant⟩' (vii.4*b*–5*a*). The warning here appears to be directed primarily at those on the verge of joining the movement who hesitated to commit themselves. *when God visits the earth*: i.e. in order to act as judge at the end of this age, but here particularly in order to punish the wicked. For the verb 'to visit' used with reference to God see above, p. 21.

vii.10–13*a*. The threat of future punishment is reinforced by the quotation of Isa. 7:17, here understood as a prophecy of punishment (see below), and by a comment intended to draw out the significance of the passage. The B-text follows the A-text as far as the middle of xix.7, but it appears that the copyist of manuscript B then omitted several lines by mistake. *There will come upon you...days such as have* ⟨*not*⟩ *come since the day that Ephraim broke away from Judah*: Isa. 7:17, also used in [xiii.23]–xiv.1. In the context of the book of Isaiah it is not clear whether these words represent a threat or a promise; only the addition at the end of the verse of 'the king of Assyria' (see the NEB footnote) makes them unambiguously a threat. Within the Damascus Document the prophecy is clearly understood as a threat of punishment referring to the contemporary situation. *When the two houses of Israel separated, it was Ephraim who broke away from Judah*: these words were apparently addressed to those who were in danger of being disheartened by the comparative weakness and insignificance of the Essene movement. 'Ephraim' and 'Judah' are the northern and southern kingdoms, but here they may also be understood to represent those outside the movement and those within it; cp. the use of 'house of Judah' as a symbolic name for the movement in IV.11. At the time of the division of the kingdom (cp. 1 Kings 12) it was the numerically strong and powerful north ('Ephraim') that was in the wrong, and by implication the same was true in the author's day of Judaism outside the Essene movement. *All the apostates were delivered up to the sword*: an allusion in the first instance to the punishment of the northern kingdom in 722 BC, but the subsequent quotation of Ezek. 9:4 in XIX.11*b*–12 suggests that the destruction of the southern kingdom in 587 BC was also in mind. The implication in any case is clear: as God had punished the apostates in the past, so he would do again.

XIX.7*b*–11*a*. The reference to the 'sword' in VII.13 (A) leads naturally into the quotation of Zech.13:7 in manuscript B. This prophecy of judgement, like Isa. 7:17, was taken to have a contemporary reference and serves to reinforce further the warning of punishment; but the last part of the verse was understood in a positive sense as an assurance of salvation. An interpretative comment follows (lines 9*b*–11*a*), just as in the case of the quotation of Isa. 7:17. For manuscript A see below. *Strike the shepherd, and the flock will be scattered*: this part of Zech. 13:7 is quoted in Matt. 26:31; Mark 14:27, where Jesus is 'the shepherd'. In the Damascus Document 'the shepherd' is not identified, but may perhaps have been understood to represent the leaders of non-Essene Judaism. *and I will turn my hand towards the little ones*: whether the 'little ones' are sheep or 'shepherd boys' (so NEB), in the Massoretic text these words continue the prophecy of judgement (hence 'against the little ones'). But in the Damascus Document the comment which follows indicates that the turning of God's hand was understood to signify divine protection, and the 'little ones' now represent the members of the movement. *Those who heed him are the poor of the flock*: a comment, perhaps originally a marginal gloss, specifying who belongs to the movement; 'him' is most probably God, and 'the poor of the flock' is used, like 'the little ones', to refer to the members. The comment has been formed from two phrases taken from Zech. 11:11 (only apparent in the Hebrew). *These will escape at the time of the visitation*: an assurance of salvation for members of the movement. *but the remainder*: Jews outside the movement. *will be handed over to the sword when the messiah of Aaron and Israel comes*: the divine visitation is linked to the coming of 'the messiah of Aaron and Israel'. The expectation is apparently of a single messianic figure, and in this the Damascus Document has a different view from that of other Qumran documents, such as the Community Rule or 4QTestimonia, in which there is the expectation of two messiahs; see the comment on 1QS IX.9*b*–11. In the Damascus Document, where the same or a similar expression also occurs in XII.23–XIII.1; XIV.19; XX.1, the Hebrew is admittedly ambiguous and could also be translated 'the messiah of Aaron and (the messiah) of Israel'; but the translation 'the messiah of Aaron and Israel' is more likely, and thus the expectation is of a single figure. A Cave 4 manuscript (4QD^b) has confirmed the reading of the Cairo manuscript A (see above, p. 13) in XIV.19, and it cannot be argued that the Hebrew text in these passages represents a mediaeval mistake. In contrast to this expectation of a single messiah the parallel passage in manuscript A (VII.18*b*–21*a*), like other Qumran documents, seems clearly to refer to two messianic figures ('the interpreter of the law' and 'the prince of the whole congregation').

XIX.11*b*–13*a*. The author quotes Ezek. 9:4 as confirmation of his interpretation of Zech. 13:7. Ezek. 9 describes in visionary form the salvation of a faithful minority and the killing of the guilty majority; the author sees this as a prefiguration of what will happen at God's future visitation. *the first visitation*: the events of 587 BC. *the avenging sword of the covenant*: taken from Lev. 26:25, also used in 1.17*b*–18*a*.

XIX.13*b*–14. A formal conclusion to the warning. Those envisaged here, a little differently from VII.9*b* = XIX.5*b*–6*a*, are members of the movement who were not steadfast in observing its laws. *these, the statutes*: 'the statutes' is most probably an explanatory gloss on 'these'; it does not occur in the parallel passage in VIII.2. 'These' refers back to the list of injunctions in VI.11*b*–VII.4*a*, and the usage is similar to that of VII. 5. *Belial*: here envisaged as the agent of God's punishment; see further the comment on IV.12*b*. The 'destroying angels' (CD II.6; 1QS IV.12) may be regarded as his minions.

VII.13*b*–VIII.1*a*. The text of A seems clearly secondary in comparison with that of B (XIX.7*b*–13*a*). Thus the A-text does not continue the warning of future punishment, but is concerned with the settlement of the movement at 'Damascus' and the coming of 'the interpreter of the law' and 'the prince of the whole congregation'; it is only in connection with 'the prince' that the theme of punishment is briefly reintroduced. Further, the statement at the end, 'These escaped at the time of the first visitation, but the apostates were delivered up to the sword', looks like an editorial link which was intended to join the A-text back to the original. It is noticeable that this link picks up the language used at the beginning of the passage (VII.13b–14a) and serves to round the passage off, but also that it seems to have been written in the light of statements in the B-text (see XIX.10–11a, 13a). Finally, the passage in A has a self-contained character and almost certainly once existed as an independent tradition. From all this it seems clear that the passage in A, known as the Amos–Numbers midrash, is secondary, and it seems most likely that it was inserted deliberately in place of the original (represented by B). A clue as to the reason for the insertion is perhaps provided by the material in which A and B overlap, namely their messianic expectations. Thus a major reason for the insertion of the midrash was probably a wish to bring the Damascus Document into line with other Qumran documents by a statement of the belief in two messiahs. From VIII.1b (= XIX.13b) onwards the two texts once more run closely parallel to one another.

VII.13b–14a. *but those who held fast escaped to the land of the north*: editorial transition to the midrash; 'the land of the north' is 'Damascus', assumed here to be a symbolic name for Qumran. The immediately preceding words, as we have seen, refer to the destruction of the northern kingdom and implicitly that of the southern kingdom, the events which marked the beginning of the exile. Through the insertion of the midrash the text moves directly from these events to the establishment of the community at Qumran; for the theological pattern see the comment on 1.5b–8a and cp. III.10b–17a, 'Through it the first ones who entered the covenant incurred guilt and were delivered up to the sword...But with those who held fast to the commandments of God...God established his covenant with Israel for ever...'

VII.14b–21a. *The Amos–Numbers midrash.* In the first part of the midrash Amos 5:27a is interpreted to mean that 'those who held fast' have been established at 'Damascus' as a community devoted to the study and observance of the law. The second part is concerned with the messianic expectations of the community. Amos 5:27a forms part of a prophecy of judgement in the book of Amos, but here it has been made a prophecy of salvation.

VII.14b–18a. *I will exile the Sikkuth of your king and the Kiyyun of your images from my tent to Damascus*: Amos 5:27a, quoted in a form different from that of the Massoretic text, and with the insertion of two phrases from Amos 5:26. 'Sikkuth' and 'Kiyyun' are the distorted forms that are used in the Massoretic text of what were most probably the names 'Sakkuth' and 'Kaiwan', both of which are known from Mesopotamian sources as names of the astral deity Saturn; cp. the RSV. But some scholars, on the basis of one element in the Septuagint, emend *sikkūth* to *sukkath*, 'tent' or 'booth', and take the second name to be a word meaning 'base' or 'pedestal'; cp. the NEB, 'the shrine of your idol king and the pedestals of your images'. However, the Septuagint did understand the text to refer to pagan deities; cp. the quotation of the text in Acts 7:42b–43. In the Damascus Document it is not quite clear how the quotation itself (lines 14b–15a) was read and understood, and 'Sikkuth' and 'Kiyyun' have been deliberately left untranslated. The situation is different in the interpretation (lines 15b–18a), where the individual elements in the text have been repeated in a slightly different form. *from my tent to Damascus*: instead of the Massoretic text 'beyond Damascus'. The 'tent' is a symbol for the temple in Jerusalem. 'Damascus' has often been thought to be a symbolic name for Qumran, and this view is adopted here; it cannot, however, be proved to be so, and, as we have seen, some scholars believe 'Damascus' to be a symbolic name for Babylon (see above, pp. 15, 49). It seems likely that it is the reference to Damascus in the Amos–Numbers midrash that underlies all the references to Damascus in the Damascus Document. *The books of the law are the booth of the king*: instead of *sikkūth*, as in line 14, the author read *sukkath* ('booth'), a variant known also from the Septuagint. The reason for the identification of 'the booth of the king' with 'the law' is not certainly known, and the same is true of the identification of 'the king' with 'the assembly' and 'the bases of the images' with 'the books of the prophets'. *as he said: 'I will raise up the booth of David which is fallen'*: Amos 9:11a, also used in 4QFlor 1–3 1.12–13. 'David' represents 'the king', i.e. 'the assembly', and the prophecy is in effect interpreted to mean that God has established (proper study and observance of) the law within the community. *The king is the assembly*: cp. the references to 'the assembly' in 1QSa 1.25b; II.4. *And the bases of the images ⟨...⟩ are the books of the prophets*: it appears that instead of *kiyyūn*, as in line 15, the author read *kēnē* ('bases'), just as above he read *sukkath* instead of *sikkūth*. A later copyist attempted to 'correct' the text and repeated the preceding words in the form 'And the Kiyyun of the images'; hence the omission marks in the translation. *whose words Israel despised*: cp. e.g. 2 Kings 17:13–14; 2 Chron. 36:15–16.

VII.18b–21a. *The star*: not mentioned in the quotation in lines 14b–15a, but taken from the immediate context of the quotation; see the NEB footnote to Amos 5:26. The reference to 'the star' serves to introduce a statement of the community's messianic expectations. The Amos–Numbers midrash was probably inserted, as we have seen, in order to correct the expectation of a single messiah in XIX.10b–11a (B). *is the interpreter of the law who will come to Damascus*: the passage could also be translated 'who came to Damascus', and 'the interpreter of the law' has sometimes been taken as the title of a figure of the past, as it is in VI.7b–8a. But the use of Num. 24:17 (see below) and the fact that 'the interpreter' is closely linked with 'the prince', who is clearly a future figure, make it much more likely that 'the interpreter of the law' is here the title of a messianic figure, most probably the messiah of Aaron of 1QS IX.11; cp. the use of the title in a messianic sense in 4QFlor 1–3 I.11. It is interesting to observe that the community's messianic expectations are associated with 'Damascus', assumed here to be a symbolic name for Qumran. *as it is written:'a star shall come forth out of Jacob, and a comet shall rise out of Israel'*: Num. 24:17, frequently interpreted in a messianic sense in this period; cp. e.g. 4QTestim 9–13; T. Jud. 24; Targum Onkelos (where the 'star' and the 'comet' are identified as 'the king' and 'the messiah'). *the prince of the whole congregation*: almost certainly another name for the messiah of Israel of 1QS IX.11; cp. the use of 'the prince of the congregation' as a messianic title in the work called 'Words of Blessing' (1QSb v.20), and the use of 'prince' to refer to the future Davidic king in Ezekiel (e.g. 34:24; 44:3). *he shall beat down all the sons of Seth*: quoted from the end of Num. 24:17. 'The sons of Seth' represent the wicked, who are to be punished by the messiah.

VII.21b–VIII.1a. *These escaped at the time of the first visitation, but the apostates were delivered up to the sword*: an editorial link intended to join the midrash to the original text. The 'these' are not 'the sons of Seth', but 'those who held fast' (VII.13), and the link reuses the language of VII.13b–14a; but it also appears that it was written in the light of XIX.10–11a, 13a, in B.

VIII.1b–2a. Virtually identical with XIX.13b–14.

A FURTHER WARNING

Manuscript A	Manuscript B

VIII.2 That will be the
day 3 when God will visit. The
princes of Judah have become
those upon whom wrath will be
poured out. 4 For they hope for
healing, but... All are rebels
inasmuch as they have not
turned aside from the way 5 of
the traitors, but have defiled
themselves in the ways of
fornication, and in the wealth of
wickedness, and in taking
revenge, and bearing one
another a grudge, 6 and hating
one another. Each man has
evaded his duty to his
blood-relation, 7 and they have
approached for lewdness, and
have acted arrogantly for the
sake of wealth and gain.

XIX.15 That will be the day
when God will visit, as he said:
'The princes of Judah have
become like those who
move 16 the boundary; upon
them I will pour out wrath like
water.' For they entered into
the covenant of
repentance, 17 but have not
turned aside from the way of
the traitors; and they have
defiled themselves in the ways
of fornication, and in the
wealth of wickedness, 18 and in
taking revenge, and bearing one
another a grudge, and hating
one another. Each man has
evaded his duty 19 to his
blood-relation, and they have
approached for lewdness, and
have acted arrogantly for the
sake of wealth and gain.

Each man has done what was
right in his own eyes 8 and each
has chosen the stubbornness of
his heart. They have not kept
away from the people and have
presumptuously acted without
restraint 9 by walking in the
way of the wicked, of whom
God said: 'Their wine is the
venom of serpents, 10 the cruel

Each man has done 20 what was
right in his own eyes and each
has chosen the stubbornness of
his heart. They have not kept
away from the people 21 and
their sin and have
presumptuously acted without
restraint by walking in the
ways of the wicked, of
whom 22 God said: 'Their wine

Manuscript A

poison of asps.' The serpents are
the kings of the peoples, and
their wine is [11] their ways; and
the poison of the asps is the
head of the kings of Greece who
will come to wreak [12]
vengeance on them. But all
these things the builders of the
wall and those who daub it with
plaster have not understood
because [13] one who raised the
wind and preached lies has
preached to them, against whose
whole congregation the anger of
God is kindled.

[14] And when Moses said:
'Not because of your
righteousness or the uprightness
of your heart are you going in
to possess these nations,[15] but
because he loved your fathers
and because he kept the
oath'[16] – such shall be the case
for the converts of Israel who
turn aside from the way of the
people. Because of God's love
for [17] the first who testified in
his favour, he loves those who
come after them, for to them
belongs [18] the covenant of the
fathers. But because of his

Manuscript B

is the venom of serpents, the
cruel poison of asps.' The
serpents [23] are the kings of the
peoples, and their wine is their
ways; and the poison of the asps
is the head [24] of the kings of
Greece who will come against
them to take vengeance. But all
these things the builders [25] of
the wall and those who daub it
with plaster have not
understood because (there is)
one who follows the wind and
raises whirlwinds and preaches
lies to men, [26] against whose
whole congregation the anger of
God is kindled.

And when Moses said [27] to
Israel: 'Not because of your
righteousness or the uprightness
of your heart are you going in
to possess these nations, [28] but
because he loved your fathers
and because he kept the
oath' – such shall be [29] the case
for the converts of Israel who
turn aside from the way of the
people. Because of God's love
for the first [30] who testified
against the people in favour of
God, he loves those who come
after them, for to them
belongs [31] the covenant of the

Manuscript A	Manuscript B
hatred for the builders of the wall, his anger is kindled. And such shall be the case [19] for all who reject the commandments of God and abandon them and turn away in the stubbornness of their heart. [20] This is the word which Jeremiah spoke to Baruch the son of Neriah, and (which) Elisha (spoke) [21] to his servant Gehazi.	fathers. But God hates and loathes the builders of the wall, and his anger is kindled against them, and against all [32] those who follow them. And such shall be the case for all who reject the commandments of God [33] and abandon them and turn away in the stubbornness of their heart.

This second warning falls into two parts. In the first the Jewish leaders of the day are condemned, and punishment at the hands of 'the head of the kings of Greece' is presented as the inevitable consequence of their behaviour. In the second those within the movement are assured of salvation, whereas God's anger is said to be aroused against those outside ('the builders of the wall'). A clue to the purpose of this material is provided by the conclusion (VIII.18*c*–19): 'And such shall be the case for all who reject the commandments of God and abandon them and turn away in the stubbornness of their heart.' It appears from these words that at the time at which this passage was composed, probably a little later than the preceding one, there was a real risk of members leaving the movement and associating once more with non-Essene Judaism; it seems likely in fact that some had already done so. This passage is directed at potential apostates and serves both as a warning that there can be no compromise with non-Essene Judaism and as a reminder that salvation lies only within the movement; those who do apostatise must expect the same punishment as Jews outside the movement.

What has been said so far applies in the first instance to the A-text. The differences between the A-text and the B in this passage are less substantial than in the preceding one, but are of significance, and the view followed here is that the A-text represents the original. The B-text is to be regarded as a later revision; some of the changes introduced into the B-text have the effect of making this passage more explicitly a warning directed at potential apostates. Two elements in the passage are probably secondary: VIII.12*c*–13 = XIX.25*b*–26*a* and VIII.20–21*a*.

VIII.2b–3a. *That will be the day when God will visit*: a link-sentence intended to join the present warning to the preceding one.

VIII.3b–13. The condemnation of the princes of Judah. The title 'the princes (or 'rulers') of Judah' is given in the quotation of Hos. 5:10 (see below): they most probably represent the leaders of contemporary Jewish society. There are significant parallels between the description of the behaviour of 'the princes' in lines 4b–9a and other parts of the exhortation. Some of the faults mentioned recall the sins described in the condemnation of non-Essene Judiasm in IV.12b–V.15a. But there are also parallels with some elements in the summary of the duties of members (VI.11b–VII.4a): 'the princes of Judah' are in effect presented as behaving in the way that members of the movement should not. It is this which indicates that this passage is aimed, not at 'the princes of Judah' themselves, but at members who were attracted by non-Essene Judaism and were tempted to abandon their commitment to the movement.

VIII.3b. *The princes of Judah have become those upon whom wrath will be poured out*: an abbreviated quotation of Hos. 5:10 which serves as an introduction to the condemnation of 'the princes of Judah'. In B the quotation has been given in full, and 'as he said' inserted to smooth the abrupt transition.

VIII.4a. *For they hope for healing, but…All are rebels*: the first words are possibly an allusion to Hos. 5:13; the omission marks reflect a corrupt and uncertain text. The quite different text of B ('For they entered into the covenant of repentance') makes what follows refer to apostates and thus makes the whole passage much more explicitly a warning directed at potential apostates.

VIII.4b–9a. *they have not turned aside from the way of the traitors*: 'the traitors' are here not a specific group, but Jews outside the movement. *have defiled themselves in the ways of fornication*: cp. IV.17, 20; VII.1. *and in the wealth of wickedness*: cp. IV.17; VI.15. *and in taking revenge, and bearing one another a grudge, and hating one another*: cp. VII.2b–3a; IX.2–8a, and more generally VI.20b–21a. *evaded his duty to his blood-relation*: cp. VI.21c–VII.1a and Isa. 58:7. *and they have approached for lewdness*: probably incest is meant; cp. Lev. 18:17; 20:14 and the attack on niece-marriage in V.7b–11a. *and have acted arrogantly for the sake of wealth and gain*: cp. the warning against carrying out certain actions 'for the sake of wealth and gain' in X.18; XI.15; XII.7. *done what was right in his own eyes*: cp. III.6. *chosen the stubbornness of his heart*: cp.II.17b–18a; III.5, 11b–12a. *They have not kept away from the people*: cp. VI.14c–15a. *and have presumptuously acted without restraint by walking in the way of the wicked*: cp. the beginning of the list of accusations, 'All are rebels inasmuch as they have not turned aside from the way of the traitors' (VIII.4b–5a).

VIII.9b–12a. *of whom God said, 'Their wine is the venom of serpents, the cruel poison of asps'*: Deut. 32:33, part of a pictorial description of the enemy nation used by God to punish his people, is quoted in the Damascus Document as referring to 'the wicked' in whose ways 'the princes of Judah' walk. The effect of the quotation and ensuing commentary is to accuse 'the princes' of following foreign – more precisely, hellenistic – ways; but this will lead inevitably to punishment at the hands of the foreigners (the Greeks). *The serpents are the kings of the peoples*: the individual elements of Deut. 32:33 are interpreted without reference to their significance in their original context. 'The peoples' could be the nations in general, but from what follows it is clear that the Greeks are really in mind. *and their wine is their ways*: thus 'the princes of Judah' are shown to follow Greek ways. *and the poison of the asps is the head of the kings of Greece*: the interpretation is based on a play on the Hebrew word *rō'š*, which can mean both 'poison' (as in Deut. 32:33) and 'head' (here in the sense 'chief'). The wording is so vague that it is impossible to say whether the author had a particular individual in mind. *who will come to wreak vengeance on them*: or 'who came'. But in the context of the passage as a whole these words make more sense as a threat than as an account of a past event.

VIII.12b. *But all these things the builders of the wall and those who daub it with plaster have not understood*: an allusion to Ezek. 13:10, already used in IV.19b. 'The builders of the wall' are ordinary Jews outside the Essene movement, and 'those who daub it with plaster' are their leaders ('the princes of Judah'); it is unlikely that there is a specific reference here to prophets, as in Ezekiel itself. The statement that they 'have not understood' may be an allusion to Deut. 32:28–9, already used in V.17a; for the importance of 'understanding' in the Damascus Document see the comment on VI.2b–3a.

VIII.12c–13. These words, like IV.19c–20a, are almost certainly secondary. They make the faults of 'the builders of the wall and those who daub it with plaster' the responsibility of an individual teacher with an organised group of followers; but there has been no reference whatever to this individual in the preceding passage. (On this figure ('one who...preached lies', i.e. 'the preacher of lies') see above, pp. 23–4.) *one who raised the wind and preached lies has preached to them*: based on Micah 2:11, but in a form different from that of the Massoretic text. *against whose whole congregation the anger of God is kindled*: see the comment on I.21*b*–II.1.

VIII.14–18*a*. Deut 9:5*a* combined with Deut. 7:8*a* is made the basis of an assurance of salvation for the members of the movement ('the converts of Israel'). *such shall be the case for the converts of Israel*: literally 'those who (re)turn of Israel'; see the comment on VI.4*b*–5. *who turn aside from the way of the people*: in contrast to 'the princes of Judah' who 'have not turned aside from the way of the traitors' (VIII.4*b*–5*a*). *the first...those who come after them*: the original members and those who joined later, a distinction similar to that in IV.2*b*–4*a* and VI.4*b*–9*a*. *for to them belongs the covenant of the fathers*: the covenant with the patriarchs, possibly an allusion to Deut. 4:31. It is the members of the movement, not those outside, who are now to inherit the blessings promised in the covenant with the patriarchs.

VIII.18*b*. *But because of his hatred for the builders of the wall, his anger is kindled*: a final reminder of the punishment awaiting those outside the movement; the structure of the sentence is parallel to that of the preceding one. In B the tone has been made much sharper ('God hates and loathes the builders of the wall'), and the addition at the end ('against them, and against all those who follow them') once again has the effect of making the whole passage refer more explicitly to apostates.

VIII.18*c*–19. A formal conclusion, similar to XIX.13*b*–14 = VIII.1*b*–2*a*; for its significance, see above, p. 66. *all who reject the commandments*: cp. XIX.5*b*. *and abandon them*: cp. I.3; III.11. *in the stubbornness of their heart*: cp. VIII.8 = XIX.20.

VIII.20–21*a*. This sentence is not in the B-text and may well be an addition. *the word which Jeremiah spoke to Baruch*: perhaps an allusion to Jer. 45:3–5. *and (which) Elisha (spoke) to his servant Gehazi*: cp. 2 Kings 5:26–7. The apparently clear allusion in this case suggests that these are both examples of judgement on unfaithful servants.

THE EXCLUSION OF APOSTATES

Manuscript A	Manuscript B
VIII.21 All the men who entered into the new covenant in the land of Damascus	XIX.33 Likewise none of the men who entered into the new covenant 34 in the land of Damascus

and turned back and acted treacherously and turned aside from the well of living waters [35] shall be counted in the assembly of the people or entered in their roll from the day of the gathering in [XX.1] of the teacher of the community until the appearance of the messiah from Aaron and from Israel.

Such shall be the case [2] for every one who enters the congregation of the men of perfect holiness, but shrinks from carrying out the precepts of the upright. [3] He is the man who is melted in a furnace. When his deeds become apparent, he shall be sent away from the congregation [4] like one whose lot had never fallen among the disciples of God. According to his unfaithfulness the men of knowledge shall reprove him [5] until the day he again stands in the assembly of the men of perfect holiness. [6] But when his deeds become apparent, according to the interpretation of the law in which the men of perfect holiness walk, [7] let no man make any agreement with him in regard to property or work, [8] because all the holy ones of the Most High have cursed him.

Such shall be the case for all among the first and the last who reject (the commandments), [9] who set idols upon their heart and walk in the stubbornness [10] of their heart; they shall have no share in the house of the law. They shall be judged in the same way as their companions who turned back [11] with the scoffers. For they spoke error against the statutes of righteousness, and rejected [12] the covenant and the agreement which they established in the land of Damascus, that is the new covenant. [13] Neither they nor their families shall have any share in the house of the law.

From the day [14] of the gathering in of the teacher of the community until the end of all the fighting men who turned back [15] with the liar (there will be) about forty years. And at that time the anger of God will be kindled [16] against Israel, as he said: 'without king or prince, without judge or [17] anyone to reprove with righteousness'. But those who turned from the transgression of Jacob, who have kept the covenant of God, will then speak to one [18] another to turn one another to righteousness that their step may hold firmly to the way of God. And God will pay heed [19] to their words and listen, and a book of remembrance will be written [before him] of those who fear God and think on [20] his name, until salvation and deliverance are revealed to those who fear [God. Then] you will again [distinguish] between the righteous [21] and the wicked, between one who serves [Go]d and one who does not serve him. And he will show steadfast love to [thousands], to those who love him [22] and heed him, for a thousand generations.

Warnings and promises continue in the final part of the exhortation (XIX.33b–XX.34), but they are of a different character from those in the preceding sections. The material divides into two parts, of which the second (XX.22b–34) repeats the pattern of the first (XIX.33b–XX.22a). Beyond this it is difficult to make precise statements about the formation of the material. So far as XIX.33b–XX.22a is concerned, the first three paragraphs, dealing with different categories of men who are to be excluded from the movement, are each introduced by a similar phrase: 'Likewise' (XIX.33b), 'Such shall be the case' (XX.1b), 'Such shall be the case' (XX.8b – not quite the same as XX.1b in the Hebrew). These look like phrases used by the editor to bind together supplementary pieces of material of diverse origin, and certainly the second paragraph (XX.1b–8a) stands apart from the rest of the passage. It deals with the temporary expulsion of erring members and is similar in character to 1QS VIII.16b–IX.2. It is not clear whether the other two paragraphs were originally written as one piece, or whether they originally belonged with the fourth paragraph; this deals with the situation following the death of 'the teacher of the community' and offers an assurance of God's love towards faithful members of the movement. However, the different elements in XIX.33b–XX.22a (apart from XX.1b–8a) appear to presuppose basically the same situation and are treated here as a unity.

The situation presupposed was one in which a significant group of members, under the leadership of 'the liar' (XX.15), had already broken away from the movement (XIX.33b–XX.1a). Other members were rebellious in their attitude, although they had not actually defected (XX.8b–13a). The movement was clearly demoralised and in danger of collapse, and this material was written to boost the morale of the members who remained faithful. It belongs, along with I.13–18a; IV.19c–20a; VIII.12c–13, to a secondary stage in the formation of the Damascus Document.

For this final part of the exhortation we are dependent on manuscript B. In A the columns containing the end of the exhortation have been lost; the text breaks off in mid-sentence at the end of column VIII.

XIX.33b–XX.1a. *The exclusion of apostates. the men who entered into*

the new covenant in the land of Damascus: cp. the similar wording in
VI.19. Here, once more, 'the land of Damascus' appears to be a
symbolic name for Qumran. *and turned back*: this verb is used twice
elsewhere in this passage of apostasy, cp. XX.10*b*–11*a*, 'who turned back
with the scoffers'; XX.14*b*–15*a*, 'who turned back with the liar'. *and
acted treacherously*: cp. the references to 'the traitors' in 1QpHab II.1,
3, 5, and see the comment on CD I.12. *the well of living waters*: the
law as understood and interpreted within the movement, cp.
III.16*b*–17*a*; VI.3*b*–5. *the assembly of the people*: i.e. the movement. *from
the day of the gathering in*: 'to be gathered to one's father's kin' is a
regular expression for death in the Old Testament, cp. Gen. 25:8, 17;
Num. 27:13. *of the teacher of the community*: or 'of the unique
teacher' – the text is uncertain. But the reference in any case is to the
figure elsewhere called 'the teacher of righteousness': see the comment
on I.10*b*–12. The implication of the present passage is that the teacher
did have the authority to readmit repentant apostates, but that after
the death of the teacher the movement felt too unsure of itself to do
so. *until the appearance of the messiah from Aaron and from Israel*: see the
comment on XIX.10*b*–11*a*.

XX.1*b*–8*a*. Temporary expulsion of disobedient members. As already
indicated, this paragraph stands apart from the surrounding material
and is similar in character to 1QS VIII.16*b*–IX.2. It provides for the
disciplining, by means of temporary expulsion, of members who
'shrink from carrying out the precepts of the upright'; the provisions
for temporary expulsion are comparable to those of 1QS VIII.16*b*–19;
VIII.24*b*–IX.2. *the men of perfect holiness*: cp. 1QS VIII.20. *the precepts of
the upright*: 'the upright' are the members of the movement (cp. 1QS
III.1; IV.22*a*), and what is at issue here is failure to observe the law as
interpreted by the movement; cp. line 6. *He is the man who is melted
in a furnace*: an allusion to Ezek. 22:22. In Ezekiel the melting is thought
of entirely as a punishment, but here the use of the imagery of refining
points to the purifying effect which the temporary expulsion was
intended to have. *he shall be sent away*: cp. 1QS VIII.22. *like one whose
lot had never fallen*: cp. the references to the 'decision' or 'lot' in 1QS
VI.16, 18, 21*b*–22*a*, which relate to the admission of new members. *let
no man make any agreement with him in regard to property or work*: cp.
1QS VIII.23*b*–24*a* (referring to the man permanently expelled), 'no
man from among the men of holiness shall have anything to do with
his property or with his counsel in regard to any matter'; also the
provisions in 1QS VIII.17*b*–18*a*, 24*b* for the exclusion 'from the purity
and from the council' of the man temporarily expelled. *the holy ones*:
i.e. the angels, cp. Dan. 4:13, 17, 23.

8*b*–13*a*. Exclusion of rebellious members. *for all among the first and the last who reject (the commandments)*: or, less certainly, 'for all who reject the first and the last'. On the former translation 'the first and the last' are the original members of the movement and those who joined later; cp. VIII.16*b*–17 = XIX.29*b*–30, 'the first... those who come after them'. On the latter 'the first and the last' is an elliptic title for the movement's laws, 'the first (rules)' being the original legislation, 'the last (rules)' legislation introduced by the teacher of righteousness; cp. XX.31*b*–32, where obedience to the teacher is mentioned immediately after instruction in 'the first rules'. *who set idols upon their heart*: based on Ezek. 14:3, 4, 7, also used in 1QS II.11–18, the cursing of those whose entry into the covenant was insincere; cp. 1QS II.11*b*–12, 16*c*–17*a*. *and walk in the stubbornness of their heart*: this originally Deuteronomistic phrase is used repeatedly in the Damascus Document and the Community Rule, but cp. here 1QS II.14*a*. *they shall have no share in the house of the law*: i.e. in the movement; cp. the references to the 'sure house' (III.19) and 'the house of Judah' (IV.11), both occurring in the context of a passage in which the law is presented as being central to the movement. *They shall be judged in the same way as their companions who turned back with the scoffers*: the fact that the rebellious members condemned in this passage are distinguished from 'their companions who turned back with the scoffers' suggests that those condemned here had not actually left the movement. The 'companions who turned back' are no doubt the same as the group of apostates mentioned in XIX.33*b*–XX.1*a*, and 'the scoffers' are presumably the nucleus of this group. It is difficult not to regard 'the scoffers', also mentioned in 4QpIsa^b II.6, 10, as the followers of the man called in 1.14 'the scoffer'. *For they spoke error against the statutes of righteousness, and rejected the covenant and the agreement*: the attitude condemned in lines 9–10*a* was matched by outward expressions of behaviour. What exactly was involved is not clear, but it was presumably some form of outspoken criticism of aspects of the movement's legislation.

13*b*–22*a*. In the period of uncertainty following the death of the teacher, faithful members of the movement are assured of God's love.

13*b*–15*a*. *From the day of the gathering in of the teacher of the community*: see the comments on XIX.33*b*–XX.1*a*. *until the end of all the fighting men*: taken from Deut. 2:14. *who turned back with the liar*: a deliberate link back to the description of the apostates in XIX.33*b*–XX.1*a*; XX.10*b*–11*a*. The leader of 'the scoffers' is here identified as 'the liar'; see above, p. 23. *(there will be) about forty years*: an allusion to the traditional length of the total time spent in the wilderness, cp. e.g. Deut. 2:7 (Deut. 2:14, referring to part of this period, has 'thirty-eight years'). Like Israel in the wilderness (cp. Num. 32:13), the faithful members of the movement had to await the death of the apostates before entering the promised land of salvation. On the other hand, it emerges from this passage that the dawning of the new era of salvation was expected within a relatively short time.

15b–17a. The forty-year period following the death of the teacher is presented as standing under God's judgement specifically because of the absence of the teacher. *as he said: 'without king or prince, without judge or anyone to reprove with righteousness'*: an adapted quotation of Hos. 3:4, in which the six terms in Hosea have been reduced to four; 'without judge or anyone to reprove with righteousness' represents an interpretation of 'without image or household gods'. In the Damascus Document all four terms refer to the teacher of the community.

17b–18a. In this period of uncertainty, without the leadership provided by the teacher, faithful members of the movement will be compelled to rely on mutual support in order to preserve their faith. *But those who turned from the transgression of Jacob*: adapted from Isa. 59:20, 'to those in Jacob who turn from transgression'; for this title for members of the movement see the comment on 11.5. *who have kept the covenant of God*: in contrast to the rebellious members who 'rejected the covenant and the agreement' (lines 11b–12a). *will then speak to one another*: quoted from Mal. 3:16a; Mal. 3:16b, 18 are used in the following lines.

18b–22a. Those who do 'hold firmly to the way of God' are assured of salvation and of God's love. *And God…think on his name*: adapted quotation of Mal. 3:16b. *a book of remembrance*: for the idea of a book in which the names of the righteous are recorded see also Exod. 32:32–3; Ps. 69:28; Dan. 12:1. *until salvation and deliverance are revealed to those who fear* [*God*: an allusion to Isa. 56:1. *Then*] *you will again* [*distinguish*]…*does not serve him*: Mal. 3:18. When salvation comes, faithful members of the movement will be recognised as such, and will be seen to be vindicated. *And he will show steadfast love…for a thousand generations*: a combined quotation of Exod. 20:6 (Deut. 5:10) and Deut. 7:9.

A FINAL WARNING AND PROMISE

xx.22[…] of the house of Peleg who went out from the holy city, 23 and relied on God at the time when Israel was unfaithful and made the sanctuary unclean, but returned again 24 to [the wa]y of the people in a fe[w] respects, [al]l of them – each according to his spirit – shall be judged in the council [25] of holiness. But when the glory of God appears to Israel, all those who have broken through the boundary of the law among those who have entered the covenant [26] shall be cut off from the mi[dst] of the camp, and with them all those of Judah who have acted wickedly [27] in the days of its trials.

But all those who hold fast to these rules, going [28] and coming in accordance with the law, who obey the teacher and confess before God (saying): 'Truly we [29] have acted wickedly, we and our fathers, in that we have walked contrary to the statutes of the covenant, righteousness [30] and truth are your judgements upon us'; who do not act presumptuously against his holy statutes, his righteous precepts, [31] and his true testimonies; who have been instructed in the first rules by which [32] the men of the community were governed; who obey the teacher of righteousness and do not reject [33] the statutes of righteousness when they hear them – they will rejoice and be glad, and their heart will be strong, and they will triumph [34] over all the sons of the earth, and God will make expiation for them, and they will see his salvation because they have taken refuge in his holy name.

The pattern of warning (xx.22b–27a) and promise (xx.27b–34) repeats that of the previous section (xix.33b–xx.22a).

22b–25a. The identity of 'the house of Peleg' (or 'the house of separation'), also mentioned in 4QpNah 3–4 iv.1a, is unknown. Furthermore, the text is damaged and the translation in part uncertain. But it appears that the concern here is only with part of the house of Peleg. Those mentioned had apparently joined the movement, but had subsequently become lax in their observance of some aspects of the movement's laws. These members were to be judged on an individual basis, and we are reminded that the Community Rule contains two passages dealing with the disciplining of members (1QS vi.24–vii.25; viii.16b–ix.2). It is not known why former members of the house of Peleg should be singled out for special mention; this passage reflects a particular moment in the history of the movement that is now obscure. *the holy city*: Jerusalem. *and relied on God*: the Hymns speak several times of relying on God's mercy or God's truth (e.g. 1QH iv.36b–37a). *at the time when Israel was unfaithful and made the sanctuary unclean*: for defiling the temple cp. v.6b–7a; xii.1b–2a. *but returned again*

to [*the wa*]*y of the people in a fe*[*w*] *respects*: in VIII.16 = XIX.29 members
of the movement were described as 'the converts of Israel who turn
aside from the way of the people'. *the council of holiness*: cp. the use
of this title in 1QS II.25; VIII.21.

25b–27a. When God appears apostates will be punished in the same
way (by death) as wrongdoers who had never joined the movement.
It is not clear whether the concern here is with the same group as in
lines *22b–25a*, or with apostates in general. *the glory of God*: i.e. God
himself; in the Old Testament God was sometimes said to manifest
himself by means of his glory (see e.g. Exod. 24:15–18; Ezek. 1:26–8).
the boundary of the law: cp. the reference to 'the boundary stone' as
a symbol for the law in 1.16. *shall be cut off*: see the comment on III.1.
from the mi[*dst*] *of the camp*: quoted from Deut. 2:14 (not apparent from
the NEB), also used in line 14 above. *all those of Judah who have acted
wickedly*: those outside the movement. *in the days of its trials*: the period
of crisis preceding the appearance of God.

27b–34. Final promise to faithful members of the movement. This
material gives the impression of having been written specifically to
form a conclusion to the exhortation (columns I–VIII; XIX–XX). *these
rules*: a reference back to the summary of the duties of members in
VI.11*b*–VII.4*a* and perhaps also a reference forward to the collection of
laws in columns IX–XVI. *the teacher*: here probably God, as the
parallelism suggests; cp. III.8. *Truly we have acted wickedly...your
judgements upon us*: the confession is similar to that in 1QS 1.24*b*–II.1*a*.
*who have been instructed in the first rules by which the men of the community
were governed*: 'the first rules' are the laws adopted by the movement
before the appearance of the teacher of righteousness; this original
legislation continues to remain in force: cp. 1QS IX.10*b*–11; CD IV.8:
XX.8*b*(?). *the statutes of righteousness when they hear them*: perhaps an
allusion to the solemn recital of the laws at ceremonies of the
movement, for example the ceremony for the renewal of the covenant.
and they will triumph over all the sons of the earth: an expression of hope
of the defeat of the nations. In the War Scroll, which depicts the final
battle to be fought against the forces of evil, the nations are allied with
the forces of evil.

The Community Rule

The Community Rule (1QS) was one of the first of the Qumran scrolls to be found and remains one of the most important. It provides a set of regulations to govern the life of a community living an independent existence and is most naturally interpreted as being intended for those members of the wider Essene movement who lived at Qumran. But it contains more than a series of rules; two obvious exceptions are the section on the two spirits, which represents an important statement of the community's beliefs, and the hymnic material with which the document ends (the latter is not translated here).

The existence of a series of headings throughout the Rule, together with the fact that the manuscript itself has been divided into paragraphs by marginal signs and by blank lines and spaces, serves to divide the document into a number of separate sections. The major divisions are as follows: statement of the aims of the community, I.1–15; entry into the community, I.16–III.12; the teaching of the community, III.13–IV.26; the common life, V.1–VII.25; programme for a new community, VIII.1–IX.26a; a liturgical calendar and concluding hymn, IX.26b–XI.22. It is difficult to believe that these sections all belonged together originally, and indeed it seems clear not only that the Rule as a whole is a composite document, but also that the major sections listed above are in some cases composed of smaller units which were originally independent. The evidence for this lies firstly in the existence of duplicate passages: there are three general statements of the aims of the community (I.1–15; V.1–7a; VIII.1–4a); the admission of new members is dealt with twice (V.20b–23a; VI.13b–23); there are two lists of punishments (VI.24–VII.25; VIII.16b–IX.2); and secondly in the existence of contradictions: most obviously, in IX.7 the priests alone have authority, while in V.2b–3a authority is shared between the priests and the laity. It is commonly thought that the oldest material in the Rule is to be found in VIII.1–IX.26a, and recently it has been argued that the Rule was composed in a series of stages on the basis of this nucleus (more precisely of VIII.1–X.8a minus some secondary material). It is not clear, however, that it is possible to arrange the material in a chronological sequence, except that VIII.1–IX.26a does seem to be earlier than the rest of the material. It seems difficult to go with confidence beyond the recognition that the Rule is a composite document, and that within the major sections units that were originally separate have sometimes been brought together because of similarities of theme or because they were thought to be appropriate to the context.

The document translated here is the manuscript of the Rule discovered in Qumran Cave 1 which is dated to 100–75 BC. But since this manuscript seems clearly not to be the autograph copy, the composition of the Rule must be placed before this, probably towards the end of the second century BC. Fragments of ten manuscripts of the Rule were found in Cave 4 (4QS^a–j) and in some cases these contain an older and better text than that found in the Cave 1 manuscript. Reference will sometimes be made to variants attested by the Cave 4 manuscripts. Fragments of a manuscript from Cave 5 (5QS) possibly, but not certainly, also belong to the Rule.

Bibliography

M. Burrows, with the assistance of J. C. Trever and W. H. Brownlee, *The Dead Sea Scrolls of St Mark's Monastery*, volume II/2: *Plates and Transcription of the Manual of Discipline*, New Haven, 1951.

P. Wernberg-Møller, *The Manual of Discipline Translated and Annotated with an Introduction* (Studies on the Texts of the Desert of Judah, 1), Leiden, 1957.

A. R. C. Leaney, *The Rule of Qumran and Its Meaning: Introduction, Translation and Commentary* (The New Testament Library), London, 1966.

J. Murphy-O'Connor, 'La Genèse littéraire de la Règle de la Communauté', *Revue Biblique* 76 (1969), 528–49.

J. Pouilly, *La Règle de la Communauté de Qumrân: son évolution littéraire* (Cahiers de la Revue Biblique, 17), Paris, 1976.

THE AIMS OF THE COMMUNITY

1.1 For [... the book of the ru]le of the community. They shall seek ² God wi[th a whole heart and soul; they shall] do what is good and right before him in accordance with that which ³ he commanded through Moses and through all his servants the prophets; they shall love all ⁴ that he has chosen and hate all that he has rejected; they shall keep away from all evil ⁵ and cling to all good works; they shall practise truth, righteousness, and justice ⁶ in the land and not continue walking in the stubbornness of a guilty heart and of lustful eyes, ⁷ committing all evil.

They shall admit into the covenant of love all those who willingly offer themselves to observe the statutes of God, [8] so that they may be joined to the counsel of God and may walk perfectly before him in accordance with all [9] the things that have been revealed at the times appointed for their revelation; and so that they may love all the sons of light, each [10] according to his lot in the plan of God, and may hate all the sons of darkness, each according to his guilt [11] in the vengeance of God.

And all those who willingly offer themselves to his truth shall bring all their knowledge, their abilities, [12] and their wealth into the community of God, that they may purify their knowledge in the truth of the statutes of God, and may order their abilities [13] according to his perfect ways and all their wealth according to his righteous counsel.

They shall not depart from any one [14] of all the commandments of God concerning their times; they shall not anticipate their appointed times, or be behind [15] in any of their feasts. They shall not turn from his true statutes to go to the right or the left.

This passage serves as an introduction to the Rule and sets out the aims and ideals of the Qumran community in general terms. The latter part of the passage (1.11*b*–15) is directed particularly at candidates for admission to the community, while the opening lines (1.1–11*a*) appear to be directed particularly at those who stand at its head.

1.1–11*a*. Since line 7 refers to responsibility for the admission of new members to the community, it would appear that lines 1–11*a* are directed in the first instance at the community's leader or leaders; but this is not quite clear because almost half of line 1 has been lost. Much of what is said in these lines in any case also applies to the community as a whole.

1*a*. There are two gaps in line 1, and it is impossible to reconstruct the text with any certainty. It has been suggested that it began, 'For [the wise leader...]' (see on III.13); this would fit well, but it is not clear how the text then continued. *the book of the ru*]*le of the community*: probable reconstruction based on a Cave 4 manuscript of the Rule.

1*b*–7*a*. Because of the gaps in line 1 it is not exactly clear how this passage links up with the words that precede; the translation offers one interpretation, but others are possible. The general sense is, however, clear; this passage describes in broad terms the duties of the members of the community. *seek God wi*[*th a whole heart and soul*: restoration based on the Cave 4 manuscripts of the Rule. The phrases 'to seek God' and 'with a whole heart and soul' both occur frequently in the later writings of the Old Testament; cp. e.g. 2 Chron. 15:12, 'And they entered into a covenant to seek guidance of (literally 'to seek') the LORD the God of their fathers with all their heart and soul.' *do what is good and right*: cp. Deut. 6:18; 12:28. *in accordance with that which he commanded through Moses and through all his servants the prophets*: cp. VIII.15–16a; CD V.21b–VI.1a. Study and observance of the word of God as revealed in the Old Testament constituted one of the most important aims of the Qumran community; see the comment on VI.6b–8a. *through all his servants the prophets*: the description of the prophets as God's servants is common in the Old Testament. For the idea of the prophets as the mediators of God's commandments see Ezra 9:10–11; Dan. 9:10. *love all that he has chosen and hate all that he has rejected*: underlying this and the comparable antithetical statements in this passage is the dualistic belief which is characteristic of the thought of the Qumran community, the belief, that is, in the radical opposition between the spirits of truth and injustice; see further on III.13–IV.26. The language used in this passage may have been inspired by Isa. 7:15–16 and Amos 5:15; cp. CD II.15. *keep away from all evil and cling to all good works*: cp. 1 Thess. 5:21–2; T. Benj. 8:1, 'And you therefore, my children, flee evil…cling to goodness and love.' *practise truth, righteousness, and justice*: cp. V.3b–4a; VIII.2; T. Benj. 10:3, 'Therefore practise truth and righteousness, each man with his neighbour, and justice.' *truth*: this word is used frequently in the scrolls, often, as here, with the underlying sense of faithfulness to God's law and sincerity in one's actions. *righteousness, and justice*: often used in combination in the Old Testament as objects of the verb 'to practise' (literally 'to do'); cp. for example Ezek. 18:5, 'Consider the man who is righteous and does what is just and right.' *and not continue walking in the stubbornness of a guilty heart*: based on language that is characteristic of the Deuteronomistic layers of Jeremiah; cp. for instance 3:17 and see the comment on CD II.17b–18.

7b–11a. A continuation of the description of the aims of the community, here presented in relation to the admission of new members. *They shall admit*: admission of new members, described in detail in VI.13b–23, was primarily the responsibility of the leader of the community, and it is possible that we should translate, 'He shall admit'. *the covenant of love*: entry into the community is presented as entry into a covenant with God, and the covenant concept is fundamental in the scrolls. The expression used here is not found in the Old Testament, but carries with it the thought that the covenant was the means by which God's love was mediated to the members of the community. *counsel of God*: the word translated 'counsel', which in the Old Testament always has this meaning, in the scrolls sometimes has the meaning 'council' (cp. for instance III. 2). Here the two senses overlap. Entry into the covenant is part of God's counsel or purpose, but at the same time brings the person who joins into membership of the council of God, here meaning the community. *all the things that have been revealed*: this probably refers to the community's interpretation of the hidden meaning of scripture (cp. v.9; CD III.13*b*–14*a*), although in IQS v.12 'the things revealed' are the clear commands of the law. *at the times appointed for their revelation*: a difficult phrase, literally 'at the times of their decree', i.e. at the times decreed for them (the 'them' being the things revealed). The passage apparently alludes to the belief of the community that its interpretation of scripture was given in a series of revelations as a result of study of the law; cp. IX.13, 'He shall do the will of God in accordance with all that has been revealed from time to time.' See also VIII.11*b*–12*a*, 15*b*. The phrase has sometimes been taken as referring to the calendar followed by the community, with a translation something like 'with regard to their appointed feasts'; but a reference to the calendar seems unlikely at this point. *sons of light…sons of darkness*: the members of the community and their opponents – in the Community Rule Jews who do not belong to the community. The expressions do not occur in the Damascus Document, but they are both used in column 1 of the War Scroll, where 'the sons of darkness' include Israel's traditional enemies and the Kittim, as well as 'those who break the covenant'; see IQM I.1–2. (The expression 'the sons of light' does not occur in the War Scroll other than in column 1.) *his lot*: or 'his destiny'; there is a strong deterministic element in the theology of the Qumran community, and this is reflected in the terminology used here. *plan*: the same word translated 'counsel' above. Alternatively the passage could be translated 'each according to his position in the council of God'; cp. CD XIII.12. *in the vengeance of God*: the vengeance which God will enact when he comes to judge the wicked; cp. IV.11*b*–14; Jer. 50:15, 28.

11*b*–13*a*. The attitude required on the part of candidates for admission to the community. *their knowledge, their abilities, and their wealth*: these words are a reminder that the group at Qumran which produced the scrolls lived a communal life and practised community of goods. This group formed a part, perhaps the most important part, of the larger Essene movement, and Philo and Josephus in their descriptions of the Essenes refer to the fact that they held their property in common; see Philo, Omn Prob Lib 77, 85–6: Josephus, *War* ii.8:3–4 (122, 124–7). The early Christians lived a similar communal life (see Acts 2:44–7; 4:32–7), but with the difference that the practice of handing property over to the Church was clearly a voluntary matter (see Acts 5:4); at Qumran the members of the community were obliged to hand over their goods.

13*b*–15*a*. The members of the community were to keep strictly to their own calendar; for the importance of the calendar within the community see the comment on CD iii.12*b*–16*a*.

15*b*. *turn...to the right or the left*: cp. Deut. 28:14.

ENTRY INTO THE COMMUNITY

The admission of members to the community, a theme that was introduced in the first section of the Rule (i.1–15; see lines 7, 11), provides the focus for the material which follows in i.16–iii.12. The first part of this (i.16–ii.18) describes the ritual for the ceremony of entry into the covenant, while the last part (ii.25*b*–iii.12) refers to those who, apparently after a probationary period, refuse to enter the covenant. The passage in the middle (ii.19–25*a*) refers to an annual assembly of all the members which seems to have taken place at the renewal of the covenant. The heading in iii.13, 'For the wise leader', clearly marks the beginning of a new section of the Rule.

THE COVENANT CEREMONY

[1.16] All those who join the order of the community shall enter into a covenant before God to do [17] all that he has commanded and not to turn back from following him through any fear or terror or trial [18] which takes place during the reign of Belial.

When they enter into the covenant the priests and the Levites shall [19] bless the God of salvation and all the deeds of his faithfulness, and all [20] those who are entering into the covenant say after them, 'Amen, Amen!'

[21] The priests recount the righteous acts of God manifested in his mighty deeds [22] and proclaim all his gracious acts of love towards Israel. And the Levites recount [23] the iniquities of the children of Israel, and all their guilty transgressions, and their sins during the reign [24] of

Belial. [And all] those who are entering into the covenant confess after them and say: 'We have committed iniquity 25 [and transgressed,] we have [sin]ned and acted wickedly, we [and] our [fath]ers before us, in that we have walked 26 [contrary to the covenant] of truth and righteous[ness…] his judgement upon us and upon our fathers, 11.1 but he has bestowed his loving grace upon us from everlasting to everlasting.'

And the priests bless all 2 the men of the lot of God who walk perfectly in all his ways and say: 'May he bless you with all 3 good and keep you from all evil. May he enlighten your heart with understanding of life and graciously bestow upon you knowledge of eternity. 4 May he lift up the face of his mercy upon you in eternal peace.'

And the Levites curse all the men 5 of the lot of Belial, and answer and say: 'Cursed be you for all your guilty deeds of wickedness. May God give you up 6 to terror at the hand of all who take vengeance, and may he visit destruction upon you at the hand of all who exact 7 retribution. Cursed be you without mercy for the darkness of your deeds, and damned be you 8 in the gloom of everlasting fire. May God not show mercy to you when you call, or forgive you by making expiation for your iniquities. 9 May he lift up the face of his anger to take vengeance on you, and may there be no peace for you in the mouth of all who make intercession.' 10 And all those who are entering into the covenant say after those who curse and those who bless, 'Amen, Amen!'

11 And the priests and the Levites shall continue and say: 'Cursed for the idols of his heart which he worships be 12 the one who enters into this covenant while placing before himself the stumbling-block of his iniquity so that he backslides because of it. When 13 he hears the terms of this covenant, he will bless himself in his heart and say, "May there be peace for me, 14 even though I walk in the stubbornness of my heart." But his spirit shall be destroyed, the dry with the moist, without 15 forgiveness. May the anger of God and the wrath of his judgements burn upon him for everlasting destruction. May all 16 the curses of this covenant cling to him. May God set him apart for evil,

and may he be cut off from all the sons of light because of his backsliding ¹⁷ from God through his idols and the stumbling-block of his iniquity. May he assign his lot amongst those who are cursed for ever.' ¹⁸ And all those who are entering the covenant answer and say after them, 'Amen, Amen!'

The ritual for the ceremony of entry into the community, with its series of blessings and curses, very obviously draws its inspiration from the covenant ceremony described in Deut. 27 and from the material in Deut. 28–30 which is likewise concerned with the covenant. The account of the ceremony is preceded by a short introductory statement (1.16–18a), and the ceremony itself is divided into five parts: praise of God (1.18b–20); recital of God's deeds on behalf of his people and confession of sin (1.21–11.1a); blessing of the righteous (11.1b–4a); cursing of the wicked (11.4b–10); cursing of those whose entry into the covenant is insincere (11.11–18). A similar kind of ritual is described in 1QM xiii.1–6.

1.16–18a. Entry into the community involved entry into a covenant to serve God faithfully. As we have already noted, the covenant concept is fundamental to the Qumran community, and in this, as in so many other matters, the community was simply appropriating to itself a basic Old Testament idea.

16–17a. *enter into a covenant*: the same Hebrew expression that is used in Deut. 29:12. *to do all that he has commanded and not to turn back from following him*: again the language reflects that of the Old Testament; for the former phrase cp. e.g. Gen. 7:5 and for the latter Num. 14:43 (NEB, 'ceased to follow').

17b–18a. *fear or terror or trial which take place during the reign of Belial*: 'the reign of Belial' is one of the names used for the present age, which was believed to be under the control of Belial; see the comment on CD vi.10. It was further believed that as this age drew to a close the members of the community would have to face various trials which would test them and show their worthiness to participate in the new age; cp. CD xx.27a; 1QH v.16; 1QM xvii.1, 8b–9. Similar ideas are to be found in the New Testament: cp. for instance Matt. 6:13; 1 Peter 1:6–7. *trial*: the Hebrew word is used in Prov. 17:3; 27:21 of a 'melting-pot' or 'crucible' in which precious metals are refined; in the scrolls it is used in a metaphorical sense of the suffering or 'trial' by which an individual is tested; cp. Mal. 3:2–3. *Belial*: see the comment on CD iv.12b.

18*b*–20. Praise of God for his actions on behalf of his people.

18*b*–19. *priests...Levites*: the community saw itself as the true Israel, the nucleus of the ideal Israel of the future, and its structure was intended to reflect that of Israel itself. Thus, like Israel, the community had its own priests and Levites who officiated at its ceremonies. From a historical point of view it is likely that a substantial number of those who established the Qumran community were priests and Levites who were dissatisfied with the conduct of religious affairs in Jerusalem. *the God of salvation*: cp. Isa. 12:2 (NEB, 'God...my deliverer'); Luke 1:47. *faithfulness*: the word elsewhere translated 'truth'; faithfulness to his own nature and to his promises to his people is what is in mind. God's deeds on behalf of his people reflect this faithfulness.

19*b*–20. *and all those who are entering into the covenant say after them, 'Amen, Amen!'*: the influence of Deut. 27:14–26 is obvious here and in the remainder of the passage. But the double 'Amen' reflects Neh. 8:6.

1.21–11.1*a*. The recital of God's deeds on behalf of his people and the acknowledgement and confession of Israel's sin, which are merely referred to here, form the actual theme of several Old Testament passages; see e.g. Ps. 106; Neh. 9:5–37; cp. Acts 7:2–53. The use made of these recitals varies, but the passage in Nehemiah belongs to the same situation as that of the Rule, i.e. a covenant ceremony; Neh. 9:5–37 forms part of Neh. 9–10 which, in the present form of the book, describes the making of a covenant.

22*b*–24*a*. *the iniquities of the children of Israel, and all their guilty transgressions, and their sins*: an adaptation of Lev. 16:21.

24*b*–25*a*. The beginning of line 25 is damaged, but the restoration is certain. The words of the confession make use of the language of such passages as Ps. 106:6:

> We have sinned like our forefathers,
>
> we have erred and done wrong.

(The close similarity of language is more obvious in the original Hebrew.) See also 1 Kings 8:47; Jer. 3:25; Dan. 9:5; cp. CD xx.28*b*–30*a*.

25*b*–26*a*. *in that we have walked [contrary to the covenant] of truth and righteous[ness*: restoration based on CD xx.29; the general sense is clear, but the exact words are uncertain.

1.26*b*–11.1*a*. [...] *his judgement upon us and upon our fathers*: the gap in line 26 is too large to be restored, but cp. CD xx.29*b*–30*a*. *but he has bestowed his loving grace upon us*: cp. Isa. 63:7. *from everlasting to* *everlasting*: the same Hebrew expression as is used for instance in Ps. 90:2; 103:17.

II.1*b*–4*a*. Blessing by the priests of the men of the lot of God; cp. Deut. 27:11–13; 28:1–6.

1*b*–2*a*. *the men of the lot of God*: 'lot' here has the sense 'portion', and the expression means 'the men who belong to God' – in contrast to 'the men of the lot of Belial' (lines 4*b*–5*a*), i.e. those who belong to Belial. The expressions 'lot of God' and 'lot of Belial' (or 'lot of darkness') also occur in the War Scroll (cp. e.g. 1.5; XIII.5*b*–6); they convey much the same as the corresponding expressions 'sons of light' and 'sons of darkness', that is they refer to the members of the community and those who are not members; in the present context 'the men of the lot of God' no doubt means in the first instance those joining the community. For the idea that men are divided into two opposing groups see the comment on III.13–IV.1; and for the idea that a particular portion of mankind belongs to God cp. Deut. 32:9; Ecclus. 17:17; but the word 'lot' is not used in these passages. *walk perfectly in all his ways*: the expression uses the language of Deuteronomy; cp. 10:12, 'to conform to all his ways'; 11:22.

2*b*–4*a*. An adaptation of the Aaronic blessing of Num. 6:24–6. The influence of the passage in Numbers can also be seen in Jub. 12:29 and in the Words of Blessing (cp. e.g. 1QSb III. 1–5). *keep you from all evil*: cp. Ps. 121:7.

4*b*–10. Cursing by the Levites of the men of the lot of Belial; cp. Deut. 27:14–26; 28:15–19.

4*b*–5*a*. The *Levites* pronounce the curses, as in Deut. 27:14. *the men of the lot of Belial*: see the comment above. In the context it is perhaps backsliders who are particularly in mind.

5*b*–7*a*. *May God give you up to terror*: for the reference to 'terror' cp. Deut. 28:25 (NEB, 'May you be repugnant'), but cp. also Jer. 29:18 (NEB, 'I...make them repugnant') and Ezek. 23:46 (NEB, 'abandon them to terror'); in these last two passages the Hebrew verb used with the word for 'terror' is the same as in the Rule. *all who take vengeance...all who exact retribution*: either angels of punishment (cp. 1 En. 62:11) or human persecutors, but more probably the former.

7*b*–8*a*. *gloom of everlasting fire*: whatever precisely is the case in lines 5*b*–7*a*, the thought here is of punishment after the judgement at the end of this age. In the literature of the intertestamental period burning in fire is the common means of punishment for the wicked; cp. for example 1 En. 90:26–7; T. Zeb. 10:3; Matt. 18:8; 25:41.

8*b*. *forgive you by making expiation for your iniquities*: cp. 1QH IV.37

and see the comment on CD 11.4*b*–5*a*. Other passages speak of the members of the community making expiation by their deeds; see the comment on v.6*a*.

9. The reverse of the blessing in line 4. *all who make intercession*: the translation is uncertain, and 'all who hold fast to the fathers' (i.e. the tradition or covenant of the fathers) would also be possible. The translation 'all who make intercession' is based on an idiom in languages cognate with Hebrew. The intercessors are assumed to be angels, and the hope expressed is that the wicked may not find peace at the last judgement through the intercession of angels. For angels as intercessors see, e.g., T. Dan 6:1; 1 En. 9:3; 15.2.

11–18. Cursing of those whose entry into the covenant is insincere.

11*b*–12*a*. *Cursed for the idols...the stumbling-block of his iniquity*: the words of the curse draw on the formula repeated in Ezek. 14:3, 4, 7; cp. verse 3, 'these people have set their hearts on their idols and keep their eyes fixed on the sinful things that cause their downfall' (the similarity of language is clearer in the original Hebrew). *which he worships*: the meaning of the text is unclear, and the translation follows a suggested emendation.

12*b*–16*ab*. *When he...sons of light*: an adaptation of Deut. 29:19–21.

12*b*–14*a*. *When he...the moist*: cp. Deut. 29:19. *But his spirit shall be destroyed, the dry with the moist*: the author is using the last words of Deut. 29:19, but the meaning is not quite clear. In literal translation Deut. 29:19 ends with the words 'to the sweeping away of moist and dry' (see the NEB footnote); but 'moist and dry' is apparently a proverbial expression for 'everything', and the sense is conveyed by the NEB, 'but this will bring everything to ruin'. In the Rule, with the exception of the word for 'his spirit', the author has taken the vocabulary from Deut. 29:19. But it is not clear whether 'the dry with the moist' is still to be understood as a proverbial expression for 'everything', which would suggest a translation, 'But his spirit shall be completely destroyed', or whether the expression is meant to convey something of the double character of the insincere member of the community. There is perhaps an allusion to this passage in 1QpHab XI.13*b*–14*a*.

14*b*–16*a*. *without forgiveness. May the anger...cling to him*: cp. Deut. 29:20*a*. *burn upon him for everlasting destruction*: see the comment on lines 7*b*–8*a*. *May all the curses of this covenant cling to him*: the text agrees with the Septuagint version of Deut. 29:20*a* rather than the Massoretic text (literally, 'and all the curse will fall heavily on him'), but for the reference to the 'covenant' see also Deut. 29:21; cp. CD 1.16*b*–17*a*.

16b. *May God set him apart...sons of light*: cp. Deut. 29:21a.

16c–17a. *because of his backsliding from God through his idols and the stumbling-block of his iniquity*: cp. Ezek. 14:3, 4, 7 and see the comment on lines 11b–12a.

17b. *his lot*: here, as in 1.10, with the meaning 'destiny' or 'fate'. *amongst those who are cursed for ever*: cp. 1 En. 27:2, which refers to the gathering together for punishment of those who are 'cursed for ever'.

THE ANNUAL RENEWAL OF THE COVENANT

II.19 Thus they shall do every year, as long as the reign of Belial lasts. The priests shall enter 20 into the order first, one after the other according to their spiritual status. And the Levites shall enter after them. 21 And thirdly all the people shall enter into the order, one after the other, by thousands, hundreds, 22 fifties, and tens, so that every man of Israel may know his own position in the community of God 23 according to the eternal plan. No man shall move down from his position, or move up from his allotted place. 24 For they shall all be in a community of truth, virtuous humility, kindly love, and right intention 25 towards one another in a holy council, and they shall all be members of an eternal fellowship.

Lines 19–25a, although thought by some scholars to refer to a separate ceremony, are best taken as a continuation of the instructions for the ceremony of entry into the covenant. They provide for an annual renewal of the covenant and thus indicate that the formal admission of new members took place once a year. This passage prescribes the hierarchical order that is to be observed when the covenant is renewed.

In the Old Testament Deut. 31:9–13 appears to legislate for the renewal of the covenant every seven years at the feast of tabernacles (or booths), and in any case scholars have believed that covenant-renewal was an important aspect of this great autumn festival. However, it seems clear that at Qumran the covenant was renewed at the feast of weeks (Pentecost, as it is called in Greek, cp. Acts 2:1); according to the calendar observed by the community this festival fell on the fifteenth day of the third month. Thus the oldest manuscript of the Damascus Document refers to a gathering of all the members in the third month; the exact day is not mentioned, but the reference is apparently to the celebration of the covenant-renewal ceremony on the occasion of the feast of weeks. More explicit is the statement of the book of Jubilees, a document closely associated with the Qumran community: 'That is why it is ordained and written on the heavenly tablets that they should celebrate the feast of weeks in this month (i.e. the third month) once a year – so as to renew the covenant each year' (Jub. 6:17). But it may be observed that 2 Chron. 15:10–13 already refers to a renewal of the covenant in the third month, apparently at the feast of weeks. In Jewish tradition the feast of weeks commemorates the giving of the law at Sinai (cp. b. Pes. 68b), and Acts 2 implicitly presents Pentecost as a new Sinai event.

II.19a. *as long as the reign of Belial lasts*: the community believed that the present age, the reign of Belial (cp. I.18a), would come to an end in a short time, and that in the new age its laws would be superseded; see further IX.10b–11.

19b–23. The order of precedence at the renewal of the covenant. *The priests shall enter into the order first*: the translation is based on the assumption that we have here a technical term for admission to the covenant (cp. I.16 and Deut. 29:12), but the translation 'shall enter in order' (or even 'shall pass by in order') would also be possible (similarly in line 21). The pre-eminent role assigned to the priests is observable here, as it is throughout the Qumran writings, and serves as a reminder of the essentially priestly character of the community. Instead of the three groups mentioned here, VI.8–9 has priests, elders, and people, while CD XIV.3–6a mentions proselytes in addition. *one after the other according to their spiritual status*: literally 'according to their spirits'. The members of the community were ranked in a strict order, each man's position in the order being determined annually on the basis of his spiritual character and his deeds; see v.20b–24a. *all the people*: the lay members of the community. *by thousands, hundreds, fifties, and tens*: the organisation of the lay members of the community was modelled on that of Israel in the wilderness: cp. Exod. 18:21; Deut. 1:15. In 1 Macc. 3:55 Judas, presented as a faithful adherent of the law, divides his army in the same way; see the Cambridge Bible Commentary on 1 Maccabees, p. 55. *Israel*: here the community is meant; it believed itself to be the true Israel. *his own position*: his rank within the community. The Hebrew expression (*bēt maʿ amād*) means literally 'the house (i.e. place) of his standing', and some scholars have thought that *maʿamād* is used here – and elsewhere in the scrolls – as a technical term with a sense comparable to that of *maʿamād* in the rabbinic writings. In this latter usage *maʿamād* has been defined as follows: 'It is the

name given to a group of representatives from outlying districts,
corresponding to the twenty-four "courses of priests". Part of them
went up to the Temple as witnesses of the offering of the sacrifices
(Ta'an. IV.2), and part came together in their own town, where they
held prayers at fixed times during the day coinciding with the fixed
times of sacrifice in the Temple' (H. Danby, *The Mishnah*, Oxford,
1933). However, it seems unlikely that the word has a comparable
technical meaning in the scrolls, particularly in view of the fact that
in line 23 *bēt ma'amād* is used synonymously with a quite different
Hebrew expression, 'his allotted place'. The position or rank of each
individual was determined by the community (v.23b–24a), but was at
the same time in accordance with God's 'eternal plan'.

24–25a. The character of the community. *a holy council...an eternal
fellowship*: both apparently intended as titles of the community. The
use of these terms, like that of 'community of God' (1.12: II.22), is an
indication that the members believed that their life already formed a
part of the life of God's heavenly council (cp. Jer. 23:18, 22); elsewhere
in the scrolls we find the idea that the angels are present in the
community; cp. for instance 1QSa II.8b–9a.

REFUSAL TO ENTER THE COVENANT

II.25 No one who refuses to enter ²⁶ [into the covenant of Go]d so that
he may walk in the stubbornness of his heart [shall enter into the
comm]unity of his truth, for III.1 his soul has spurned the disciplines
involved in the knowledge of the precepts of righteousness; he has not
devoted himself to the conversion of his life, and with the upright he
shall not be counted. ² His knowledge, his abilities, and his wealth shall
not be brought into the council of the community, for he ploughs with
wicked step, and defilement ³ accompanies his conversion. He shall not
be justified when he follows the stubbornness of his heart; for he regards
darkness as the ways of light. In the spring of the perfect ⁴ he shall
not be counted. He shall not be made clean by atonement, or purified
by waters for purification, or made holy by seas ⁵ and rivers, or purified
by any water for washing. Unclean, unclean shall he be as long as he
rejects the precepts ⁶ of God by refusing to discipline himself in the
community of his counsel. For it is through a spirit of true counsel with
regard to the ways of man that all ⁷ his iniquities shall be wiped out
so that he may look on the light of life. It is through a holy spirit uniting

him to his truth that he shall be purified from all [8] his iniquities. It is through a spirit of uprightness and humility that his sin shall be wiped out. And it is through the submission of his soul to all the statutes of God [9] that his flesh shall be purified, by being sprinkled with waters for purification and made holy by waters for cleansing.

Let him, therefore, order his steps that he may walk perfectly [10] in all the ways of God in accordance with that which he commanded at the times (when he made known) his decrees, without turning to right or left, and without [11] going against any one of all his commandments. Then he will be accepted through soothing atonement before God, and it will be for him a covenant [12] of the eternal community.

This passage is directed in the first instance against those who, apparently at the end of their probationary period, refused to enter the covenant. Membership of the community involved entry into the covenant, and no one who refused to participate in the covenant ceremony, and to take upon himself the obligations of the covenant, could be a community member (cp. I.16–18*a*). But it becomes apparent that what is at issue here is not just a formal refusal to enter the covenant, but rather the attitude of the person entering, which must be one of complete sincerity (cp.II.11–18). For the insincere person the purificatory rites of the community would be of no effect. In contrast the person whose conversion was completely sincere is given an assurance that these rites would cleanse him, and that he would receive divine forgiveness and acceptance; for him entry into the covenant would mean membership of God's eternal community.

II.25*b*–III.1. *walk in the stubbornness of his heart*: see on I.6. *his soul has spurned...the precepts of righteousness* (or 'judgements of righteousness'): this passage, together with the verb 'refuse' (II.25), draws on the vocabulary of Lev. 26:43, 'because they rejected my judgements and spurned my statutes'. *the upright*: the members of the community.

III.2–3*a*. *His knowledge, his abilities, and his wealth*: see on I.11*b*–12*a*. *the council of the community*: an expression used frequently in the Community Rule to refer to the whole community (see for instance VI.10, 12–13, 14; cp. 1QpHab XII.4); in line 6 the synonymous expression 'the community of his counsel (or 'council' – see the comment on I.8)' is used. *for he ploughs* (literally 'for his ploughing is'): a metaphor no doubt based on Hos. 10:13. *with wicked step*: or perhaps 'in the mud of wickedness'.

3*b*–4*a*. *In the spring*: a symbolic name for the community; cp. 'the

spring of Jacob' as a symbolic name for Israel in Deut. 33:28 (where
the NEB paraphrases as 'the tribes of Jacob'). According to line 19 the
generations of truth come from 'a spring of light'. *the perfect*: the
members of the community; cp. 'the perfect of way' (IV.22a) and 'the
men of perfect holiness' (VIII.20).

4b–6a. An allusion to the washing rites practised by the community.
According to Josephus (*War* II.8.5 (129)) the Essenes took purificatory
baths each day before their common meal, and this practice may well
be particularly in mind in v.13. But from the present passage it appears
that a ritual bath also formed part of the covenant ceremony.
Instructions about the water to be used in such a rite are given in CD
x.10–13, and amongst the many cisterns at Qumran two basins have
been identified which served as baths and were perhaps used for ritual
baths. In the present passage it is important to observe that the
purificatory rites were thought to have no effect unless accompanied
by the appropriate inner disposition, that is one of sincere and
wholehearted repentance, and of humble submission to God inspired
by a spirit of true counsel and of holiness (see lines 6b–9a). The use
of a washing rite (or 'baptism') as part of a ceremony of admission
was not unique to the Qumran community amongst the Jews of that
time: converts to Judaism were immersed as part of the rites of
admission to the Jewish faith; for the baptism of John see Mark 1:2–8
(and parallels), and for Christian baptism such passages as Acts 2:37–41;
Rom. 6:1–4; 1 Pet. 3:21.

4b–5a. *waters for purification*: the Hebrew is literally 'waters of
impurity', i.e. to remove impurity, and the expression occurs frequently in Num. 19, where NEB renders as 'water of purification' (for
instance at verses 9, 13); Num. 19:1–10 describes the rite for preparing
the ashes used in the water. *water for washing*: the expression as such
does not occur in the Old Testament, but the Hebrew reflects the
language of the expression 'to bathe in water' which occurs frequently
in Lev. 14–16 (as 14:9; 15:5).

5b–6a. *Unclean, unclean shall he be as long as he rejects the precepts of
God*: the language is drawn from Lev. 13:45–6, but here it is not the
one who suffers from a malignant skin-disease who is unclean, but the
one who 'rejects the precepts (or 'judgements') of God'; for the latter
expression cp. line 1 and Lev. 26:43. *by refusing to discipline himself*: cp.
line 1. *in the community of his counsel*: see the comment on lines 2–3a.

6b–7a. *a spirit of true counsel*: cp. Isa. 11:2. The term 'spirit' is used
in lines 6, 7 and 8 to refer to the disposition of the individual, and what
is in mind here is proper understanding of *the ways of man*, that is of

man's spiritual constitution and behaviour (cp. lines 20–21a). *the light of life*: the expression occurs in Job 33:30; Ps. 56:13; John 8:12. Here the light is the enlightenment which the member receives within the community. For the expression used here contrast line 3, 'for he regards darkness as the ways of light'.

7b–8a. *a holy spirit*: see on 6b–7a. However, a variant reading has 'his spirit of holiness', and the passage would then refer to the spirit given to the community by God.

8b–9a. *that his flesh shall be purified*: the author reverts again to language which in the Old Testament is used of disease and various types of uncleanness (cp. Lev. 13–15; Num. 19, and lines 4b–6a). The particular expression here employs language which is used in Lev. 15:13 of a man with a discharge, and in 2 Kings 5:10 in relation to skin-disease. *waters for purification*: see the comment on lines 4b–5a.

9b–12. A concluding exhortation directed towards the person joining the community. *at the times (when he made known) his decrees*: literally 'at the times of his decrees'; see the comment on 1.9. *without turning to right or left*: cp. 1.15b. *through soothing atonement*: based on the Old Testament expression 'a soothing odour' (cp. for example Exod. 29:18, 25, 41; Ezek. 20:41). In the context we are perhaps to understand that the atonement is effected not by sacrifice, but through the right behaviour and the correct inward disposition; cp. viii.3, 'pay for iniquity by the practice of justice', where 'pay for' is from the same Hebrew verb as 'be accepted' in the present passage. *and it will be for him a covenant of the eternal community*: based on Num. 25:13, where the Hebrew reads literally, 'and it will be for him...a covenant of the eternal priesthood'.

THE TEACHING OF THE COMMUNITY

The section which begins with a new heading in iii.13 and ends in iv.26 – another new heading follows immediately in v.1 – clearly forms a self-contained element in the Community Rule. It is fundamentally important inasmuch as it sets out explicitly ideas about the nature of man which, although implicit elsewhere in the Qumran writings, are nowhere else expressed in such clear terms. For convenience the passage is divided into three parts: iii.13–iv.1; iv.2–14; iv.15–26.

THE TWO SPIRITS

III.13 For the wise leader that he may instruct and teach all the sons of light about the history of all the sons of men 14 according to all the kinds of spirits revealed in the character of their deeds during their generations, and according to their visitation of chastisement as well as 15 their times of reward.

From the God of knowledge comes everything that is and will be. Before they existed he fixed all their plans, 16 and when they come into existence they complete their work according to their instructions in accordance with his glorious plan, and without changing anything. In his hand 17 are the laws for all things, and he sustains them in all their concerns.

He created man to rule 18 the world, and he assigned two spirits to him that he might walk by them until the appointed time of his visitation; they are the spirits 19 of truth and of injustice. From a spring of light come the generations of truth, and from a well of darkness the generations of injustice. 20 Control over all the sons of righteousness lies in the hand of the prince of lights, and they walk in the ways of light; complete control over the sons of injustice lies in the hand of the angel 21 of darkness, and they walk in the ways of darkness. It is through the angel of darkness that all the sons of righteousness go astray, 22 and all their sins, their iniquities, their guilt, and their deeds of transgression are under his control 23 in the mysteries of God until his time. All their afflictions and their times of distress are brought about by his rule of hatred, 24 and all the spirits of his lot make the sons of light stumble. But the God of Israel and his angel of truth help all 25 the sons of light.

He created the spirits of light and of darkness, and upon them he founded every deed,26 [and upon] their [ways] every work [...] God loves one for all IV.1 eternity, and he delights in all its actions for ever; the other — he loathes its counsel and hates all its ways for ever.

After a heading (III.13—15a), and a statement about the predetermination of all things by God (III.15b—17a), the author begins to set out his beliefs about the nature of man. Basic to these beliefs is the conviction that there are two opposing forces in the world, the spirits

of truth and of injustice, and that all men are under the control of one
or the other (III.17b–21a); further that the behaviour and future destiny
of an individual depend on which spirit controls him (IV.2–14). Side
by side with the idea that men are assigned to one spirit or the other
there is found the belief that men are influenced by both spirits, and
in this way an attempt is made to take account of the fact that men
are a mixture of both good and evil. Thus the wicked behaviour of
righteous men is said to be caused by the angel of darkness (a name
used for the spirit of injustice; see III.21b–25a). Elsewhere it is said that
the two spirits struggle within the heart of man, and that a man's
behaviour is proportionately good or evil according to which spirit
predominates in him (IV.23b–25a; cp. IV.15–18a).

The belief that there is a conflict in this world between the opposing
forces of good and evil is called dualism. But the dualism of the
Community Rule is not absolute inasmuch as no independent existence
is ascribed to the principle of evil. Thus on the one hand it is said that
God created the spirits of both light and darkness (i.e. truth and
injustice; see III.25). On the other hand it is said that God has assigned
an end to the existence of injustice, and that thereafter truth will prevail
for ever (IV.18b–23a). The dualistic beliefs of the community are seen
here to be linked intimately to its expectation that God would shortly
intervene in the world to destroy evil, and to establish a new era in
which his rule would be undisputed.

Dualistic beliefs are widely presupposed in Jewish and Christian
writings of the period, but they are rarely presented in such an explicit
form as in the Community Rule; see, however, Ecclus. 33:7–15;
42:24; T. Jud. 20:1–2 (cp. verse 1, 'Understand then, my children, that
two spirits attend on man, the *spirit* of truth and the *spirit* of error');
T. Asher 1:3–6:6. Elsewhere within the Qumran writings, it is perhaps
in the War Scroll that dualistic ideas are most prominent. It may be
noted here that there are affinities between the passage on the two spirits
in the Community Rule (III.13–IV.26) and the passages on the Two
Ways that are to be found in early Christian writings (cp. Epistle of
Barnabas 18–21; Didache 1–6).

The explanation of human behaviour in terms of an explicit dualism
represents a new development in Judaism, but the background to the
ideas of the Community Rule can be found within the Old Testament
itself. The Old Testament often speaks of God's spirit which stirs men
to action (cp. e.g. Judg. 14:6; 1 Sam. 10:10), but it also knows of spirits
that are to some extent independent of him (cp. e.g. 2 Kings 19:7;
Num. 27:16); it can even speak of God sending an evil (1 Sam.

16:14–16) or a lying (1 Kings 22:21–3) spirit. The doctrine of the two spirits in the Rule may be seen as a development of these Old Testament ideas, a development perhaps influenced by the dualistic beliefs of Zoroastrianism, the religion of ancient Iran. The development of the doctrine may be compared with the emergence of the idea of Satan (1 Chron. 21:1) or Belial (see the comment on CD IV.12*b*) as an independent being opposed to God, and with a host of subordinates at his command; it may also be related to the growth after the exile in the importance attached to angels as agents of God. As an explanation of human behaviour the doctrine of the two spirits in the Rule may be compared with the idea found in the rabbinic writings of the two inclinations, the evil and the good (see the comment on v.4*b*–5).

III.13–15*a*. *An introduction to the teaching which follows*. *For the wise leader*: the Hebrew word (*maskīl*) occurs a number of times in the scrolls (cp. e.g. IX.12, 21; CD XII.21; also Dan. 11:33, 35; 12:3). In the scrolls the term appears to be used as one of the titles for the lay leader of the community who in VI.14 is called 'the officer in charge at the head of the many'. *history*: literally 'generations' (*tōlēdōt*), the same word that occurs in such passages as Gen. 2:4; 5:1; 6:9 (seen more obviously in the RSV than the NEB). In the Community Rule the term is used to refer not to a 'history' in our sense of the term, but rather to an account of men's character, a description of their nature – and the term has in fact sometimes been translated as 'nature'. *according to all the kinds of spirits*: men are under the control of either the spirit of truth or that of injustice, but are also thought to be influenced by both spirits in varying degrees; it is thus possible to think of them possessing different kinds of spirits. The use of the word 'kinds' (cp. Gen. 1:11–12, 21, 24–5), linked to the use of the word 'generations' (*tōlēdōt*), suggests an allusion to the creation narrative (Gen. 1:1–2:4*a*). *during their generations*: throughout the history of mankind. The Hebrew word used (*dōrōt*) is not the same as the one translated 'history' (literally 'generations') in the previous line. *their visitation of chastisement as well as their times of reward*: a reference to God's future intervention to punish the wicked and to reward the good. The 'visitation' of those whose lives are dominated by the spirit of truth and of those dominated by the spirit of injustice is described in IV.6*b*–8, 11*b*–14.

15*b*–17*a*. *God, the source of all existence, has predetermined everything that happens in the universe*. The determinism that in a variety of ways frequently finds expression in the scrolls and in other Jewish writings of the period, is here presented within a cosmological framework; cp. 1QH 1.7–20; Ecclus. 16:26–8; 1 En. 2:1–5:3. *the God of knowledge*: a title for God taken from 1 Sam. 2:3 which also occurs in the Hymns (e.g. 1.26). *Before they existed*: the author seems to have in mind not just the actions of human beings, but everything that happens – all things take place in accordance with the *plans* which God laid down in advance. *they complete their work…in accordance with his glorious plan*: cp. 1 En. 5:2, 'his works (are) before him in each succeeding year, and all his works serve him and do not change, but as God has decreed, so everything is done'.

III.17b–IV.1. The author begins to set out his teaching about the two spirits.

17b–19a. *He created man to rule the world*: a further allusion to the creation narrative, cp. Gen. 1:26–8 and see also Ps. 8:6; Wisd. of Sol. 9:2–3. *his visitation*: i.e. God's visitation at the end of this age; cp. CD XIX.10, and for the thought of God 'visiting' mankind see the comment on CD 1.7a.

19b. *From a spring of light…from a well of darkness*: a metaphorical description of the origins of those who are under the control of the spirits of truth and of injustice respectively. The symbolic use of the terms 'light' and 'darkness' is entirely natural in itself and finds many parallels of various kinds in biblical writings: cp. for instance such passages as Isa. 9:2; Ps. 107:10, 14; the use of 'light' in the sense 'prosperity, blessing' in Isa. 56–66 (e.g. 58:8, 10); the idea of the law as a light expressed in such passages as Pss. 19:8; 119:105; 2 Esdras 14:20–1; T. Levi 19:1; and the thought of Jesus as 'the light of the world' (John 8:12; 9:5).

20–21a. *sons of righteousness…sons of injustice*: the community no doubt referred these terms, like the comparable expressions 'sons of light' and 'sons of darkness' (1.9–10), to themselves and their opponents. *prince of lights*: the spirit of truth. For the title cp. CD v.18; 1QM XIII.10; a comparison of the latter passage with 1QM XVII.6b–8a suggests that the prince of light(s) was identified with the archangel Michael (cp. for example Dan. 12:1; 1 En. 9:1; Rev. 12:7). In line 24 the title 'angel of truth' is also used. *the angel of darkness*: the spirit of injustice, apparently identified with Belial (cp. 1.17b–18a; CD v.18; 1 QM XIII.10b–12a; and see the comment on CD IV.12b. *and they walk in the ways of darkness*: perhaps based on Prov. 2:13.

21b–25a. The division of mankind into two groups under the respective control of the spirits of truth and injustice is here modified in that the sins of the righteous are attributed to the influence upon them of the angel of darkness. It thus appears that men are affected by

both spirits, and that their behaviour is determined by whichever spirit
is predominant in them: cp. iv.15–18a, 23b–25a. *in the mysteries of God*:
the sins of the righteous are in accordance with God's mysterious
purposes. The word for 'mystery' or 'secret' (*raz*), found also in the
Aramaic portion of Daniel (e.g. 2:47; 4:9), is used frequently in the
scrolls with reference to God; according to 1QpHab vii.4–5a it was
to the teacher of righteousness that God made known 'all the mysteries
of the words of his servants the prophets'. *until his time*: the time of
God's visitation. *hatred*: the Hebrew word (*maśṭēmāh*),used also in CD
xvi.5; 1QM xiii.4, 11, suggests a deliberate link with the proper name
Mastema which is known from other sources (e.g. Jub. 10:8) as a name
for Belial. *and all the spirits of his lot*: like Belial in the Testaments of
the Twelve Patriarchs (cp. e.g. T. Reub. 2:1–2 and 3:3–6) the angel
of darkness has at his disposal a host of subordinate spirits. *But the God
of Israel and his angel of truth help all the sons of light*: for the thought
cp. 1QM xiii.10; xvii.6b.

   iii.25b–iv.1. *He created the spirits of light and of darkness*: despite his
dualistic views, the author retains the basic Jewish belief in one God;
the spirit of darkness is not completely independent, but owes its origin
to God. For the symbolism of light and darkness see the comment on
iii.19b.

THE TWO SPIRITS: THEIR WAYS AND THEIR VISITATION

iv.2 These are their ways in the world: to enlighten the heart of man,
to make level before him all the ways of righteousness and of truth,
and to instil in his heart reverence for the precepts 3 of God, a spirit
of humility, patience, abundant compassion, eternal goodness, insight,
understanding, strong wisdom which trusts in all 4 the deeds of God
and relies on the abundance of his kindness, a spirit of knowledge with
regard to every plan of action, zeal for the precepts of righteousness,
a holy purpose 5 with a constant mind, abundant kindness towards all
the sons of truth, a glorious purity which loathes all the impure idols,
circumspection 6 linked to discernment in all things, and concealment
of the truth of the mysteries of knowledge. These are the counsels of
the spirit for the sons of truth in the world.

   The visitation of all those who walk in it will be healing, 7 abundant
peace with long life, fruitfulness with every everlasting blessing, eternal

joy with life for ever, and a crown of glory [8] with a garment of honour
in eternal light.

[9] To the spirit of injustice belong greed, slackness in the service of
righteousness, wickedness and falsehood, pride and haughtiness, lying
and deceit, cruelty [10] and great hypocrisy, impatience and abundant
folly, zeal for insolence, abominable deeds committed in a spirit of lust,
impure ways in the service of uncleanness, [11] a blaspheming tongue,
blind eyes, a deaf ear, a stiff neck, a stubborn heart causing a man to
walk in all the ways of darkness, and an evil cunning.

The visitation [12] of all those who walk in it will be abundant
chastisements at the hand of all the destroying angels, eternal destruction
brought about by the anger of the avenging wrath of God, perpetual
terror, and everlasting shame [13] with the ignominy of destruction in
the fires of darkness. And all the times of their generations (will be
spent) in sorrowful mourning and bitter distress in the abysses of
darkness until [14] they are destroyed without remnant or survivor for
them.

In two parallel passages the author now contrasts the behaviour and
the fate of those dominated respectively by the spirit of truth and the
spirit of injustice. This material may be compared with Gal. 5:16–25,
where a contrast is drawn between 'the kind of behaviour that belongs
to the lower nature' and 'the harvest of the Spirit'; cp. also Rom.
1:29–31.

iv.2–6a. It is possible that a phrase, comparable to that of line 9,
which served to make clear that lines 2–6a deal with the ways of the
spirit of truth, has dropped out of line 2.

2. *to make level before him*: perhaps an allusion to Isa. 40:3 (quoted
in viii.14), but 'before him' refers here to man, not God; cp. Ps. 5:8.
Throughout this passage allusions to the Old Testament may be
discerned, but only a few instances can be noted here.

4. *a spirit of knowledge*: cp. Isa. 11:2, a passage which may more
generally be in mind here.

5. *a constant mind*: an expression unique in the Old Testament to Isa.
26:3 (NEB, 'Thou dost keep in peace men of constant mind'); cp.
viii.3; 1QH 1.35; ii.9, 36. *circumspection*: the Hebrew expression is taken
from Mic. 6:8 (NEB, 'to walk wisely').

6a. *concealment of the truth of the mysteries of knowledge*: according to

Josephus (*War* II.8.7 (141)) the Essenes were 'to conceal nothing from the members of the sect and to report none of their secrets to others, even though tortured to death.' *the spirit*: i.e. of truth.

6b–8. The author uses a number of familiar Old Testament concepts to describe the eternal bliss which awaits those who walk in the spirit of truth; cp. the description of the new age in 1 En. 10:16–11:2. *healing*: cp. Jer. 14:19; Mal. 4:2. *long life*: frequently mentioned in the Old Testament as a sign of divine favour; cp. for instance Ps. 21:4. *fruitfulness*: likewise frequently mentioned as one of the blessings given by God (e.g. Deut. 7:13); cp. 1 En. 10:17–18, where it is seen as one of the blessings of the new age. *a crown of glory*: a symbol of divine favour: cp. Ps. 8:5; T. Benj. 4:1; 1 Pet. 5:4. *a garment of honour*: cp. 1 En. 62:15. *in eternal light*: cp. the description of the new Jerusalem in Isa. 60:19–20, and similarly Rev. 22:5.

9–11a. Reminiscences of the language of the Old Testament can again often be discerned: a few are noted here. *a spirit of lust*: cp. Hos. 4:12 (NEB, 'a spirit of wantonness'); 5:4. *impure ways in the service of uncleanness*: illegitimate worship is meant: cp. Ezek. 36:17–18. *and an evil cunning*: the Hebrew word for 'cunning' ('*ormāh*) is the same as that used for 'discernment' in line 6 (cp. the negative and positive meanings of this same word in Josh. 9:4 (NEB, 'a ruse') and Prov. 1:4 ('shrewdness')). Here, as elsewhere in this passage, the language used in the list of the ways of the spirit of injustice mirrors that in the list of the ways of the spirit of truth.

11b–14. The eternal punishment which awaits those who walk in the spirit of injustice. *the destroying angels*: cp. CD II.6 and the frequent references in 1 En. 37–71 to 'angels of punishment' (e.g. 53:3). *in the fires of darkness*: darkness and fire are also associated in II.8a (cp. 1 En. 103:7–8); see the comment on II.7b–8a for the theme of burning as the means of punishment for the wicked. *in the abysses of darkness*: cp. Jub. 7:29; 2 Pet. 2:4 for the thought of hell as an abyss of darkness. But the passage could also be translated 'in calamities of darkness'. *until they are destroyed without remnant or survivor for them*: based on Ezra 9:14, also used in CD II.6b–7a.

THE TWO SPIRITS: THE END OF INJUSTICE

IV.15 The history of all the sons of men is constituted by these (two spirits): in their (two) classes all their hosts in their generations have an inheritance, and in their ways they walk. All the work [16] which they do (is carried out) in relation to their (two) classes, depending on

whether a man's inheritance is great or small, for all the times of
eternity. For God has established them in equal parts until the last
time, [17] and has put eternal enmity between their (two) classes. An
abomination to truth are the actions of injustice, and an abomination
to injustice are all the ways of truth; there is a fierce [18] struggle between
all their principles, for they do not walk together.

But God in his mysterious insight and glorious wisdom has assigned
an end to the existence of injustice, and at the appointed time [19] of the
visitation he will destroy it for ever. Then truth will appear in the world
for ever, for it has defiled itself in the ways of wickedness during the
reign of injustice until [20] the time decreed for judgement. Then God
will purify by his truth all the deeds of man and will refine for himself
the frame of man, removing all spirit of injustice from within [21] his
flesh, and purifying him by the spirit of holiness from every wicked
action. And he will sprinkle upon him the spirit of truth like waters
for purification (to remove) all the abominations of falsehood (in
which) he has defiled himself [22] through the spirit of impurity, so that
the upright may have understanding in the knowledge of the Most
High and the perfect of way insight into the wisdom of the sons of
heaven. For it is they whom God has chosen for the eternal
covenant, [23] and to them shall all the glory of Adam belong. There
shall be no more injustice, and all the deeds of deceit shall be put to
shame.

Until now the spirits of truth and injustice struggle in the hearts of
men, [24] and they walk in wisdom or in folly. According to a man's
inheritance in truth and righteousness, so he hates injustice; and
according to his share in the lot of injustice he acts wickedly through
it and so [25] loathes truth. For God has established them in equal parts
until the decreed end and the renewal. And he knows the work of their
deeds for all the times [26] [of eternity], and he has given them as an
inheritance to the sons of men that they may know good [and evil,
and that he may deter]mine the fates of every living being according
to the spirit within [him at the appointed time...of the] visitation.

The last part of the teaching on the two spirits falls into three sections:
lines 15–18a describe the activity of the spirits in the lives of men,

picking up the theme of iii.21b–25a that men are affected by both spirits; lines 18b–23a provide a statement about the end of the existence of injustice and the inauguration of the new era; finally, the teaching on the two spirits is recapitulated in lines 23b–26.

iv.15–18a. The activity of the two spirits in the lives of men.

15a. *The history*: literally 'the generations' (*tōlēdōt*); see the comment on iii.13–15a. *in their (two) classes*: the class (or group) of the spirit of truth and the class of the spirit of injustice. *all their hosts in their generations*: all mankind throughout history. The use of the word 'hosts' may be a reminiscence of Gen. 2:1 (NEB, 'with all their mighty throng'). The word for 'generations' (*dōrōt*) is the same as that used in iii.14 and iv.13; elsewhere in this passage the word is *tōlēdōt*.

15b–16a. *All the work which they do*: literally 'All the work of their deeds'. *(is carried out) in relation to their (two) classes*: all human actions are carried out under the influence of either the spirit of truth or the spirit of injustice. Men have within them a mixture of both spirits, and the character of their actions – like their assignment to the class of the spirit of light or of injustice – depends on which of the two spirits is dominant in them (cp. lines 23b–25a). *depending on whether a man's inheritance is great or small*: i.e in each of the two spirits. The language used is taken from Num. 26:56, part of a passage dealing with the inheritance of the land by the tribes.

16b–17a. *For God has established them*: i.e. the spirits of truth and injustice. *in equal parts*: the Hebrew expression occurs in Exod. 30:34. It is apparently used here to indicate that both spirits exercise an influence on man in this age, although the description of this age as the 'reign of Belial' (or some similar expression; see the comment on CD vi.10) makes clear that in this age the spirit of injustice was thought to have the upper hand. This situation would only be reversed at *the last time* when God would intervene to inaugurate the new age; this intervention is described in lines 18b–23a.

17b–18a. *between all their principles*: literally 'precepts, laws' – the precepts of the spirits of truth and of injustice.

18b–23a. God's visitation to destroy injustice and to inaugurate the new era.

19b–20a. *the reign of injustice*: an expression synonymous with 'the reign of Belial'; cp. 1.18a and see the comment on CD vi.10.

20b–21a. *will purify by his truth all the deeds of man and will refine for himself the frame of man*: two different words are used for 'man' here, but in both cases with a collective meaning. The author is thinking of the purification of a righteous remnant (i.e. the members of the community) after the destruction of wickedness and of wicked men.

21b–22a. *And he will sprinkle upon him the spirit of truth*: for the thought cp. Joel 2:28–9. *like waters for purification*: the same expression that is used in III.4, 9; see the comment on III.4b–5a. *the upright…the perfect of way*: the author is again no doubt thinking of the members of the community: cp. III.1, 3b. *the knowledge of the Most High*: the knowledge which God gives; the expression occurs in Num. 24:16. *the wisdom of the sons of heaven*: the wisdom possessed by the angels; for 'sons of heaven' as a term for 'angels' cp. 1 En. 6:2.

22b–23a. *For it is they whom God has chosen*: the divine choice of Israel (cp. e.g. Deut. 7:6), and of various groups and individuals within the nation, is an important theme within the Old Testament. The members of the community claimed this status for themselves and even referred to themselves as 'the chosen' (cp. VIII.6b; IX.14c; 1QpHab X.13); in contrast the wicked are those whom God 'did not choose' (CD II.7b). *and to them shall all the glory of Adam belong*: see the comment on CD III.19–20a.

23b–26. A summary of the teaching on the two spirits.

23b–24a. *the spirits of truth and injustice struggle in the hearts of men*: see the comment of III.21b–25a; IV.15–18a.

25b. *For God has established them in equal parts*: see the comment on lines 16b–17a. *the renewal*: for the theme of renewal cp. e.g. Isa. 43:19; 65:17; 1 En. 91:16; Rev. 21:5, 'Then he who sat on the throne said, "Behold! I am making all things new!"'

25c–26. *the work of their deeds*: the deeds of the two spirits; the same phrase is used in 15b–16a, but there with reference to the deeds of men. *that they may know good [and evil*: perhaps an allusion to Gen. 2:9. *the fates*: literally 'the lots', cp. I.10; II.17b. [*him at the appointed time…of the] visitation*: the general sense is clear, but the text cannot be restored with any certainty.

THE COMMON LIFE

Columns V–VII contain a series of rules governing the internal life of the community. A number of rubrics occur within the text, and with the aid of these, and on the basis of common content, the material may be divided into the following sections; v.1–7a, statement of principles; v.7b–20a, the binding oath; v.20b–VI.8a, rules for the organisation of the life of the community; VI.8b–13a, rules for a session of the many; VI.13b–23, rules for the admission of new members; VI.24–VII.25, the penitential code. As will become apparent, it is difficult to think that this material is all of one piece; it appears rather to have been put together from several sources.

PRINCIPLES GOVERNING THE LIFE OF THE COMMUNITY

v.1 This is the rule for the men of the community who willingly offer themselves to turn back from all evil and to hold fast to all that he has commanded as his will.

They shall separate themselves from the congregation [2] of the men of injustice and shall form a community in respect of the law and of wealth. They shall be answerable to the sons of Zadok, the priests who keep the covenant, and to the multitude of the men [3] of the community who hold fast to the covenant; on their word the decision shall be taken on any matter having to do with the law, with wealth, or with justice. Together they shall practise truth and humility, [4] righteousness and justice, kindly love and circumspection in all their ways. Let no man walk in the stubbornness of his heart so as to go astray after his heart [5] and his eyes and the thought of his inclination! Rather they shall circumcise in the community the foreskin of their inclination and of their stiff neck that they may lay a foundation of truth for Israel, for the community of the eternal covenant. [6] They shall make expiation for all those who willingly offer themselves to holiness in Aaron and to the house of truth in Israel, and for those who join them in community. In lawsuits and judgements [7] they shall declare guilty all those who transgress the statutes.

Lines 1—7a of column v serve as an introduction to the rules which follow; it may be compared with the introductions in I.1—15 and VIII.1—4a. It states in summary form the principles which should govern the life of the community and touches on a number of matters which are elsewhere developed at greater length. Three manuscripts of the Rule discovered in Cave 4 provide a shorter, and apparently older, version of the material in this column.

v.1a. The heading. Two of the three Cave 4 manuscripts mentioned above have a different heading, 'Interpretation (i.e of the law) for the wise leader concerning the men of the law who willingly offer themselves...'; cp. the description of the Hasidim (in Greek

'Hasidaeans') in 1 Macc. 2:42, 'It was then that they were joined by a company of Hasidaeans, stalwarts of Israel, every one of them a volunteer in the cause of the law.'

1b–2a. They shall separate themselves from the congregation of the men of injustice: the necessity for separation from those who were not members of the community is treated in detail in lines 10b–20a; see the comment there. *the congregation of the men of injustice*: non-members of the community, those under the control of the spirit of injustice (cp. III.17b–21a). But the description of them as a 'congregation' may indicate that a particular group is in mind. *and shall form a community in respect of the law and of wealth*: concern for the law (cp. vi.6b–8a) and the sharing of property (see on 1.11b–13a) are here presented as the basis of the life of the community. *the law (tōrāh)*: both here and in line 3 the Mosaic law is meant.

2b–3a. They shall be answerable to the sons of Zadok, the priests…and to the multitude of the men of the community: authority in the community is here seen to be shared between the priests and the whole body of full members, cp. v.21b–22; vi.18b–19a. However, in ix.7 ultimate authority rests with the priests, and the pre-eminent position of the priests within the community is in any case clear throughout the Qumran writings (cp. e.g. vi.3b–5a). 'Sons of Zadok' is used in the scrolls interchangeably with 'sons of Aaron' as a title for the priests (cp. line 2 with line 21; 1QSa 1.23 with 24), except that in CD iv.3b–4a 'sons of Zadok' is a symbolic title for the whole community. The background to the use of this title is to be found in the Old Testament.

Zadok, often thought to have been priest of the Jebusite shrine at Jerusalem before David conquered the city, appears in 2 Sam. 8:17 without any explanation as one of David's priests, the other being Abiathar. In the struggle for power at the end of David's reign Zadok supported Solomon and became chief priest (1 Kings 1:7–8; 2:26–7, 35), and according to the genealogy of 1 Chron. 6:3b–15 the office remained in this family until the exile. The reform programme of Ezek. 40–8 stated that only the descendants of Zadok should have the right to officiate as priests in the temple at Jerusalem (Ezek. 44:6–31: see verse 15). The background to this claim for an exclusive status has been thought to lie in the attempt in the reign of Josiah to centralise worship in Jerusalem; the legislation of Deut. 18:6–8 had provided that the Levites, here meaning the priests from the shrines outside Jerusalem, who lost their status should be allowed to officiate at the central sanctuary, but 2 Kings 23:8–9 indicates that the priests in Jerusalem prevented this. The passage in Ezekiel represents a reaffirmation of the claims of the descendants of Zadok, but it is not clear how far in the post-exilic period they were able to maintain their exclusive position in the temple at Jerusalem. The Priestly Writing uses the more general title 'sons of Aaron' for the priests (for their position see Num. 3:5–10; 18:1–7), and 1 Chron. 24 knows of two priestly lines descended from Aaron, those of Eleazar, the supposed ancestor of Zadok, and of Ithamar (cp. 1QM XVII.2–3), whose line is traced to Ahimelech, the son of Abiathar. However, according to Num. 25:10–13 the covenant of priesthood was made only with Phinehas, the son of Eleazar, and it is through this line that Zadok's genealogy is traced back to Aaron in 1 Chron. 6:3b–15, 49–53 – in reality, as we have seen, Zadok was probably not even an Israelite. A similar importance is attached to Zadok and Phinehas in Ecclesiasticus: the covenant of priesthood made with Phinehas is mentioned in 45:23–4 and in the Hebrew version of 50:24 (see the Cambridge Bible Commentary on Ecclesiasticus, p. 253); and in a psalm which is found only in the Hebrew version between 51:12 and 13 God is praised as the one who 'chose the sons of Zadok to be priests'. So far as the scrolls are concerned, the use of the title 'sons of Zadok' constitutes a claim that the priests within the community represented the true continuation of the legitimate priestly line, an attitude no doubt governed by the view that the priests in Jerusalem were illegitimate and unworthy holders of office. *the multitude of the men of the community*: 'multitude' is used here, and in v.9, 22; VI.19 (but translated as part of line 18), apparently in the same sense as the term 'the many', that is to refer to the whole body of the full members of the community. In a similar way the Greek word *plēthos* (literally 'multitude') is used in Acts to refer to the Christian community; cp. e.g. Acts 15:30 (NEB, 'the congregation'). For 'the many' see on VI.1b. *the decision shall be taken*: literally 'the fixed rule of the lot shall fall'; but it is unlikely that a literal casting of lots (cp. for instance Num. 33:54; Josh. 16:1) is meant. The idea underlying this figurative use of language is that the decisions of all the full members are as authoritative as the old sacred lot.

3b–4a. *justice, kindly love and circumspection*: the Hebrew of these words, together with 'they shall practise', is a quotation from Mic. 6:8 (NEB, 'to act justly, to love loyalty, to walk wisely').

4b–5. *Let no man walk in the stubbornness of his heart so as to go astray after his heart and his eyes and the thought of his inclination!*: cp. 1.6: CD II.16a. 'Stubbornness of heart' is characteristic of the language of the Deuteronomistic layers of the book of Jeremiah (e.g. 3:17); for the reference to the heart and eyes cp. Num. 15:39; Ezek. 6:9. The concept of the 'inclination' (Hebrew *yēṣer*) may be compared with the rabbinic idea of the two inclinations, the evil and the good; here the thought is of an evil inclination. For the two inclinations cp. also the passage on the two spirits (III.13–IV.26); see above p. 96. *they shall circumcise...the foreskin of their inclination and of their stiff neck*: the law of circumcision (Gen. 17:9–14) is given a spiritual interpretation in terms similar to those of Deut. 10:16, 'you must circumcise the foreskin of your hearts and not be stubborn (literally 'not make your neck stiff') any more', cp. Deut. 30:6; Jer. 4:4; 1QpHab XI.13. *lay a foundation of truth for Israel*: as the following phrase makes clear, 'Israel' in this passage means the true Israel which consisted of the members of the community.

6a. *They shall make expiation*: through their right behaviour the members of the community make expiation for the sins committed by those who belong to it; cp. VIII.6b, 10a; IX.4–6, and see III.6b–8a, for the idea that a man's sins will only be wiped out if he shows a proper disposition. But in other passages it is God who 'makes expiation for' men's sin; see for example II.8b; CD II.5; 1QH IV.37. *to holiness in Aaron...to the house of truth in Israel*: cp. VIII.5b–6a, 8b–10a; IX.6. Holiness and truth (or 'faithfulness') are the qualities to be shown by the priests ('Aaron') and laity ('Israel') respectively within the community.

6b–7a. The duties of members included participation in the trial and sentencing of wrongdoers within the community; cp. the list of punishments in VI.24–VII.25.

THE BINDING OATH

v.7 These are their rules of conduct, according to all these statutes, when they are admitted to the community.

Everyone who joins the council of the community ⁸ shall enter into the covenant of God in the presence of all those who willingly offer themselves. He shall undertake by a binding oath to return to the law of Moses with all his ⁹ heart and soul, following all that he has commanded, and in accordance with all that has been revealed from it to the sons of Zadok, the priests who keep the covenant and seek his will, and to the multitude of the men of their covenant ¹⁰ who together willingly offer themselves for his truth and to walk according to his will.

He shall undertake by the covenant to separate himself from all the

men of injustice who walk [11] in the way of wickedness. For they are
not counted in his covenant because they have not sought or consulted
him about his statutes in order to know the hidden things in which
they have guiltily gone astray, [12] whereas with regard to the things
revealed they have acted presumptuously, arousing anger for judgement and for taking vengeance by the curses of the covenant to bring
upon themselves mighty acts of judgement [13] leading to eternal
destruction without a remnant.

He shall not enter the waters in order to touch the purity of the men
of holiness, for men are not purified [14] unless they turn from their evil;
for he remains unclean amongst all the transgressors of his word. No
one shall join with him with regard to his work or his wealth lest he
burden him [15] with iniquity and guilt. But he shall keep away from
him in everything, for thus it is written, 'You shall keep away from
everything false.' No one of the men of the community shall
answer [16] to their authority with regard to any law or decision. No
one shall eat or drink anything of their property, or take anything at
all from their hand, [17] except for payment, as it is written, 'Have no
more to do with man in whose nostrils is breath, for what is he worth?'
For [18] all those who are not counted in his covenant, they and
everything that belongs to them are to be kept separate. No man of
holiness shall rely on any deeds [19] of vanity, for vanity are all those
who do not know his covenant. He will destroy from the earth all those
who spurn his word; all their deeds are impure [20] before him, and all
their wealth unclean.

We have already seen (1.16–III.12) that membership of the community
involved entry into the covenant. This section deals with two of the
obligations to which the member bound himself in the covenant by
a solemn oath: the obligation to return to the law of Moses (lines
7c–10a) and the obligation to keep separate from the men of injustice
(lines 10b–20a).

v.7b. A heading for the section which follows. *their rules of conduct*:
literally 'the rules of their ways', cp. IX.21b.

7c–8a. *Everyone who joins the council of the community shall enter into
the covenant*: cp. 1.16.

8b–10a. *He shall undertake by a binding oath*: in the light of CD xv.7b–10a it would appear that the candidate swore this oath on the day he offered himself for membership and was examined by the officer in charge (cp. VI.13b–15a). Josephus (*War* II.8.7 (139–42)) also refers to an oath sworn by the candidate, but this seems to have been at a later stage in the process of admission to membership; the oath sworn on admission forms an exception to the statement in *War* II.8.6 (135) that the Essenes avoid the use of oaths. The text of the Rule contains an implicit allusion to Num. 30, which deals with the fulfilment of vows and oaths; the word translated 'binding' only occurs in the Old Testament in Num. 30, and the expression 'binding oath' only in Num. 30:13 (more obvious in the RSV than the NEB). *to return to the law of Moses with all his heart and soul*: cp. CD XV.8–10, 12; XVI.1–2; the covenant is understood as a continuation and renewal of the Mosaic covenant, and so the person entering the community has to take upon himself the obligation to return to the law of Moses, cp. 1.2–3. *with all his heart and soul*: this phrase, or rather one virtually identical with it, is characteristic of the language of Deuteronomy and the Deuteronomistic history; cp. for instance Deut. 4:29; 2 Kings 23:25. The second of these passages as a whole is in fact similar to the passage in the Rule. *following all that he has commanded*: i.e. that God has commanded, cp. e.g. 1.3, 17. *and in accordance with all that has been revealed from it to the sons of Zadok...and to the multitude of the men of their covenant*: this qualification is important – what is required is obedience to the law as understood and interpreted by the community; for the importance of the study of the law see VI.6b–8a. *the sons of Zadok...the multitude*: see the comment on lines 2b–3a.

10b–20a. The second obligation which the person entering the community took upon himself was to keep separate from the men of injustice. In the post-exilic period the Jews were called upon to separate themselves from the peoples of the land (Ezra 6:21; 9:1; 10:11; Neh. 9:2; 10:28), but it is perhaps of more relevance to note that within the Jewish nation Aaron and his sons were set apart for the service of God (1 Chron. 23:13), and that the Levites, who are said to belong to God, were also to be kept separate (Num. 8:14 – in all these passages the same Hebrew verb (*bādal*) is used as in the Rule). Like the Pharisees, the Qumran community appears as a group concerned to observe strictly the laws of ritual purity, and the demand for separation was no doubt based on a desire to avoid contamination through contact with outsiders, who were regarded as unclean; but in making this demand the community was merely appropriating to itself the priestly and levitical ideals of the Old Testament. The regulations of columns v–vii appear to suggest that separation did not exclude all contact with outsiders, and some at least of the material seems to be directed at those who were living amongst their fellow Jews; in columns viii–ix the demand for separation involves withdrawal into the wilderness (viii.13–14).

11b–13a. *For they are not counted in his covenant*: for the expression cp. line 18. *because they have not sought or consulted him about his statutes*: a quotation from Zeph. 1:6, but interpreted by the addition of 'about his statutes' to refer to the study of the law, cp. vi.6b–8a. *in order to know the hidden things...whereas with regard to the things revealed they have acted presumptuously*: an allusion to Deut. 29:29. The 'hidden things' are the secrets of the law disclosed by study, and the 'things revealed' are the clear commands of the law. The failure of 'the men of injustice' consists both in the fact that they have not studied the law in order to discover the commands which they have unknowingly transgressed, and in the fact that they have transgressed the clear commands of the law. *presumptuously*: literally 'with a high hand'; the author appears to be drawing on the use of this expression in Num. 15:30, where a distinction is drawn (in verses 27–31) between sins committed inadvertently and those committed presumptuously. *arousing anger for judgement and for taking vengeance*: perhaps based on Ezek. 24:8. *by the curses of the covenant*: cp. ii.16a and Deut. 29:21. *mighty acts of judgement*: cp. Exod. 6:6; 7.4.

13b–20a. These lines appear at first sight to provide details about the way in which the person joining the community was to keep separate from the 'men of injustice'. This can clearly be seen to be the case for lines 15b–18a, while lines 18b–20a form an appropriate homiletic conclusion to this section. But lines 13b–15a, although dealing with the theme of separation, interrupt the natural flow of the passage. In the first place, it is difficult to interpret lines 13b–14a as referring to the person joining the community; within its context this sentence is most naturally taken as referring to one of the 'men of injustice', although closer examination suggests that it is really concerned not with the total outsider but rather with the person whose conversion is insincere (see below). Secondly, it may be observed that the 'men of injustice' are spoken of in the plural in lines 10b–13a, and that plural forms are also used of the wicked in lines 15b–18a, but that the singular is used of the wicked in lines 13b–15a. Finally, these internal indications of a break in the sequence are confirmed by the external form of the manuscript: a space has been left in the middle of the line, between 13a and 13b, and there is a paragraph sign in the margin. Recognition of the abrupt transition between 13a and 13b led one scholar to the view that lines 13b–15a were an interpolation, and more recently it has been argued that this interpolation continues down as far as vi.8a. Such a view is not impossible, and it would help to explain the fact that one particular subject, the admission of new members, is treated more than once within columns v–vii (cp. v.20b–23a with vi.13b–23). But it may be questioned whether all the material in v.13b–vi.8a belongs to the same redactional layer, and it is perhaps more sensible simply to recognise that a number of different sources have been brought together in the compilation of columns v–vii. From this perspective it may be seen that lines 13b–15a were included because they illustrated the theme of separation. The question whether lines 15b–20a originally followed directly on 13a, or belonged with 13b–15a, may be left open; but in any case it may be noticed that the words of line 18, 'For all those who are not counted in his covenant, they and everything that belongs to them are to be kept separate', link back clearly to those of lines 10b–11a.

13b–15a. Similarities with the theme of ii.11–18 and ii.25b–iii.12 (see especially iii.4b–6a) suggest that this passage was originally concerned with the person whose conversion was insincere. Such a person was not to be allowed to participate in the washing rites of the community because these were of no effect unless accompanied by the appropriate inner disposition. Further, the members of the community were to keep away from such a man; it is this point, the demand for separation, which led to the inclusion of this passage here.

13b–14a. *He shall not enter*: it is difficult to think that the subject of this sentence is the candidate who has just taken the oath on joining the community. *the waters*: apparently an allusion to the washing rites which, according to Josephus, preceded the daily common meal; see the comment on iii.4b–6a. *the purity*: or 'the pure thing'; usage in the rabbinic writings indicates that the word refers to the ritually clean articles and, particularly, to the ritually clean food of the community. What is at issue here is exclusion from the common meal of the community. *the men of holiness*: a title used here, and in viii.17, 20, 23; ix.8, for the members of the community.

14b–15a. *lest he burden him with iniquity and guilt*: based on Lev. 22:16. *for thus it is written*: the demand for separation is reinforced by the quotation of Exod. 23:7 which in the Hebrew reads literally, 'You shall keep away from a false thing', whereas the Greek (the Septuagint) and the Rule have 'You shall keep away from everything false.'

15b–16a. Separation from outsiders in matters of law.

16b–17a. Separation from outsiders with regard to food and goods.

No one shall eat or drink anything of their property: the concern to preserve
the ritual purity of the community through avoiding contact with
non-members is apparent here. *except for payment*: goods that are
purchased are treated differently from those received as gifts, the idea
perhaps being that change of ownership altered the status of the object
with regard to its purity. This rule presupposes that some members of
the movement of which the group at Qumran formed a part were
living amongst their fellow Jews and had money available to buy
goods; cp. CD xiii.14–15 and the comment on 1.11*b*–13*a*. *as it is
written, 'Have no more to do with man…for what is he worth?'*: Isa. 2:22,
a verse which occurs in the Hebrew Old Testament, but not the
Septuagint, is used to support the demand for separation. There is a
conscious word-play in lines 17–18 inasmuch as the Hebrew verb
translated 'to be worth' is the same as the one in line 18 (cp. line 11)
translated 'to be counted'.

17*b*–18*a*. Cp. lines 10*b*–11*a*, 'He shall undertake…to separate
himself from all the men of injustice…For they are not counted in his
covenant.'

18*b*–19*a*. *man of holiness*: cp. line 13*b*. *vanity*: those outside the
covenant are described in language used in the Old Testament of
idolatry (e.g 2 Kings 17:15) and of the worthlessness of human
existence (e.g. Eccl. 1:2).

19*b*–20*a*. *those who spurn his word*: based on Jer. 23:17, but in the
form known from the Septuagint (and adopted by the NEB), not the
Massoretic text.

THE ORGANISATION OF THE LIFE OF THE COMMUNITY

v.20 When a man enters into the covenant to act according to all these
statutes that he may join the congregation of holiness, they shall
examine 21 his spirit in common, distinguishing between one man and
another, with respect to his insight and his deeds in regard to the law,
under the authority of the sons of Aaron who have willingly offered
themselves in the community to establish 22 his covenant and to pay
attention to all his statutes which he has commanded men to perform,
and under the authority of the multitude of Israel who have willingly
offered themselves to return in the community to his covenant. 23 They
shall register them in the order, one before another, according to their
insight and their deeds, that they may all obey one another, the one
of lower rank obeying the one of higher rank.

They shall [24] review their spirits and their deeds every year that they may promote each man according to his insight and the perfection of his way, or demote him according to his perversity.

They shall reprove [25] one another in tr[uth], humility, and kindly love towards man. Let no man speak to his neighbour in anger or in complaint [26] or with a [stiff] neck [or in a jealou]s spirit of wickedness, and let him not hate him[...] of his heart. But let him reprove him on the same day lest [VI.1] he incur guilt because of him. And let no man bring a matter against his neighbour before the many except after reproof before witnesses.

In these (ways) [2] shall they all walk in all their dwelling-places, each with his neighbour.

The one of lower rank shall obey the one of higher rank in regard to work and money.

Together they shall eat, [3] together they shall pray, and together they shall take counsel.

In every place where there are ten men from the council of the community, let there not be lacking among them a man [4] who is a priest; they shall sit before him, each according to his rank, and in the same order they shall be asked their counsel in regard to any matter.

When they prepare the table to eat or the new wine [5] to drink, the priest shall first stretch out his hand to bless the first fruits of the bread and the new wine... [6] ...

In the place where there are ten men let there not be lacking a man who studies the law day and night [7] continually, one man being replaced by another. And the many shall watch together for a third of all the nights of the year to read the book, to study the law, [8] and to pray together.

The rules in v.20*b*–vi.8*a* are somewhat miscellaneous in character, and it is plausible to think that material of diverse origin and date has been brought together.

v.20*b*–23*a*. Admission of new members. This subject is also dealt with in vi.13*b*–23, a fact which points to the composite character of the Rule as a whole. Precise rules of procedure are laid down in vi.13*b*–23, whereas the present passage is couched in general terms. It speaks of an examination by the whole community of the person aspiring to membership and is perhaps to be compared with the examination described in vi.15*b*–16*a*, which occurred at the beginning of the second period of probation. Alternatively it might be compared with the examination by the officer in charge (vi.13*b*–14*a*) at the very beginning of the process of admission, but only if it be assumed that this took place in the presence of all the full members.

20*b*–22. *When a man enters into the covenant*: cp. the description of the covenant ceremony in 1.16–iii.12. *the congregation of holiness*: only used here in the Community Rule as a title for the community, but cp. 1QSa 1.9, 12*b*–13*a*, and the title 'men of holiness' in line 13*b* above; 'congregation' is used frequently with reference to the community in the Rule of the Congregation (1QSa). *they shall examine his spirit...with respect to his insight and his deeds in regard to the law*: for the wording cp. vi.14, 17, 18. *his spirit*: literally 'their spirit', an inconsistency in the use of singular and plural forms. *in common*: or 'in the community'. *his insight and his deeds in regard to the law*: insight into the law in order to know how properly to observe it. As in the case of the Pharisees, study and observance of the law appear repeatedly throughout the scrolls as fundamental to the aims of the community. *the sons of Aaron...the multitude of Israel*: see the comment on lines 2*b*–3*a* and note that the title 'sons of Aaron' is used here for the priests.

23*a*. As we saw in the comment on ii.19*b*–23, the members of the community were ranked in a strict order. The present passage refers to the assignment of new members to their place in that order; cp. vi.22. *their insight and their deeds*: i.e. in regard to the law.

23*b*–24*a*. *They shall review their spirits and their deeds every year that they may promote...or demote*: perhaps best taken of an annual examination and classification of all the members. Alternatively it might refer to the annual examination of those in the process of becoming members: cp. vi.13*b*–23.

v24*b*–vi.1*ab*. Reproof of fellow members. The structure of this section calls for comment inasmuch as it appears to be divided into two quite separate parts. The first sentence (v.24*b*–25*a*) is linked grammatically with what precedes. There is then a space in the middle of line 25, and a paragraph sign in the margin; this, combined with the change in grammatical construction, suggests the start of a new section. In fact it appears that the reference to the annual examination of members led, not unnaturally, to the thought of the reproof of those found wanting (v.24*b*–25*a*). This topic was then expanded by means of an interpretative comment (v.25*b*–vi.1*ab*) based on Lev. 19:17–18, a passage also used as the basis of CD ix.2–8*a*.

v.24b–25a. *in tr[uth], humility, and kindly love*: cp. II.24.

v.25b–26a. *or with a [stiff] neck [or in a jealou]s spirit of wickedness*: the restoration is based on, but not identical with, the reading of one of the Cave 4 manuscripts. *and let him not hate him* [...] *of his heart*: cp. Lev. 19:17a, 'You shall not nurse hatred against your brother' (literally 'You shall not hate your brother in your heart').

v.26b–vi.1a. *lest he incur guilt because of him*: cp. Lev. 19:17b, which might be translated, 'lest you incur blame because of him' (cp. the translation in the NEB footnote).

vi.1b. This rule envisages three stages in the reproof of a fellow member: in private, before witnesses, and before the many; it has been compared with the three stages of reproof laid down in Matt. 18:15–17. *the many*: a technical term, used frequently in columns vi–vii of the Rule and in some other passages (e.g. viii.19; CD xiii.7), to refer to the full members of the community. The same Hebrew word (*rabbîm*) was also used in the rabbinic writings to refer to the members of the associations in which the Pharisees were organised. *before witnesses*: cp. Deut. 19:15.

1c–8a. The regulations in this passage appear to be directed at members of the Essene movement who lived, not at Qumran, but amongst their fellow Jews; they envisage a basic organisation of the members in groups of ten. A general similarity between the aims and ideals of the Essene movement and those of the Pharisees has often been observed, but such a comparison seems particularly apposite here inasmuch as the Pharisees organised themselves in associations or fellowships (*habûrôth*) whose members took upon themselves the obligation to observe strictly the laws of ritual purity; it is this kind of communal organisation which seems to be presupposed in this section of the Rule. The particular character of the regulations in lines 1c–8a, together with the occurrence of a new heading (1c–2a), suggests that material from a source different from that of the surrounding passages is being used here.

1c–2a. A heading for what follows. *in all their dwelling-places*: Josephus reports that the Essenes 'occupy no one city, but settle in large numbers in every town' (*War* ii.8.4 (124)). Similarly Philo (Apologia pro Iudaeis, as quoted in Eusebius, Praeparatio Evangelica viii.11.1) states that they 'live in many cities of Judaea and in many villages and grouped in great societies of many members'. As indicated above, lines 1c–8a appear to be concerned with those members of the wider Essene movement who lived, not at Qumran, but amongst their fellow Jews.

2b. *The one of lower rank shall obey the one of higher rank*: cp. v.23a;

II.23*b*. *work*: The Hebrew word could also be translated 'property' (cp. Exod. 22:8, 11).

3*b*–4*a*. *In every place where there are ten men*: cp. CD XII.23*b*–XIII.2*a*, which states more explicitly that ten is the minimum needed to form a group. Josephus alludes to such a group of ten in his account of the Essenes: 'if ten sit together, one will not speak if the nine desire silence' (*War* II.8.9 (146)). The rabbinic writings likewise regard ten men as the minimum needed to perform certain religious activities; cp. Mishnah, Meg. IV.3; Sanh. 1.6; Ab. III.6, 'If ten men sit together and occupy themselves in the law, the Divine Presence rests among them.' *let there not be lacking...a man who is a priest*: the same rule is found in greater detail in CD XIII.2*b*–7*a*. In the present passage the duties of the priest are defined as presiding at meetings of the group and at the common meal. *they shall sit before him, each according to his rank*: a further indication of the hierarchical structure of the community; cp. line 2*b*.

4*b*–5*a*. The common meal. An account of the common meal of the Essenes, and of the washing rite which preceded it, is given by Josephus in *War* II.8.5 (129–31); as in the Rule, the meal was preceded by a prayer spoken by the priest. The regulation in the Rule is similar, although less detailed, to that given in the Rule of the Congregation for the meal to be eaten in the last days in the presence of the priest-messiah and the messiah of Israel (1QSa II.11*b*–22); this suggests that in some sense the common meal was seen as an anticipation of the meal to be eaten in the messianic era. *to bless the first fruits of the bread and the new wine*: or 'to bless at the beginning the bread and the new wine'. The saying of grace before meals is a common Jewish and Christian practice: cp. Mishnah, Ber. VI–VIII, which prescribes the forms of blessing to be said over food of various kinds, and Matt. 14:19. After 'new wine' the copyist by mistake repeated in lines 5*b*–6*a* the words of line 5*a*.

6*b*–8*a*. Study of the law. These lines epitomise the importance attached by the Qumran community to the study of the Old Testament, particularly the Mosaic law. Study of the law was essential if one was to know how to obey it, and study and observance of the law constituted the ideal on which the community's existence was based – as they also formed the ideal for other Jewish groups of the day, notably the Pharisees.

6*b*–7*a*. *the law*: the Mosaic law (Hebrew *tōrāh*). *day and night*: cp. Josh. 1:8; Ps. 1:2. The former passage in particular seems to underlie the whole context in the Rule (more obvious in the Hebrew than the NEB translation). *one man being replaced by another*: the text is uncertain, and the translation is based on an emendation; 'concerning the duties of one man towards another' would also be a possibility.

7b–8a. for a third of all the nights of the year: most probably a third of each night, rather than one night in three. The suggestion that the members were divided into three groups in order to ensure that watch was maintained throughout the night has nothing in the text to support it. *the book*: the law of Moses, cp. 'book of the law' in Josh. 1:8. *the law*: a different word (*mišpāṭ*) from the one used in line 6*b* (*tōrāh*). What is in mind here is the content of the Pentateuch.

RULES FOR A SESSION OF THE MANY

VI.8 This is the rule for a session of the many. Each (shall sit) according to his rank. The priests shall sit in the first seats, the elders in the second, and then the rest 9 of all the people shall sit, each according to his rank. In the same order they shall be asked for judgement, or concerning any counsel or matter which has to do with the many, each man offering his knowledge 10 to the council of the community. No man shall interrupt his neighbour's words before his brother has finished speaking, or speak before one registered in rank 11 before him. A man who is asked shall speak in his turn. In a session of the many no man shall say anything which is not approved by the many and, indeed, by the overseer 12 of the many. Any man who has something to say to the many, but is not entitled to question the council 13 of the community, shall stand on his feet and say, 'I have something to say to the many.' If they tell him to speak, he shall speak.

The heading in 8*b*, together with the paragraph sign in the margin, indicates the beginning of a new section; it is concerned in the first instance with procedure at meetings of the members of the community (lines 8*b*–13*a*).

VI.8c–9a. The priests shall sit in the first seats: cp. line 4*a*. *priests... elders... the rest of all the people*: the comparable passage in II.19*b*–23 refers to priests, Levites and 'all the people'; it is not clear whether the substitution of 'elders' for 'Levites' indicates a different structure for the community, or whether it merely reflects a difference of nomenclature. For the position and authority of 'elders' see Num. 11:16–17, 24–30.

9*b*–10*a*. *In the same order they shall be asked*: cp. line 4*a*.

10*b*–11*a*. *interrupt his neighbour's words*: cp. VII.9*c*.

11*b*–12*a*. *the overseer of the many*: from this passage it appears that the overseer (Hebrew *mᵉbaqqēr*) controlled the meetings of the members. It seems likely that he was the same person as the one called in line 14 'the officer in charge (Hebrew *pāqīd*) at the head of the many' who was responsible for the admission of new members, but it is not clear whether he is also to be identified with 'the overseer of the property of the many' (lines 19*b*–20*a*). Elsewhere in the Rule reference is made to 'the wise leader' (Hebrew *maskīl*); his duties included the pastoral oversight of the members of the community and the admission of new members (IX.14*b*–21*a*), and it seems that he is the same as the one called in column VI 'the overseer of the many' and 'the officer in charge'. References to the overseer (*mᵉbaqqēr*) are also to be found in the Damascus Document, which, as we have seen, is concerned with the groups of Essenes who lived amongst their fellow Jews in the towns and villages of Palestine, rather than with the group at Qumran. Here two passages are particularly important. The first (XIII.2*b*–20*a*) appears to be directed at the individual groups and prescribes that for each there shall be a priest and an 'overseer of the camp'. The references to the priest remind us of what is said in 1QS VI.3*b*–4*a* about the priest attached to the group of ten; the duties of the overseer are similar to those of the wise leader (*maskīl*) in 1QS IX.14*b*–21*a* and again include pastoral oversight and the admission of new members. The second passage in the Damascus Document (XIV.6*b*–12*a*) is concerned with the movement as a whole. It again mentions two officers, a priest and an 'overseer of all the camps'; their responsibilities were for the whole movement, but their duties are only briefly defined. The Damascus Document mentions the overseer in several other passages and also includes two references (XII.21; XIII.22) to the wise leader (*maskīl*). From all these references it appears that the movement as a whole, and each individual group of which it was composed, were controlled by two officers, a priest and an overseer; the second of these was also called 'the wise leader' and (in one passage) 'the officer in charge'. Not much is said about the duties of the priest, and he seems to have been the less important figure of the two. By contrast the overseer exercised considerable powers over the members and may also have been responsible for financial matters (cp. 1QS VI.19*b*–20*a*).

THE ADMISSION OF NEW MEMBERS

VI.13 Anyone who willingly offers himself from Israel 14 to join the council of the community, the officer in charge at the head of the many shall examine him with respect to his insight and his deeds. If he is suited to the discipline, he shall admit him 15 into the covenant that he may return to the truth and turn aside from all injustice, and shall instruct him in all the rules of the community.

And afterwards, when he comes to stand before the many, they shall all be asked 16 about his affairs, and as the decision is taken on the advice of the many, he shall either draw near or keep away. If he draws near to the council of the community, he shall not touch the purity 17 of the many until they have examined him with respect to his spirit and his deeds while he completes a full year, nor shall he have any share in the wealth of the many.

18 When he has completed a year in the midst of the community, the many shall be asked about his affairs with respect to his insight and his deeds in regard to the law. If, on the advice of the priests and the multitude of the men of their covenant, the decision is taken for him 19 to draw near to the fellowship of the community, both his wealth and his property shall be handed to the overseer 20 of the property of the many; he shall enter it in the account with his own hand, but shall not spend it on the many. He shall not touch the drink of the many until 21 he has completed a second year in the midst of the men of the community.

When he has completed a second year, he shall be examined on the authority of the many. If the decision is taken for him 22 to draw near to the community, they shall register him in the order of his rank amongst his brothers, with respect to law, judgement, purity, and for pooling his wealth. His counsel 23 and his judgement shall be available to the community.

One of the most important matters which meetings of the full members had to determine was the admission of new members, and it is perhaps hardly surprising, therefore, that the statement of the procedure for the conduct of meetings of the community (lines 8*b*–13*a*) should be followed – without any break in the manuscript – by a statement of the procedure for the admission of new members (lines 13*b*–23; cp. v.20*b*–23*a*). According to the rules laid down in this passage admission to full membership of the community took more than two years. Those who desired to join were first examined by 'the officer in charge at the head of the many', and, if thought suitable, were admitted into the covenant (lines 13*b*–15*a*). There then followed a period of probation of unspecified length at the end of which the candidate was examined by 'the many', that is by the whole body of full members (lines 15*b*–17). If the candidate was confirmed in membership at this stage, he then had to undergo two further years of probation, with an examination by 'the many' at the end of each, before being finally admitted to full membership (lines 18–21*a*, 21*b*–23). The privilege of participation in the rites of the community (the 'purity' and the 'drink') was not granted immediately, but only by degrees after the completion of the successive stages of probation, and the same was also true with regard to the pooling of the candidate's property with that of the community.

In the *War* (II.8.7 (137–42)) Josephus gives an account of the procedure for admission to the Essene movement which has been compared with the procedure in the Rule. The passage is as follows:

> A candidate anxious to join their sect is not immediately admitted. For one year, during which he remains outside the fraternity, they prescribe for him their own rule of life...Having given proof of his temperance during this probationary period, he is brought into closer touch with the rule and is allowed to share the purer kind of holy water [i.e. to participate in the washing rites], but is not yet received into the meetings of the community. For after this exhibition of endurance, his character is tested for two years more, and only then, if found worthy, is he enrolled in the society. But, before he may touch the common food, he is made to swear tremendous oaths. (*War* II.8.7 (137–9))

It is possible to read the two accounts in such a way as to ignore the differences between them, and equally in such a way as to make too much of them; but neither method is very helpful. In comparing the two accounts it had to be borne in mind that the Rule was written for the internal use of the community at Qumran, whereas Josephus was writing, at least one hundred and fifty years later, for outsiders (the Romans) about the larger Essene movement; and further, that many details in the two accounts are unclear. There are differences between the two accounts, perhaps the most striking of which is that Josephus speaks of an initial period of probation of one year spent 'outside', whereas in the Rule the length of the initial period is unspecified and the candidate appears already to be in some sense within the community. But both accounts then describe a further two-year period of probation. While one should not seek to gloss over the differences between the two accounts, it does seem clear that they are speaking about essentially the same procedure.

VI.13*b*–15*a*. The initial period of probation. *the officer in charge at the head of the many*: 'the officer in charge' was responsible for the admission of new members and thus is apparently to be identified with the person called 'the wise leader' in IX.12–21 (cp. lines 15*b*–16*a*). The duties of the latter were similar to those of 'the overseer of the camp' mentioned in CD XIII.7*b*–20*a* (cp. lines 11–13), and this suggests that 'the officer in charge' was the same as 'the overseer of the many' (lines 11*b*–12*a* above; see the comment there). The use of the phrase 'at the head of the many' may indicate that the examination was conducted at a meeting of the full members. *shall examine him with respect to his insight and his deeds*: i.e. in regard to the law, cp. V.20*b*–21*a*. *he shall admit him into the covenant*: what this involved is not entirely clear. In the light of CD XV.7*b*–10*a* the candidate will have sworn the oath mentioned in V.8*b* above on the day that he was examined by the officer in charge. In any case the candidate at this stage became in some sense a member of the community. But he was still very far from being a full member, and his acceptance was subject to confirmation by the many at a later stage (lines 15*b*–16*a*). It is perhaps because his position was still uncertain that Josephus can speak of the candidate spending the initial period of probation 'outside'. *that he may return to the truth and turn aside from all injustice*: cp. V.8, 10, 'to return to the law of Moses...to separate himself from all the men of injustice'.

15*b*–17. The second period of probation: first year. *and as the decision is taken*: literally 'and as the lot falls' (similarly in lines 18, 21*b*–22*a*); see the comment on V.3*a*. *advice*: the word elsewhere translated 'counsel/council'. *he shall not touch the purity of the many*: during the first year of the second period of probation the candidate was presumably admitted to some privileges of membership, but we are only told of the ones from which he was excluded. Two things are mentioned: the purity and the sharing of property. In the Rule the word 'purity' or 'pure thing' refers to the ritually clean articles and particularly the ritually clean food of the members of the community, as the parallel usage in the rabbinic writings makes clear (see the comment on V.13*b*–14*a*). What is being said here is that at this stage the candidate was still not permitted to share in the common meal

of the community. *nor shall he have any share in the wealth of the many*:
the candidate retained his own property and was not yet entitled to
benefit from that of the community. For the sharing of property by
the community see the comment on 1.11*b*–13*a*.

18–21*a*. The second period of probation: second year. *advice*: a
different word from that used in line 16. *the priests and the multitude of
the men of their covenant*: see the comment on v.2*b*–3*a*. *both his wealth
and his property shall be handed to the overseer of the property of the many*:
in this final stage of probation the candidate's property was handed over
to the community, but was still kept separate. It is not clear whether
'the overseer of the property of the many' was the same as the one
called above 'the overseer of the many' (lines 11*b*–12*a*) and 'the officer
in charge' (line 14). *He shall not touch the drink of the many until he has
completed a second year*: it may be assumed that the candidate was now
allowed to attend the common meal ('the purity of the many'), but
he was still not permitted to touch 'the drink'. From the rabbinic
writings we know that the Pharisees believed that liquids were
susceptible to ritual impurity to a higher degree than solid food, and
that candidates for admission to the Pharisaic associations (*ḥabūrōth*)
were not allowed to handle liquids during the first stage of initiation.
The same kind of attitude towards liquids underlies the legislation of
the Rule. Those who were not yet full members, even though in the
final stage of their probation, were not permitted to touch the drink
shared by the full members in order that there should be no risk that
the full members should be rendered ritually unclean by those who
had not attained to the same degree of purity as themselves.

21*b*–23. Full membership. *they shall register him in the order of his rank*:
cp. II.19*b*–23; v.23*a*. *with respect to law, judgement, purity, and for pooling
his wealth*: an allusion to important aspects of the life of the
community – the study of the law, the giving of legal decisions,
participation in the common meal and the sharing of property.

THE PENITENTIAL CODE

VI.24 These are the rules by which they shall judge at a community
inquiry according to the cases.

If a man is found among them who has knowingly lied 25 about
wealth, they shall exclude him from the purity of the many for one
year, and he shall be fined a quarter of his food.

Whoever answers 26 his neighbour with obstinacy or speaks to him impatiently, ig[nor]ing the dignity of his companion by rebelling against the command of his neighbour who is registered before him, 27 [has] taken the law into his own hands. He shall be fined for on[e] year [...

Who]ever affirms anything by the name of the one honoured above all th[ose who are honoured...] VII.1 If he has blasphemed, either through being terrified by distress or for whatever reason he may have, while he is reading the book or praying, they shall exclude him, 2 and he shall never return to the council of the community. If he has spoken in anger against one of the priests registered in the book, he shall be fined for one year 3 and excluded on his own from the purity of the many. But if he spoke through inadvertence, he shall be fined for six months.

Whoever lies knowingly 4 shall be fined for six months.

The man who knowingly and without cause insults his neighbour shall be fined for one year 5 and excluded.

Whoever speaks deceitfully to his neighbour or knowingly acts deceitfully shall be fined for six months. If 6 he is negligent towards his neighbour, he shall be fined for three months. But if he is negligent with regard to the wealth of the community so that he causes its loss, he shall restore it 7 in full. 8 If he is unable to restore it, he shall be fined for sixty days.

Whoever bears a grudge against his neighbour without cause shall be fined for six months/one year. 9 And likewise for anyone who avenges anything himself.

Whoever speaks with his mouth anything foolish: three months.

For the one who interrupts his neighbour's words: 10 ten days.

Whoever lies down and falls asleep during a session of the many: thirty days. And likewise for the man who leaves a session of the many 11 without permission and without reason as many as three times in one session – he shall be fined for ten days, but if he leaves while they are standing, 12 he shall be fined for thirty days.

Whoever goes naked before his neighbour without being compelled to do so shall be fined for six months.

13 A man who spits into a session of the many shall be fined for thirty days.

Whoever brings his hand out from beneath his garment and [14] is so raggedly dressed that his nakedness is seen shall be fined for thirty days.

Whoever guffaws foolishly shall be fined for thirty [15] days.

He who brings his left hand out to gesticulate with it shall be fined for ten days.

The man who goes about slandering his neighbour [16] shall be excluded from the purity of the many for one year and fined. But a man who goes about slandering the community shall be sent away from them [17] and shall never return.

The man who makes complaints about the authority of the community shall be sent away and shall not return. But if it is against his neighbour that he makes complaints [18] without cause, he shall be fined for six months.

The man whose spirit so deviates from the fundamental principles of the community that he betrays the truth [19] and walks in the stubbornness of his heart, if he returns, he shall be fined for two years. In the first year he shall not touch the purity of the many, [20] and in the second he shall not touch the drink of the many, and he shall sit behind all the men of the community. When he has completed [21] two years, the many shall be asked about his affairs. If they allow him to draw near, he shall be registered in his rank, and afterwards he may be asked about judgement. [22] But no man who has been in the council of the community for ten full years [23] and whose spirit turns back so that he betrays the community, and who leaves [24] the many to walk in the stubbornness of his heart, shall ever return to the council of the community. Anyone from the men of the commun[ity who has any]thing to do [25] with him in regard to his purity or his wealth whi[ch...] the many, his sentence shall be the same: he shall be sent [away].

The last part of the material relating to the internal life of the community (columns V–VII) provides a list of punishments for various offences that might be committed by members of the community. This section is clearly set off from what precedes by a new heading (VI.24a), a paragraph sign in the margin, and the leaving blank of most of VI.23 and the beginning of VI.24. The offences, which are listed in a somewhat haphazard order, are miscellaneous in character, but they all reflect the circumstances and tensions of life within the community. The punishments vary enormously in severity and range from total expulsion to a ten-day penance whose exact nature is not made clear. Judged by this scale of punishments the most serious offences were blasphemy, slandering the community, making complaints about the authority of the community, and leaving the community after being a member for ten years.

This is not the only list of punishments to be found in the scrolls. Material of a similar character occurs in VIII.16b–IX.2, a fact which points to the composite form of the Rule as a whole. In addition the beginning of a list of punishments has survived in CD XIV.18–22, but unfortunately the text is damaged and in any case breaks off after a few lines. The literary form of the list of punishments is that of casuistic law; it is reminiscent, for example, of much of the material in the so-called Book of the Covenant (Exod. 20:22–23:33; see e.g. 21:12–27).

In column VII a number of surprising gaps have been left in the manuscript, of which the most obvious is a three-line space between lines 6 and 8 (the one word in line 7 was written in by a second copyist). It seems likely that the copy from which our manuscript was made was faulty or illegible at this point, and that the gaps were left so that corrections and additions could be inserted at a later stage. In fact, several corrections were made to the manuscript by a second copyist.

VI.24b–25a. *lied about wealth*: most probably, lied about the amount of his personal possessions which were supposed to be handed to the overseer of the property of the many (VI.19b–20a); cp. Acts 5:1–11, although in this story the offence is not so much the lie about property as the attempt to deceive the Holy Spirit. *they shall exclude him from the purity of the many*: namely from the common meal: see the comment on VI.15b–17. We should perhaps assume that exclusion meant that he returned to the status of those on probation. *for one year*: lying about property is treated more seriously than lying about other matters, for which the punishment lasts for six months (VII.3b–4a). However, in CD XIV.20–1 the person who lies about property is only punished for six days.

25b–27a. *the dignity*: the translation assumes, not implausibly, a metaphorical meaning for a word which means literally 'foundation'. Some scholars emend the text to read 'the discipline'. *[has] taken the law into his own hands*: literally 'his own hand [has] saved him', an expression used in a similar idiomatic way in 1 Sam. 25:26 (NEB, 'from giving vent to your anger'), 31, 33. *He shall be fined*: it is not clear whether we are to assume that the fine consisted of the loss of a quarter of his food, as in line 25. Also, a more neutral translation, 'He shall be punished', would be possible. The same applies in all the following cases.

VI.27b–VII.3a. *Who]ever affirms anything by the name of the one honoured above all th[ose who are honoured...]*: the offence in this case is the use of the name of God in oaths, cp. CD xv.1–5a; Ecclus. 23:9–11; Matt. 5:33–7. The Old Testament basis of the prohibition is Lev. 19:12, 'You shall not swear in my name with intent to deceive and thus profane the name of your God.' *the name of the one honoured above all th[ose who are honoured...]*: or 'the honoured name for any [...]'. The text is damaged, and it is not clear how it continued; it may be that there was a reference to a punishment at the end of the line. The first line of the next column apparently begins to deal with another, albeit related, offence. *If he has blasphemed*: literally 'If he has cursed', but it is clear that cursing God is meant, cp. Lev. 24:15–16. *the book*: i.e the book of the law, the Pentateuch: cp. VI.7b–8a. *they shall exclude him, and he shall never return to the council of the community*: in Lev. 24:16 the penalty for blasphemy is death. *If he has spoken in anger against one of the priests*: the fact that abuse of the priests is linked with the offences of misuse of the divine name in oaths and of cursing God serves once more to emphasise the pre-eminence of the priests within the community. *registered in the book*: hardly the book of the law, as in line 1. Presumably the reference is to a list compiled by the community.

VII.5b–8a. *If he is negligent*: or perhaps 'If he acts fraudulently'. *he shall restore it in full*: cp. Lev. 6:5 (NEB, 'make full restitution'); Lev. 6:1–5 provides a biblical parallel to the offences in these lines. The fact that the member was potentially able to make restitution suggests either that he retained some personal possessions or that he could earn money. But the details are unclear.

8b–9a. *Whoever bears a grudge... anyone who avenges anything himself*: cp. Lev. 19:18; CD ix.2–8a. Some scholars have restored the text of CD xiv.22 (see above, p. 125) on the basis of this passage, but the restoration is quite uncertain. *six months/one year*: 'one year' has been inserted as a correction, thus indicating a change of practice, but 'six months' has not been deleted.

9c–10a. *interrupts his neighbour's words*: cp. VI.10b.

10b–12a. *and without reason*: or perhaps 'or who falls asleep' – in the Hebrew a difference in the reading of only one letter. *while they are standing*: perhaps for prayer.

13a. *A man who spits*: cp. Josephus, *War* II.8.9 (147), '(The Essenes) are careful not to spit into the midst of the company or to the right.'

13b–14a. *hand*: a euphemism for the male sexual organ.

15b. *brings his left hand out to gesticulate with it*: the translation 'gesticulate' is not certain, but in any case there seems to underlie this passage the basic notion that the left is the unfavoured and unacceptable side. In contrast, Josephus tells us that the Essenes did not spit to the right (see above). The Therapeutae (a Jewish sect in some ways similar to the Essenes) indicated difficulty in understanding 'by a gentler movement of the head and by pointing with a finger-tip of the right hand' (Philo, Vit Cont 77).

15c–17a. *The man who goes about slandering*: cp. Lev. 19:16.

17b–18a. *makes complaints*: the word is used in the Old Testament to refer to Israel 'complaining' or 'murmuring' in the wilderness, cp. e.g. Exod. 15:24. *authority*: literally 'foundation', cp. VI.26.

18b–25. *fundamental principles*: literally 'foundation'. *and walks in the stubbornness of his heart*: cp. I.6. *In the first year he shall not touch the purity of the many, and in the second he shall not touch the drink of the many*: i.e. he had to repeat the second stage of the probationary period: cp. VI.15b–23. This regulation is less severe than that of VIII.20–IX.2, where there is no possibility at all of readmission for the man who sins presumptuously; in the present passage the possibility of readmission is only denied to the man who leaves after having been a member for ten years. For 'purity' and 'drink' see the comments on VI.15b–17, 18–21a.

PROGRAMME FOR A NEW COMMUNITY

The last part of the Community Rule to be studied here (VIII.1–IX.26a) appears to go back to the time before the Qumran community came into existence. In all probability it presents the programme or manifesto of a group which, at the time when the material was first set down in writing, had not yet come into being, but which was shortly to form the nucleus of the Qumran community. The material divides clearly into two parts, the first (VIII.1–IX.11) being concerned with the group as a whole, the second (IX.12–26a) with its leader. For convenience VIII.1–IX.11 has been divided here into three sections: VIII.1–16a; VIII.16b–IX.2; IX.3–11.

PREPARING THE WAY OF GOD

VIII.1 In the council of the community (there shall be) twelve men and three priests, perfect in all that has been revealed from the whole 2 law, that they may practise truth, righteousness, justice, kindly love, and circumspection one towards another; 3 that they may preserve faithfulness in the land by a constant mind and a broken spirit; that they may pay for iniquity by the practice of justice 4 and (the endurance of) the distress of affliction; and that they may walk with all men according to the standard of truth and the rule of the time.

When these exist in Israel, 5 the council of the community shall be established in truth as an eternal plant, a holy house for Israel and a most holy assembly 6 for Aaron, witnesses of truth for the judgement and chosen by the will (of God), that they may make expiation for the land and pay 7 the wicked their reward. It shall be the tested wall, the precious corner-stone, whose foundations shall neither 8 shake nor stir from their place. (It shall be) a most holy dwelling 9 for Aaron, with eternal knowledge of the covenant of justice, and shall offer a soothing odour; and (it shall be) a house of perfection and truth in Israel 10 that they may establish the covenant according to the eternal statutes. And they shall be accepted to make expiation for the land and to determine the judgement of wickedness; and there shall be no more injustice.

When these have been established in the fundamental principles of the community for two years in perfection of way, 11 they shall be set apart as holy within the council of the men of the community. And nothing which was hidden from Israel, but found by the man 12 who studies shall he hide from these through fear of an apostate spirit.

When these exist as a community in Israel 13 in accordance with these rules, they shall separate themselves from the settlement of the men of injustice and shall go into the wilderness to prepare there the way of him, 14 as it is written: 'In the wilderness prepare the way of ...., make level in the desert a highway for our God.' 15 This (way) is the study of the law w[hich]h he commanded through Moses, that they should act in accordance with all that has been revealed from time to time [16] and in accordance with what the prophets revealed by his holy spirit.

This material, and particularly lines 1—4*a*, has sometimes been thought to refer to an inner 'council of the community' (line 1), consisting of twelve laymen and three priests, which is supposed to have controlled the affairs of the community. But such a governing body is not otherwise mentioned in the scrolls, and elsewhere in the Rule 'council of the community' means the whole community (see for instance III.2); there is no reason to think the expression has a different meaning here. It seems most likely, in fact, that this material represents the programme of a group that was about to be formed and was to become the nucleus of the Qumran community. The passage is marked by a high idealism, suggesting a movement in its infancy, and in the great bulk of the material there is little concern with the kind of detailed rules that are characteristic of columns V—VII. The aim of the group was to prepare the way for God's coming by withdrawing into the wilderness to live a life of perfection in accordance with the law. It believed that the community would constitute the true temple, and implicit in all this material is a condemnation of the state of affairs in the Jewish community in general, and in the temple at Jerusalem in particular. This material thus appears to be the oldest in the Rule and to go back to the period shortly before the Qumran community came into existence; it may be regarded as reflecting the aims and ideals of conservative Jews who were disturbed by the way in which the Maccabean leaders were conducting affairs, and whose decision to withdraw into the wilderness was motivated by the desire to be able to observe strictly God's laws in the way that they believed to be right. It probably dates from the middle of the second century BC.

The structure of the passage relating to the community as a whole (VIII.1—IX.11) calls for comment. It is divided in the first instance by the threefold occurrence of the introductory formula 'When these exist in Israel' (VIII.4*b*, 12*b*; IX.3). But two other introductory formulas also occur: VIII.10*b*, 'When these have been established in the fundamental principles of the community', the introduction to VIII.10*b*—12*a*; and VIII.20, 'These are the rules', the introduction to VIII.20—IX.2. Furthermore, although it lacks an introductory formula, VIII.16*b*—19 is set off in the manuscript from what precedes and follows. In fact, as will be indicated below, there are reasons for thinking that the three passages just mentioned (VIII.10*b*—12*a*; VIII.16*b*—19; VIII.20—IX.2) belong to a

second stage in the composition of this material. In the first half of
column VIII a number of spaces have been left, and corrections inserted,
as in column VII; see the comment on p. 125 above.

VIII.1–4a. An introduction which summarises the character and
purpose of the group. It may be noted that this is the third such
introduction in the Rule: cp. I.1–15 and V.1–7a. *the council of the
community*: see the comment above. *(there shall be) twelve men and three
priests*: the community was to consist of fifteen men; the 'twelve' and
the 'three' are best understood as providing for one representative for
each of the secular tribes and one for each of the three clans of the tribe
of Levi (cp. Num. 3:17) – an Israel in miniature. (It was at one time
thought that the three were included within the twelve, but this is quite
unlikely.) The preponderance of priests is again indicative of their
pre-eminence within the community. *perfect in all that has been revealed
from the whole law*: cp. I.8b–9a; V.8b–9a. *that they may practise...justice,
kindly love, and circumspection*: a quotation of Mic. 6:8, also used in
V.3b–4a. *that they may preserve faithfulness*: i.e towards God; cp. Isa.
26:1–3, which seems to be in mind in the present passage (see below).
by a constant mind; the Hebrew expression occurs in the Old Testament
only in Isa. 26:3 (NEB, 'men of constant mind'); see the comment
on IV.5. *and a broken spirit*: a quotation from Ps. 51:17; what is meant
is an attitude of humility and of reliance on God. *that they may pay
for iniquity*: the phrase is used in Lev. 26:41, 43 (NEB, 'accept their
punishment in full', 'pay in full the penalty'). By the practice of
justice and the endurance of affliction the community would atone for
sin; see further the comment on line 6b, and for the idea that the
acceptance of suffering in some sense atones for sin cp. 2 Macc. 7:37–8.
and the rule of the time: i.e the rule appropriate to a particular time: cp.
IX.12.

4b–10a. These lines continue the description of the character of the
community. When it came into existence, the community would take
the place of the temple; the members would atone for the sins of Israel
and would be involved in the punishment of the wicked.

4b–5a. *When these exist in Israel*: 'these' could be 'these men' (the
fifteen mentioned in line 1) or 'these things', but with little real
difference in meaning. The use of the formula in VIII.12b and IX.3,
where 'these' more naturally refers to the members of the community,
suggests that the first view is to be preferred. *the council of the community
shall be established*: at the moment when this material was first set down
in writing the community was still in an embryonic state. It would
become a reality when the fifteen men with the qualities described in

lines 1–4a existed as a group. *as an eternal plant*: plant imagery is widely used in the scrolls and elsewhere; see the comment on CD 1.7b–8a.

  5b–6a. a holy house for Israel and a most holy assembly for Aaron: 'Israel' and 'Aaron' in this passage represent the lay and priestly elements within the community, and 'a holy house' means 'a temple' (cp. 1 Chron. 29:3 (NEB, 'sanctuary')); the point being made is that the community, when it came into existence, would constitute for its members the true (spiritual) temple, and would, by implication, take the place of the temple in Jerusalem which was regarded as defiled (cp. CD IV.17b–18a; v.6b–7a; 1QpHab XII.7b–9a). For the thought of the community as a temple cp. 1 Cor. 3:16; 2 Cor. 6:16. *a most holy assembly for Aaron*: literally 'an assembly of the holy of holies for Aaron'; a reference to the holy of holies is certainly intended. 'The holy of holies' (or 'the most holy place', as the Hebrew expression is sometimes rendered) was the inner room of the tabernacle (Exod. 26:33–4), and similarly of the temple (1 Kings 6:16), into which the high priest alone went, and he only on the day of atonement (Lev. 16:11–17; cp. Ecclus. 50:5). It is thus entirely appropriate that the holy of holies of the temple formed by the community should be linked specifically with the priests in the community.

  6b–7a. witnesses of truth for the judgement and chosen by the will (of God): the idea that the righteous are chosen by God to act as his witnesses at the judgement is found also in the fragmentary Aramaic version of 1 En. 93:10, according to which the elect are chosen as 'witnesses of truth' or 'witnesses of righteousness' (the expression is lacking in the Ethiopic version of the verse). There is an interesting correction in the manuscript of the Rule; the text originally had 'and those who choose the will (of God)' (cp. IX.17b–18a), but this was subsequently altered to 'chosen by'. *that they may make expiation for the land*: within the temple formed by the community the members make expiation for Israel, not by sacrifice, but by the practice of justice and endurance of affliction; cp. lines 3b–4a, 10b; IX.4–6. 'The land' means the land of Israel, but even more the inhabitants (cp. e.g. Zech. 12:12 for this usage), and this section of the Rule has a more idealistic view than v.6a, where the community only makes expiation on behalf of the members. *and pay the wicked their reward*: the members of the community share in the punishment of the wicked, a theme which is elaborated at length in the War Scroll (cp. 1QM XI.13–14a).

  7b–8a. It shall be the tested wall, the precious corner-stone, whose foundations shall neither shake nor stir from their place: the author applies to the community the prophecy of Isa. 28:16:

Look, I am laying a stone in Zion, a block of granite,
a precious corner-stone for a firm foundation;
he who has faith shall not waver.

The words 'a block (literally 'stone') of granite' were traditionally understood to mean 'a tested stone' (cp. RSV), and that understanding has been followed here. In fact the author of the Rule substituted the word 'wall' for 'stone', perhaps thinking of the members of the community as forming a protective enclosure. The Hebrew word rendered in the NEB as 'waver' is the same as the one here translated as 'stir'. In the New Testament this passage is applied to Jesus (cp. Rom. 9:32b–33; 10:11; 1 Pet. 2:4–6); the Targum interprets it as referring to the messiah.

8b–10a. The symbolism of the temple as the community is continued (cp. lines 5b–6a); once again the priests ('Aaron') are associated specifically with the holy of holies, and the laity ('Israel') with the temple in general ('house of perfection and truth'). *a most holy dwelling*: or 'a dwelling of the holy of holies'; see the comment on lines 5b–6a. The word 'dwelling' is used of the Jerusalem temple in 2 Chron. 36:15 (NEB, 'dwelling-place'). One of the Cave 4 manuscripts of the Rule has 'refuge' (a difference of only one letter in Hebrew). *with eternal knowledge*: the translation is based on a minor emendation; the text reads 'in the knowledge of all'. *of the covenant of justice*: the meaning of the expression is not entirely clear, but perhaps the thought is of the covenant made with the priesthood (cp. Num. 25:13; Neh. 13:29) which is now to be re-established within the community. *and shall offer a soothing odour*: 'a soothing odour' is mentioned frequently in texts dealing with sacrifice in the Old Testament (e.g. Exod. 29:18), but we should not think here of a literal offering of sacrifice; rather it is the practice of righteousness by the members of the community which constitutes the 'soothing odour'. See further the comment on III.11. *house of perfection and truth*: 'house' means temple; the lives of those who make up this temple will be characterised by perfection and truth: cp. line 1. *that they may establish the covenant according to the eternal statutes*: the founding of the community is presented as the re-establishment of God's covenant with Israel. *And they shall be accepted to make expiation…to determine the judgement of wickedness*: these words (together with 'and there shall be no more injustice': cp. IV.23) are written in above the line as a correction; they represent a variant of the thought of lines 6b–7a. Of the two Cave 4 manuscripts that are extant for this passage, one contained the additional words, but the other did not.

10*b*–12*a*. These lines are set off as a separate paragraph in the manuscript and have an introduction of their own which differs from that used elsewhere in this passage (VIII.4*b*, 12*b*; IX.3). Furthermore the content of these lines seems slightly out of place in their present context. The passage as a whole appears to represent the programme or manifesto of a community that was still in an embryonic state, and it speaks in fairly general terms. In contrast lines 10*b*–12*a* deal with the period of probation (two years) to be served by new members of a community that seems already to be in existence; they are most naturally to be compared with VI.13*b*–23 (cp. line 21). For these reasons it is plausible to think that lines 10*b*–12*a* belong to a second stage in the formation of this passage; their content is closely related to that of lines 16*b*–19, and it may be, as has been suggested, that they originally formed the introduction to the latter passage. In any case it is possible to see why these lines might have been inserted in their present context inasmuch as there are similarities with the thought and language of the preceding lines; cp. the key-words 'fundamental principles' (literally 'foundation'), 'perfection', 'holy'.

10*b*–11*a*. *be set apart as holy within the council*: i.e. become a full member of the community.

11*b*–12*a*. No aspect of the community's teaching was to be withheld from full members even though there was the risk that they might subsequently apostatise; contrast IX.17*a*. According to Josephus (*War* II.8.7. (141)) the Essenes had to swear 'to conceal nothing from the members of the sect and to report none of their secrets to others'. *nothing which was hidden from Israel*: see the comment on v.11*b* about 'the hidden things'. *found by the man who studies*: i.e. the law: cp. VI.6*b*–7*a*. The reference is probably to any member involved in the study of the law, rather than to a particular official within the community, or, as a cryptic name, to a particular individual ('the man who studied').

12*b*–16*a*. The prophecy of Isa. 40:3 is applied literally to the community: when it came into existence, the members were to withdraw into the wilderness in order to prepare there for God's coming. This paragraph forms the continuation of the material in lines 1–10*a*.

12*b*–14. *When these exist as a community in Israel in accordance with these rules*: cp. line 4*b* and IX.3. 'In Israel' and 'in accordance with these rules' have been written in as corrections above the line; neither phrase occurs in the two Cave 4 manuscripts which are extant for this passage. *they shall separate themselves from the settlement of the men of injustice*: cp.

v.1*b*–2*a*, and for the theme of separation see the comment on v.10*b*–20*a*. The demand for complete withdrawal that is made here no doubt reflects a profound dissatisfaction with the state of affairs in Jerusalem, with its corrupt priests and defiled temple, and a conviction that it was impossible in that environment to serve God in the way that they believed to be right, or to preserve the holiness of the community from contamination. *and shall go into the wilderness*: it is difficult to dissociate this passage from the occupation of the site at Qumran which began in the latter part of the second century BC; as we have seen, the contents of the Rule are most naturally interpreted as being intended specifically for the group which lived a quasi-monastic existence at this site. The immediate justification for the withdrawal into the wilderness is provided by Isa. 40:3, but it is important to bear in mind that the wilderness was the traditional place of refuge throughout Israel's history (cp. e.g. Judg. 20:47; 1 Macc. 2:27–30). According to Hos. 2:14 Israel was to be allured into the wilderness in order to make a new beginning. The ministry of John the Baptist in the wilderness is linked to Isa. 40:3 (cp. Mark 1:2–5 and parallels; John 1:19–23), and it was in the wilderness that Jesus was tempted (Mark 1:12–13 and parallels). *to prepare there the way of him*: what the community understood by 'preparing the way' is made clear in lines 15–16*a*. *the way of him*: the Hebrew text of Isa. 40:3 has 'the way of Yahweh' (NEB, 'a road for the LORD'), but out of a reverential desire to avoid the use of the divine name the personal pronoun 'him' has been substituted for 'Yahweh' in this line, and four dots have been used instead of the name in the quotation in the following line. The use of dots in this way is attested in other passages in the scrolls. In other cases the name was, out of reverence, written in the old Hebrew script instead of the familiar square characters that are used for most of the scrolls (see the comment on 1QpHab VI.14). These practices may be compared with the devices adopted by the Massoretes to avoid pronouncing the name 'Yahweh' (see E. B. Mellor (ed.), *The Making of the Old Testament* (The Cambridge Bible Commentary), Cambridge, 1972, pp. 143–4). It is noticeable that the non-biblical scrolls (e.g. the Community Rule, the Damascus Document) avoid using this name for God. In the present passage the word for 'him' does not have the regular form of the personal pronoun, but was perhaps deliberately given a slightly different form; one of the Cave 4 manuscripts has a variant reading, 'the way of truth'.

15–16*a*. *This (way) is the study of the law...that they should act*: preparing the way for God is interpreted metaphorically as the study and observance of the law, a reminder once again of the importance attached to this by the community; cp. VI.6*b*–8*a*. *the law w[hic]h he commanded through Moses...what the prophets revealed*: cp. I.2*b*–3*a*. *all that has been revealed from time to time*: the revelations received by the community through their study of the law; cp. IX.13*a*. It may be noted here that one of the Cave 4 manuscripts – more precisely, the oldest manuscript of the Rule known to exist – omits VIII.15*b*–IX.11.

COMMUNITY DISCIPLINE

VIII.16 No man from among the men of the community, the covenant 17 of the community, who presumptuously leaves unfulfilled any one of the commands shall touch the purity of the men of holiness, 18 or know any of their counsel, until his deeds have been cleansed from all injustice by walking in perfection of way. Then they shall admit him 19 to the council on the authority of the many, and afterwards he shall be registered in his rank. In accordance with this rule (they shall treat) all who join the community.

20 These are the rules by which the men of perfect holiness shall walk with one another. 21 Everyone who joins the council of holiness, (the council) of those who walk in perfection of way in accordance with what he has commanded – every man of them 22 who transgresses a word from the law of Moses presumptuously or negligently shall be sent away from the council of the community 23 and shall never return; no man from among the men of holiness shall have anything to do with his wealth or with his counsel in regard to any 24 matter. But if he acted through inadvertence, he shall be excluded from the purity and from the council, and they shall consult the rule: 25 'He shall not judge anyone, or be asked for any counsel for two years.' If his conduct is perfect 26 in session, in study, and in council [according to the man]y, if he does not sin inadvertently again throughout two 27 years – IX.1 because it is for one sin of inadvertence that he is punished for two years, whereas the one who acts presumptuously shall never return. Only the one who sins inadvertently 2 shall be tested for two years with regard to the perfection of his way, and his counsel on the authority of the many, and afterwards he shall be registered in his rank in the community of holiness.

The material in VIII.16*b*–IX.2 is different in character from that which surrounds it; whereas the latter appears to be the idealistic programme of a community in an embryonic state of existence, VIII.16*b*–IX.2 presupposes the existence of the group and provides a code of discipline to deal with the mundane reality that some members might not live up to the high ideals which the community set itself. For this reason it seems likely that VIII.16*b*–IX.2, like VIII.10*b*–12*a*, belongs to a second stage in the formation of this section of the Rule, and that it is a little later than the surrounding material. Here it may be recalled that the oldest manuscript of the Rule omits the whole of VIII.15*b*–IX.11. This omission by one of the manuscripts from Cave 4 extends beyond the passage with which we are immediately concerned and is capable of being explained in more than one way; but it does, at the very least, lend weight to the view that columns VIII–IX are not all of one piece. The lines which immediately precede VIII.16*b*–IX.2 are concerned with the study and observance of the law which God commanded; it is plausible to think that VIII.16*b*–IX.2 was inserted in its present position because of its concern with the related theme of the non-observance of God's commands (cp. VIII.16*b*–17, 22).

The code of discipline falls into two parts, and a difference of practice is observable in them. Lines 16*b*–19 are set off as a separate paragraph in the manuscript and deal with the case of the man 'who presumptuously leaves unfulfilled any one of the commands'; such a man was to be excluded from the community until by his deeds he had given clear evidence of his repentance. A new heading, comparable to that of VI.24, introduces VIII.20–IX.2, which is even more clearly set off in the manuscript as a separate paragraph. According to this rule anyone who 'transgresses a word from the law of Moses presumptuously or negligently' was to be permanently expelled, whereas a man who acted through inadvertence was to be excluded for two years, during which time he was to be tested. The difference between the punishments in VIII.16*b*–19 and VIII.20–IX.2 has led some scholars to think that the former passage is concerned with breaches of the community's own rules, the latter with breaches of the Mosaic law. But given that the two paragraphs are quite separate, and that the second has a new introduction, it is perhaps more natural to think that the differences in the punishments merely reflect a change of practice over a period of time.

The legislation in this section, particularly VIII.20–IX.2, is comparable to that of VI.24–VII.25, but differs from the latter both in its length and in its character. Whereas VI.24–VII.25 provides a comprehensive list of punishments for a series of specific offences, VIII.16*b*–IX.2 speaks only in general terms of disobeying the law. These differences suggest that VI.24–VII.25 belongs to a later stage in the community's existence, to a time when it had become larger and more institutionalised.

VIII.16*b*–19. *the men of the community, the covenant of the community*: one of the Cave 4 manuscripts, perhaps correctly, has 'the men of the covenant of the community'. *presumptuously*: see the comment on v.12. *leaves unfulfilled any one of the commands*: apparently based on Josh. 11:15. *shall touch the purity of the men of holiness*: the offender reverts to the status of a candidate for membership during his period of probation; see the comment on VI.15*b*–17. *or know any of their counsel*: the offender was not allowed to participate in meetings of the full members. *they shall admit him*: a form of the word translated 'draw near' in VI.16–22; VII.21.

20–24*a*. *These are the rules*: the same formula is used at the beginning of the list of punishments in VI.24–VII.25. *and shall never return*: cp. VII.2, 17, 24. *no man...shall have anything to do with his wealth or with his counsel*: cp. VII.24*b*–25.

VIII.24*b*–IX.2. *But if he acted through inadvertence*: cp. VII.3. *and they shall consult the rule*: the following words are to be understood as a quotation of one of the rules of the community. One of the Cave 4 manuscripts has a variant for these words which would make the translation read, 'he shall be excluded from the purity, and from the council, and from judgement; he shall not judge...'. *If his conduct is perfect in session, in study, and in council...throughout two years*: although the offender was excluded from the council (line 24), that is he no longer had the status of a full member, but reverted to that of a candidate on probation, he was apparently present at various meetings of the community at which his conduct could be tested by the full members (cp. IX.1–2). Rules for a 'session' are given in VI.8*b*–13*a*, and by 'study' we should probably think of communal study of the law (cp. VIII.15; VI.6*b*–8*a*). But the details are not clear, and the meaning is uncertain because the sentence lacks an apodosis. An emendation based on a reading in a Cave 4 manuscript would give the sense, 'If his conduct is perfect, he shall return to the (court of) inquiry (cp. VI.24) and to the council [on the authority of the man]y, provided that he does not sin inadvertently again throughout two years.' The Cave 4 manuscript has a shorter text: '(Then) he shall return to the (court of) inquiry and to the council, provided that he does not sin inadvertently again throughout two years.' *punished*: the word translated 'fined' in VI.24–VII.25; see the comment on VI.25*b*–27*a*.

THE COMMUNITY'S SACRIFICE

XI.3 When these exist in Israel in accordance with all these rules as a foundation of the spirit of holiness in eternal truth, **4** to make expiation for the guilt of transgression and the unfaithfulness of sin, and that the land may be accepted without the flesh of burnt-offerings and without the fat of sacrifice – and the proper offering **5** of the lips is like a soothing (odour) of righteousness, and perfection of way like an acceptable freewill offering – at that time the men of the community shall separate themselves **6** as a holy house for Aaron, that they may be united as a holy of holies, and as a house of community for Israel, for those who walk in perfection. **7** Only the sons of Aaron shall rule in matters of justice and wealth, and on their word the decision shall be taken with regard to every rule of the men of the community. **8** And the wealth of the men of holiness who walk in perfection – their wealth shall not be mixed with the wealth of the men of deceit who **9** have not made their way clean by separating themselves from injustice and by walking in perfection of way. They shall not depart from any counsel of the law to walk **10** in all the stubbornness of their heart, but they shall be governed by the first rules in which the men of the community began to be instructed **11** until the coming of the prophet and the messiahs of Aaron and Israel.

This material forms the continuation of VIII.1–10a, 12b–16a. Lines 3–6 take up anew the theme of the community as the true temple; lines 7–11 provide a few practical rules for the administration of the community that was about to come into existence.

IX.3–6. These lines add little to what has already been said in VIII.1–10a except to emphasise that within the temple formed by the community a life of perfection would take the place of sacrifice. *When these exist in Israel in accordance with all these rules*: cp. VIII.4b, 12b. *to make expiation...and that the land may be accepted*: cp. VIII. 3b–4a, 6b–7a, 9, 10. *without the flesh of burnt offerings and without the fat of sacrifice – and the proper offering of the lips is like a soothing (odour) of righteousness, and perfection of way like an acceptable freewill offering*: despite some uncertainties of translation these words seem to constitute a clear statement that prayer and right behaviour would take the place of sacrifice as the means of effecting atonement; cp. VIII.3b–4a and such passages as Hos. 6:6; Amos 5:21–4; Heb. 13:15–16. The attitude of the community towards sacrifice was no doubt governed by its belief that the temple in Jerusalem and its priesthood were defiled, but the War Scroll envisages that sacrifices would be offered again in the future (cp. II.5). Within the wider Essene movement the situation is less clear. Philo states that the Essenes 'have shown themselves especially devout in the service of God, not by offering sacrifices of animals, but by resolving to sanctify their minds' (Omn Prob Lib 75). According to Josephus (*Ant.* XVIII.1.5 (19)) the Essenes sent offerings to the temple, but apparently did not offer sacrifices there; the evidence for the latter point is, however, unclear. The Damascus Document appears in VI.11*b*–14*a* to prohibit visiting the temple; in contrast CD XI.17*b*–21*a* envisages both that the members of the movement would send offerings to the temple, and that they would themselves offer sacrifices. See the comment on CD VI.11*b*–14*a*. *the proper offering of the lips is like a soothing (odour)*: cp. such passages as Ps. 69:30–1; 107:22. *a holy house for Aaron...a house of community for Israel*: see the comment on VIII.5*b*–6*a*; in the light of the parallels in VIII.5*b*–6*a*, 8*b*–9 'a house of community' no doubt means the temple formed by the community.

7. *Only the sons of Aaron shall rule*: contrast v.2*b*–3*a*, where the joint rule of priests and laity perhaps represents later practice; see the comment there. The authority possessed by 'the many' in such passages as VI.15*b*–16*a*; VIII.18*b*–19 should also be noted. *the decision shall be taken*: literally 'the lot shall fall', cp. v.3*a*.

8–9*a*. *their wealth shall not be mixed with the wealth of the men of deceit*: cp. v.16*b*–17*a*.

9*b*–11. *the first rules*: perhaps best taken as referring to the legislation given before the decision was made to establish the community at Qumran; cp. CD XX.31*b*–32*a*, which similarly refers to 'the first rules'. It is to be assumed, however, that the content of this section of the Rule (VIII.1–X.8*a*), and indeed of the Rule as a whole, reflects the character of 'the first rules'. According to the present passage 'the first rules' would be superseded in the messianic era. *until the coming of the prophet and the messiahs of Aaron and Israel*: messianic expectations were widespread amongst Jews and Christians in the intertestamental period, and in that they contain such expectations the Qumran writings are entirely typical of their age and environment (see the Cambridge Bible Commentary on 2 Esdras, pp. 166–70). But the beliefs reflected in the Rule, and in some, at least, of the other scrolls, are distinctive: it was expected that there would be, not one messiah, but two, and that the coming of these messiahs would be preceded by that of a prophet. The

latter belief is found in 1 Macc. 4:46; 14:41, and is also known from
the New Testament, where it is based both on the expectation that God
would raise up a prophet like Moses (Deut. 18:15–19; cp. John 1:21;
Acts 3:22), and on the expectation that God would send Elijah before
him (Mal. 3:1; 4:5; cp. Matt. 11:7–15; 17:10–13; Mark 6:14–16); it
is to be observed that Deut. 18:18–19 is used in 4QTestimonia, a
document which reflects the same messianic expectations as the Rule
(see below, pp. 264–5).

The two messiahs are said to be 'of Aaron and Israel'; from this
we are to understand that one is a priest, the other a lay figure or, more
precisely, a prince. In 1QSa II.11*b*–22 it is clear that the priestly messiah
had precedence over the lay messiah, just as in the community the
priests had pre-eminence over the laity. The roots of the belief in two
messiahs are to be found in the Old Testament in the prophecies of
the exilic and early post-exilic period. Thus Ezekiel alludes to the
restoration of the Davidic monarchy (34:23–4; 37:22–5), but it is
significant that in his programme for the new community (chapters
40–8) a limited role is assigned to the prince in relation to worship (cp.
45:16–17; 46:1–18). Ezra 3–6 mentions Zerubbabel, the prince, and
Joshua, the priest, as being jointly involved in the rebuilding of the
temple in the early post-exilic period; in Hag. 2:23 and Zech. 4;
6:9–14 they are presented in somewhat exalted terms – almost as
messianic figures. Here it may be observed that although in its present
form Zech. 6:9–14 refers only to the crowning of Joshua, the priest,
it seems likely that this narrative originally mentioned the crowning
of both Joshua and Zerubbabel. Against the background provided by
these passages the emergence of the belief in two messiahs becomes
intelligible. Further, the pre-eminent position assigned to the messiah
of Aaron reflects the whole tendency of post-exilic Judaism, in which
the monarchy disappeared, and the high priest took over the functions
of the king. As a parallel to the belief in a priestly and royal messiah
reference may be made to the importance attached to the joint activity
of Levi and Judah in the Testaments of the Twelve Patriarchs; but the
messianic beliefs attached to these figures (cp. e.g. T. Levi 18; T. Jud.
24) belong to the Christian stage in the composition of this complex
work. Within the scrolls the belief in two messiahs is clear in the Rule
and in some other writings, particularly 4QTestimonia; for the
expectations of the Damascus Document see above, pp. 50, 60, and 63.

THE WISE LEADER

ix.12 These are the statutes by which the wise leader shall walk with every living being according to the rule appropriate to each time and according to the weight of each man.

13 He shall do the will of God in accordance with all that has been revealed from time to time.

He shall learn all the wisdom which has been found throughout time and 14 the statute of time.

He shall separate and weigh the sons of righteousness according to their spirit.

He shall keep firm hold of the chosen ones of the time in accordance with 15 his will, in accordance with what he has commanded.

He shall administer justice to each man according to his spirit. He shall admit him according to the cleanness of his hands and cause him to approach according to his insight. 16 And likewise his love and his hatred.

He shall not argue or quarrel with the men of the pit, 17 but shall hide the counsel of the law in the midst of the men of injustice.

He shall admonish with true knowledge and righteous judgement those who choose 18 the way, each man according to his spirit and according to the rule of the time.

He shall guide them with knowledge and likewise instruct them in the mysteries of wonder and truth in the midst 19 of the men of the community that they may walk perfectly with one another in all that has been revealed to them. This is the time to prepare the way 20 to the wilderness, and he shall instruct them in everything that has been found to be done at this time, and to separate themselves from every man who has not turned his way 21 from all injustice.

These are the rules of conduct for the wise leader in these times with regard to his love and his hatred. (He shall maintain) eternal hatred 22 towards the men of the pit in a spirit of secrecy. He shall leave to them wealth and wages, like a slave to his master and an oppressed man before 23 the one who rules over him. He shall be a man zealous for the statute and its time, until the day of vengeance. He shall do the will (of God) in everything he undertakes 24 and in everything he

controls, as he has commanded. He shall willingly delight in everything
that happens to him, and have no pleasure in anything except the will
of God. ²⁵ [In al]l the words of his mouth he shall delight and shall
not desire anything which he has not command[ed], but shall watch
continually [fo]r the decision of God. ²⁶ [...] he shall bless his maker,
and in everything which happens he shall rec[ount...

The section dealing with the wise leader (ix.12–26a) is closely linked
to what precedes. It describes the qualities which the leader of the new
community must possess and the responsibilities which he would have.
The latter include the exercise of pastoral oversight, the selection and
admission of new members, and the avoidance of contact with
outsiders.

ix.12. A heading, almost identical to CD xii.20b–21. *the wise leader*:
see the comments on iii.13–15a; vi.11b–12a. As was indicated earlier,
it seems that 'the wise leader' was one of the titles of the person called
in column vi 'the overseer of the many' and 'the officer in charge'.
*shall walk with every living being according to the rule appropriate to each
time*: cp. viii.4a. *the weight*: a common metaphor for the worth of an
individual: cp. e.g. Dan. 5:27; 1 En. 41:1, 'I saw...how the deeds of
men are weighed in the balance.'

13a. *in accordance with all that has been revealed from time to time*: cp.
viii.15b and the comment on that passage.

13b–14a. *the statute of time*: the meaning of the phrase is not entirely
clear, but there is perhaps an allusion to the idea that every action has
an appropriate time for its performance; cp. line 12, 'according to the
rule appropriate to each time', and Eccles. 3:1–8.

14b. *separate and weigh the sons of righteousness*: it was the responsibility
of the leader to select the members of the new community. The word
translated 'righteousness' has a slightly anomalous form and has been
emended by some scholars to read 'Zadok' (see the comment on
v.2b–3a). It may well be that a play on the two words 'righteousness'
and 'Zadok' was intended (the words are very similar in Hebrew), but
the evidence of one of the Cave 4 manuscripts confirms the translation
'righteousness'.

14c–15a. *the chosen ones of the time*: those chosen by God at that
particular moment to form the new community. But they can also be
described as 'those who choose the way' (lines 17b–18a); cp. in viii.6b
the two readings, 'chosen by the will (of God)' and 'those who choose
the will (of God)'.

15b–16a. *admit*: cp. vi.13b–15a, which deals with the responsibility of 'the officer in charge' for the admission of new members. The word here translated 'admit' is a form of the same word that is translated 'draw near' in vi.16–22; vii.21. *And likewise his love and his hatred*: i.e. both would be based on the character of the man with whom he was dealing, on his spirit, the cleanness of his hands, his insight.

16b–17a. *the men of the pit*: i.e. of Sheol; see the comment on CD vi.14c–15a. The translation 'the men of destruction' would also be possible. *shall hide the counsel of the law*: see the comment on viii.11b–12a, and for 'counsel of the law' cp. line 9.

17b–18a. *admonish*: the same word that is translated 'argue' in the previous line. *those who choose the way*: that is the way of obedience to the law within the community; for the use here of 'the way' see the comment on CD i.13–16a. It is interesting to observe that one of the Cave 4 manuscripts has the variant reading 'those chosen of the way'. *the rule of the time*: i.e. appropriate to the time.

19b–21a. *This is the time*: these words read like a challenge; those who formed the community were being urged to recognise that the moment for action had come. *to prepare the way to the wilderness*: cp. Isa. 40:3. A link back to viii.12b–14 is obviously intended, but it is noticeable that here it is a case of preparing the way to the wilderness (cp. viii.13), not in the wilderness (viii.14). This suggests that withdrawal into the desert still lay in the future. One of the two Cave 4 manuscripts extant for this passage does have 'in the wilderness', but this looks like a harmonisation with the biblical text. *found*: through the study of the law, cp. viii.11b–12a.

21b. *These are the rules*: another heading introduces a further statement about the leader of the community.

21c–22a. *in a spirit of secrecy*: a further allusion to the demand that the teaching of the community should not be communicated to outsiders, cp. lines 16b–17a.

22b–23a. *He shall leave to them wealth and wages*: he is to show a disregard for personal possessions.

23b. *zealous for the statute and its time, until the day of vengeance*: the meaning and translation are uncertain. 'The statute and its time' perhaps alludes to the idea that each action commanded by the law has its own appropriate moment for fulfilment, cp. viii.4a; ix.12. Alternatively the passage could be translated 'the statute whose time is for the day of vengeance', referring to the duty of the leader to play his part in the future punishment of the wicked.

23c–24a. *the will (of God)*: the sense is clear from Isa. 61:2, on which this passage seems to be based (cp. the 'day of vengeance'); what the NEB translates as 'the LORD's favour' was understood to mean 'the LORD's will'.

25. *his mouth*: i.e. God's mouth. *shall watch continually [fo]r the decision of God*: apparently an allusion to the seeking of God's will through study of the law.

26a. *he shall rec[ount*: the sentence will have ended with something like 'his wonders'.

The last part of the Community Rule (IX.26b–XI.22) is not translated here. Apart from two linking sentences (IX.26b–X.1a and X.8b), it consists of a liturgical calendar (X.1b–8a) and a hymn (X.9–XI.22). The latter is similar in character to the hymns of the community in the Hymn Scroll (1QH; see below, pp. 157–82). The former prescribes the times at which prayer is to be offered, and some scholars have thought that it was at one time the last part of the Programme for the New Community (VIII.1–IX.26a); this is by no means certain, but in any case the liturgical calendar probably had an independent existence at an earlier stage.

The Rule of the Congregation

The Rule of the Congregation (1QSa) is so called because of the frequency with which it refers to the group with which it is concerned as 'the congregation' (contrast the single reference to 'the congregation of holiness' in the Community Rule (1QS v.20b)). It is concerned with the education and career of the members of the congregation and with the administration of certain aspects of its life. As such the Rule of the Congregation may be compared with the Community Rule and the Damascus Document. But whereas these two latter documents reflect the actual life of the Essene movement in the various different forms which it assumed, the Rule of the Congregation is said to be for 'the end of days' (I.I). It is, that is to say, concerned with the life of the community in the new age, the messianic age, and indeed a major concern of this document is with the positions to be occupied by the priest-messiah and the messiah of Israel in the messianic age; for this reason this documents is also known as the Messianic Rule. Because of its future concerns the Rule of the Congregation may be seen to have close affinities with the War Scroll (1QM, not translated here), which lays down the rules of conduct and the tactics to be followed in the last great battle against the forces of evil. The Rule of the Congregation draws its inspiration from the presentation of Israel in the Priestly material in Exodus, Leviticus and Numbers as a 'congregation', an organised religious community. The legislation it contains and the language used are largely drawn from these biblical books, as the many parallels indicate. The Rule thus presents an ideal constitution for the life of the congregation in the new age. However, despite this future concern, it is to be assumed that the legislation in the Rule bore some relation to the actual life of the group which lies behind it. Like the Damascus Document, the Rule of the Congregation provides for a community which included married members and children (and thus not for a community following almost a form of monastic existence, as appears to be the case for the bulk of the Community Rule); the Rule of the Congregation specifically deals with the education of children and the marriage of members.

The Rule of the Congregation was copied in the same manuscript as the Community Rule, and by the same copyist, as a kind of appendix (the same is also true of another work, Words of Blessing (1QSb), not translated here). It was no doubt added after the Community Rule because its character as a piece of legislation made it seem appropriate to include it. As we have seen, the manuscript dates from approximately 100–75 BC, but the work itself may be older.

Bibliography

D. Barthélemy, 'Règle de la Congrégation (1QSa)', in D. Barthélemy and J. T. Milik, *Qumran Cave 1* (Discoveries in the Judaean Desert, 1), Oxford, 1955, 108–18 and plates XXIII–XXIV.

INTRODUCTION

1.1 This is the rule for the whole congregation of Israel at the end of days, when they are admitted [to the community to wa]lk 2 in accordance with the law of the sons of Zadok, the priests, and of the men of their covenant who have turn[ed aside from walking in] the way 3 of the people. They are the men of his counsel who have kept his covenant in the midst of wickedness in order to make expiat[ion for the land].

4 When they join, they shall assemble them all, including children and women, and shall read in [their] h[earing] 5 [a]ll the statutes of the covenant, and they shall instruct them in all their rules lest they stray in [their] e[rrors].

1. 1–3. An extended title. *the whole congregation of Israel*: this title for the community has been taken over from the Priestly material in the Pentateuch, where 'congregation' is a term frequently used to refer to Israel as a religious community in the period of the exodus and the wilderness wanderings; cp. for example Exod. 12:3, 'speak to the whole congregation (NEB 'community') of Israel'. *at the end of days*: see above, p. 145. *in accordance with the law of the sons of Zadok, the priests, and of the men of their covenant*: authority appears to be shared between the priests and the laity, as is the case for the most part in the Community Rule; see the comment on 1QS v.2b–3a. 'The sons of Zadok' (1.2, 24; II.3) is used here interchangeably with 'the sons of Aaron' (1.16, 23; II.13) as a title for the priests. For 'the men of their covenant' cp. the formula 'the multitude of the men of their covenant'

in 1QS v.9; vi.19 (translated here in line 18). *who have turn[ed aside from walking in] the way of the people*: cp. CD viii.16 = xix.29. *in the midst of wickedness*: the present age, which was thought to be under the control of the forces of evil; see the comments on 'the reign of Belial' (1QS 1.17*b*–18*a*) and 'the time of wickeness' (CD vi.10). *the men of his counsel*: 'his' must refer to God, even though God is not mentioned. *in order to make expiat[ion for the land]*: cp. 1QS viii.6*b*, 10*a*.

4–5. Public reading of the terms of the covenant to new members. These lines have been inspired by Deut. 31:11–12, part of the passage referring to the renewal of the covenant every seven years; this raises the possibility that the ceremony to which allusion is made here may be that of the entry into (and renewal of) the covenant. Alternatively, these lines merely refer to the instruction of new members. *When they join*: literally 'When they come'. *them all*: literally 'all those who are joining' or 'all those who come'. *and they shall instruct them in all their rules*: cp. 1QS vi.15*a*, where the instruction is the responsibility of 'the officer in charge at the head of the many'.

THE EDUCATION AND CAREER OF MEMBERS

1.6 This is the rule for all the hosts of the congregation, for all who are native Israelites.

From [his] you[th] 7 they shall teach him the book of meditation, and according to his age they shall instruct him in the statutes of the covenant. He shall [receive] 8 [ins]truction in their rules for ten years […]…

At the age of twenty years [he shall be] 9 registered that he may enter (his) allotted place in the midst of his family (and) join the congregation of holiness. He shall not [approach] 10 a woman to have intercourse with her before he is fully twenty years old, when he shall know [good] 11 and evil. Then she may be accepted to testify against him in respect of the precepts of the law and to be present at the proclamation of decisions.

12 When he is fully…At the age of twenty-five years he may come to take his place among the 'foundations' of the congregation 13 of holiness to undertake the service of the congregation.

At the age of thirty years he may approach to plead in lawsuits 14 and judgements, and to take his place among the heads of the thousands of Israel, the commanders of hundreds, the commanders of fifties, [15] [the commanders] of tens, the judges and the officers of the tribes, in all their families, [under the author]ity of the sons [16] [of Aar]on the priests and of all the heads of families of the congregation who have been chosen to preside at services, [17] [to go ou]t and to come in at the head of the congregation. According to his insight and the perfection of his way he shall brace himself in (his) positi[on to per]form [18] the service assigned to him in the midst of his brethren. They shall honour one man more than another [according to whether] (he has) much or little.

[19] When a man is advanced in years, they shall assign (him) his duties in the [serv]ice of the congregation in proportion to his strength.

No man who is simple [20] shall be allowed to hold office in the congregation of Israel, (or) to defend a case, or to carry any responsibility in the congregation, [21] or to take part in the war for crushing the nations. His family shall merely register (him) in the army register, [22] and he shall do his service in forced labour in proportion to his ability.

The sons of Levi shall serve, each in his position, [23] under the authority of the sons of Aaron to lead the whole congregation in and out, each man in order, under the direction of the heads [24] of families of the congregation; (they shall serve) as commanders, judges and officers, according to the number of all their hosts, under the authority of the sons of Zadok the priests [25] [and of all the he]ads of families of the congregation.

A new heading and a paragraph sign in the margin mark this section off from the one that precedes. It is mainly concerned with the education (until the age of twenty) and the various stages in the career of members of the community; lines 19b–25a deal with the position of two particular groups, simpletons and Levites. This section may be compared with CD x.6b–10a and xiv.6b–10a, which specify age-limits for judges, the priest who enrols the many, and the overseer of all the camps; with 1QM vi.13b–vii.3a, which similarly specifies age-limits for different categories of service in the army; and with passages in the Old Testament that prescribe age-limits of various kinds (see below).

  1.6a. *for all the hosts of the congregation*: like Israel in the wilderness the congregation is thought of as being organised as an army. A division into thousands, hundreds, fifties and tens is envisaged in 1.14*b*–15*a*; 1.29*b*–II.1*a*; cp. Exod. 18:21; Deut. 1:15; 1QS II.21*b*–22*a*. *for all who are native Israelites*: quoted from Lev. 23:42. Implicit in these words is the claim that the community represents the true Israel, the ideal which all Jews should follow.

6b–8a. Instruction in the Pentateuch and in 'the statutes of the covenant' began in infancy and was followed by ten years' instruction in the community's rules. *the book of meditation*: mentioned also in CD X.6; XIII.2, and thought to be a name for the Pentateuch. Alternatively it has been suggested that it is a name for the Temple Scroll. *the statutes of the covenant*: the terms of the covenant by which the community was bound. *their rules*: the community's own regulations, perhaps much the same as is meant by 'the statutes of the covenant'. *for ten years*: the fact that the next stage in the career of a member began at twenty suggests that instruction in the community's rules began at the age of ten. The text immediately following is damaged and uncertain.

8b–11. *At the age of twenty years [he shall be] registered*: twenty was the minimum age at which Israelites were included in the census; see Exod. 30:14; 38:26; Num. 1:3; 1 Chron. 27:23. The 1QSa text draws on the two Exodus passages. *join the congregation of holiness*: cp. 1QS V.20*b*. *to have intercourse with her*: the language is based on the Hebrew expressions used in Num. 31:17, Judg. 21:12. *when he shall know [good] and evil*: indicating that he has reached the age of moral discernment; the expression is used in this sense in Deut. 1:39. *Then she may be accepted to testify against him*: this passage apparently indicates that on marriage a woman acquired a certain status within the community, including the right that in legal cases her testimony against her husband would be accepted. But a reference to the man's wife is very surprising, and the interpretation of the passage is disputed. It should perhaps be emended to read: 'Then (i.e. at twenty) he shall be accepted to testify in accordance with the precepts of the law and to be present at the proclamation of decisions.' *the precepts of the law...the proclamation of decisions*: a distinction is made once more between the legislation of the Pentateuch and the community's own legal 'decisions' or 'rules' (as the word could also be translated).

12–13a. *When he is fully...At the age of*: the copyist apparently made a mistake and so started again. *At the age of twenty-five years he may come to take his place*: in Num. 8:24, on which this passage is based, Levites begin their service at the age of twenty-five, but in Num. 4:3, 23 they begin at the age of thirty. *the 'foundations'*: used here in a

transferred sense to refer to the lower ranks within the community:
cp. the use of 'pillars' to refer to the leaders of the community in Gal.
2:9. Elsewhere in the scrolls 'foundation' is used in a transferred
sense – a little differently from here – in 1QS VI.26; VII.17, 18.

13b–18. A member could only begin to hold office within the
community at the age of thirty; cp. again Num. 4:3, 23. This corresponds
to what is said in CD XIV.6b–10a about the minimum age of the priest
who enrols the many and of the overseer of all the camps, but in CD
X.6b–7a it is said that judges should be between twenty-five and sixty
years old. *among the heads of the thousands of Israel…the officers of the*
tribes: for this list of officers cp. Deut. 1:15. *the heads of families of the*
congregation: the same phrase as in Num. 31:26 (NEB, 'the heads of
families in the community'), used to refer to the leading lay figures.
who have been chosen: literally 'for whom the lot falls'; see on 1QS
VI.16. *[to go ou]t and to come in at the head*: the expression is probably
taken from Num. 27:17, where it is used with reference to Joshua;
but cp. also 1 Sam. 18:16. The thought in the first instance is of the
military leader who 'goes out' and 'comes in' at the head of his forces.
According to his insight and the perfection of his way: the same formula
as in 1QS V.24a. *he shall brace himself*: literally 'strengthen his loins',
cp. Nahum 2:1. *They shall honour one man more than another*: for the
ranking of members cp. 1QS II.19b–23; v.23–24a. *[according to whether]*
(he has) much or little: i.e. in proportion to his insight and the perfection
of his way.

19a. When a man is advanced in years: CD X.6b–10a; XIV.6b–10a
prescribe definite upper age-limits (sixty or fifty), as do Num. 4:3, 23;
8:25 (fifty). *they shall assign (him) his duties…in proportion to his strength*:
Num. 8:26 likewise envisages some limited continuation of service:
'He may continue to assist his colleagues in attendance in the Tent of
Presence but shall perform no regular service.'

19b–22a. Simpletons. *shall be allowed*: literally 'shall enter into the
lot'; see on 1QS VI.16. *to take part in the war for crushing the nations*:
the War Scroll lays down the rules for the conduct of this war and the
tactics to be adopted. *His family shall merely register (him)*: or 'He shall
merely register his family.'

22b–25a. The Levites exercise control in the community under the
supervision of the priests and the leading lay figures ('the heads of
families of the congregation'). *to lead the whole congregation in and out*:
i.e. to exercise control; for the language cp. again Num. 27:17 (NEB
here, 'to lead them out and bring them home') and see the comment
on line 17. *under the direction of the heads of families of the congregation*:

the lay leaders (cp. line 16). It is twice stated that the Levites act under the supervision of both the priests and the lay leaders. *according to the number of all their hosts*: i.e. the number of Levitical officials is in proportion to the total numbers in the community.

ADMISSION TO MEETINGS

[1.25] If the whole assembly is summoned, whether for judgement, or [26] for a council of the community, or for mobilisation for war, they shall hallow them for three days so that every one who attends may be [27] rea[dy…].

These are the men who shall be summoned to the council of the community from the age of tw…

All [28] the wi[se men] of the congregation, those who have understanding and knowledge, the perfect of way and the able-bodied mén, together with [29] [the commanders of the tri]bes and all their judges and officers, and the commanders of thousands, and the commanders [of hundreds], [11.1] fifties, and tens, and the Levites, (each) i[n] his [divis]ion of service – these [2] are the men of renown, those called to the assembly, who shall gather for the council of the community in Israel [3] before the sons of Zadok the priests.

No man afflicted by any form of human uncleanness [4] shall enter the assembly of God; no man afflicted by (any of) these shall [5] hold a position in the congregation.

No one afflicted in his body, crippled in his feet or [6] his hands, lame, or blind, or deaf, or dumb, or afflicted in his body with a physical defect [7] visible to the eye, or an old and tottery man unable to keep still in the midst of the congregation [8] – none of these shall en[ter] to take their place [in] the midst of the congregation of the men of renown because the angels [9] of holiness are [in] their [congregat]ion. If [one of] them has something to say to the council of holiness, [10] they shall question [him] privately; but the man shall [no]t enter into the midst [of the congregation] because [11] he is afflicted.

A space in the middle of the line marks the beginning of a new section, which is primarily concerned to list the categories of those who may, and may not, be present at meetings of the members.

1.25*b*–27*a*. Meetings of the members for whatever purpose had to be preceded by rites of purification. *or for a council of the community*: 'the council of the community' is used frequently in the Community Rule (e.g. III.2) as a term for the whole body of members; in the Rule of the Congregation the expression is used rather to refer to a meeting of the members. *or for mobilisation for war*: cp. again the War Scroll. *they shall hallow them for three days*: like Israel at the foot of Mount Sinai, cp. Exod. 19:10–11, 14–15. *rea[dy...]*: the immediately following word is damaged and uncertain.

27*b*. *from the age of tw...*: for whatever reason the copyist broke off in the middle of a word (apparently 'twenty') and left a blank space; perhaps he originally intended to alter the text at a later stage.

1.27*c*–11.3*a*. The list of those who may attend divides into two. The first series of terms is general and refers to the ordinary members in terms of their intellectual, spiritual and physical qualities; the second series designates specific office-holders. *All the wi[se men]...those who have understanding and knowledge*: perhaps taken from Deut. 1:13, where the same combination of terms occurs (more obvious in the Hebrew than in translation). *the perfect of way*: cp. 1QS IV.22*a*; 1QH 1.36. *the able-bodied men*: or 'the fighting men', an expression used frequently in the Old Testament (e.g. Judges 3:29; 2 Sam. 24:9); cp. 1QM II.8; VI.13. *and all their judges...the commanders [of hundreds], fifties, and tens*: cp. 1.14*b*–15*a*. *and the Levites*: cp. 1.22*b*–25*a*. *the men of renown, those called to the assembly*: the expressions are taken from Num. 16:2 (NEB, 'conveners of assembly and men of good standing'), but used here in the reverse order; cp. lines 11, 13. *before the sons of Zadok the priests*: the pre-eminent position of the priests is once again noticeable.

11.3*b*–11*a*. Those excluded from meetings include both those affected by ritual uncleanness and those suffering from a physical defect.

3*b*–5*a*. *shall enter the assembly of God*: based on the formula used five times in Deut. 23:1–3 (RSV, 'shall enter the assembly of the LORD').

5*b*–9*a*. *crippled in his feet*: cp. 2 Sam. 4:4; 9:3. *lame, or blind, or deaf, or dumb, or...with a physical defect*: a combination of terms taken from Lev. 21:18 and Exod. 4:11; the former verse occurs in a passage (Lev. 21:16–23) which lists those prohibited from undertaking priestly functions: contrast Luke 14:21. *because the angels of holiness are [in] their [congregat]ion*: the same reason in a matter involving ritual impurity is given in 1QM VII.6, the underlying principle being that the holiness conferred on the community by the presence of the angels must not be contaminated in any way. This is an extension of the principle in Deut. 23:14, where it is said that God goes about in the camp, and for that reason the 'camp must be kept holy for fear that he should see something indecent and go with you no further': in the scrolls angels take the place of God because in this period God becomes increasingly transcendant. In 1QS XI.7b–9a the members of the community are companions of the angels. For the reference to the angels cp. also 1 Cor. 11:10.

PRECEDENCE IN THE MESSIANIC AGE

II.11 [The ses]sion of the men of renown [called to] the assembly of the council of the community, when [12] [the priest-]messiah shall summon them.

[The priest] shall enter [at] the head of the whole congregation of Israel, and (then) all [13] [his brethren, the sons] of Aaron the priests, [those called] to the assembly, the men of renown; and they shall sit [14] be[fore him, each] (in the place) appropriate to his honour. And afterwards [the messi]ah of Israel [shall enter], and the heads [of the clans of Israel] shall sit before him, [15] [ea]ch (in the place) appropriate to his honour, according to [his position] in their camps and on their marches. And all [16] the heads of fa[milies of the congreg]ation together with the wise men [of the congregation of holiness] shall sit before them, each (in the place) appropriate to [17] his honour.

[When] they gather [for the] common [tab]le, [or to drink the new] wine, and the common table is prepared, [18] [and the] new wine [mixed] for drinking, [let no] man [stretch out] his hand over the first fruits [19] of bread and [new wine] before the priest; for [it is he who] shall bless the first fruits of bread [20] and new win[e, and shall] first [stretch out] his hand over the bread. And afterwa[rds] the messiah of Israel [shall str]etch out his hands [21] over the bread. [And afterwards] the whole congregation of the community [shall ble]ss, ea[ch (in the order) appropriate to] his honour.

It is in accordance with this statute that they shall proceed [22] at every me[al at which] at least ten men [g]ather.

This final section deals with precedence at meetings and at the common meal in the messianic age; it may be compared with parts of the material in column VI of the Community Rule, namely lines 8b–13a and 4b–5a.

II.11b–12a. A form of heading, for which cp. 1QS VI.8b. *the men of renown [called to] the assembly*: cp. above, line 2. *when [the priest-]messiah shall summon them*: the translation is very uncertain because the manuscript is difficult to read at this point, and there are several gaps. The translation adopted here follows one proposal for restoration that seems plausible, but other scholars have restored the text quite differently. Despite this uncertainty, there can be no question that the rules which follow provide in the first instance for the circumstances of the messianic age; cp. 'at the end of days' in I.1. *[the priest-]messiah*: or 'the anointed [priest]' (the same Hebrew expression that is used in Lev. 4:3, 5, 16). The reference – assuming the restoration is correct – is to the figure called in 1QS IX.11 'the messiah of Aaron'.

12b–17a. Precedence at meetings. In the messianic age the order of precedence is to be: the priest-messiah and his entourage, the messiah of Israel and his entourage, the heads of families and the wise men of the congregation. The pre-eminence of the priest-messiah over the lay messiah is noticeable here, as it is also in the section dealing with the common meal (lines 17b–21a). In the regulations in QS VI.8b–13a, which presumably reflect actual practice at a particular stage in the community's history, the order of precedence is: priests, elders, the rest of the people.

12b–14a. *[The priest]*: the restoration is uncertain, but makes sense in the context; cp. the reference to 'the priest' (that is the priest-messiah) in line 19. *[those called] to the assembly, the men of renown*: cp. Num. 16:2 and line 2. *each] (in the place) appropriate to his honour*: for this emphasis on the strict observance of rank cp. e.g. 1QS V.23–24a; VI.9b–11a.

14b–15a. *[the messi]ah of Israel*: cp. line 20 and 1QS IX.11. *according to [his position] in their camps and on their marches*: according to the kind of ideal arrangements indicated in Num. 2 and 10:11–28.

15b–17a. *the heads of fa[milies of the congreg]ation*: the leading lay figures, cp. 1.16. *the wise men*: used here as a term for the ordinary members, cp. 1.28.

17b–21a. The common meal. There is an obvious similarity with the much less detailed regulation in 1QS VI.4b–5a, which again presumably reflects actual practice in the community. The similarity suggests that the community's common meal was in some sense seen as an anticipation of the common meal of the messianic age. In the present passage the pre-eminence of the priest-messiah over the lay messiah is quite explicit. *the priest*: i.e. the priest-messiah.

21b–22a. As in 1QS VI.3b–4a, 6b–7a; CD XII.23b–XIII.2a, ten is the minimum needed to form a group. The various links that we have seen to exist with the Community Rule and the Damascus Document suggest that the legislation of the Rule of the Congregation, although intended for the last days, bore some relation to actual practice within the community which lies behind it.

The Hymns

The Qumran writings include a number of works that are poetic or liturgical in character, such as the Psalms Scroll from Cave 11 or the Words of Blessing. The former work (11QPsª) contains not only forty-one biblical psalms, but also seven apocryphal psalms and a piece in prose about David's compositions (11QPsª DavComp); four of the apocryphal psalms were known already, but three are 'new'. The combination within the same collection of biblical and apocryphal psalms is to be observed. The latter work (1QSb) – copied out, like the Rule of the Congregation (1QSa), in the same manuscript as the Community Rule (1QS) as an appendix – consists of a series of blessings that were to be pronounced by 'the wise leader' (Hebrew *maskīl*; see above, pp. 96, 118); he was to bless in turn all the members of the community, the high priest, the priests, and the prince of the congregation. It appears that this work was intended for use in the messianic age, and that the blessings for the high priest and the prince were for the figures referred to elsewhere as the messiahs of Aaron and Israel. But this work may also have been used in the liturgical services of the community in anticipation of the messianic age. However, the most important of the poetic and liturgical writings consists of a collection of psalms of thanksgiving (Hebrew *hōdāyōt*), often referred to in English as the Hymns.

The manuscript of this work (1QH) was one of the first of the scrolls to be discovered; it dates from the first century AD. The manuscript has been badly damaged and in its present form consists of eighteen incomplete columns and a number of fragments. Only the first three columns, which are representative of the collection as a whole, have been translated here. Other manuscripts of this work are also known.

The psalms in this collection are written in a style similar to that of the biblical psalms and are often heavily dependent on Old Testament material for their imagery, language and vocabulary. The opening words of a number of the psalms have been lost, but in the majority of cases where the beginning has survived a standard introductory formula has been used, 'I thank you, O Lord.' In a few cases other introductory formulas are found: 'I thank you, my God' (XI.3, 15) and

'Blessed are you, O Lord' (e.g. v.20). The regular occurrence of the introductory formula 'I thank you, O Lord' is linked to the fact that many of the psalms belong to the literary type known as the individual song of thanksgiving; but this form has been used with a certain freedom and has often been combined – as is also the case in the Old Testament – with elements of the lament form. Other psalms may be classified as hymns (for instance column 1). Many of the psalms in the collection have a learned character, and in this respect, as in others, they are similar to other psalms from the period, such as the psalms in Ecclesiasticus or the collection known as the Psalms of Solomon (see volume 4 in this series, *Outside the Old Testament*, pp. 159–77).

It has often been assumed that all the psalms in this collection were composed by the same person, and further that the author was the teacher of righteousness. On this basis the attempt has been made to use these psalms as a source from which information about the character and career of the teacher may be drawn. It is, however, by no means clear that all the psalms were composed by the same person, much less that they were all composed by the teacher of righteousness. Furthermore, the fact that these psalms make extensive use of traditional imagery, language and vocabulary drawn from the Old Testament makes it very difficult to use them as a source for biographical information. There are some psalms behind which a distinct personality does seem to stand, and it is possible – but no more than this – that these should be regarded as psalms composed by the teacher of righteousness (cp. e.g. 11.7–19); but for the rest the psalms must be regarded as of unknown authorship. It is not clear whether the psalms in this collection were intended for private use or for use in the liturgical services of the community, but probably both should be envisaged. Like the biblical psalms, these psalms were capable of being used by individuals and by groups in a variety of circumstances.

Bibliography

E. L. Sukenik, *The Dead Sea Scrolls of the Hebrew University*, Jerusalem, 1955.

S. Holm-Nielsen, *Hodayot: Psalms from Qumran* (Acta Theologica Danica, 2), Aarhus, 1960.

M. Delcor, *Les Hymnes de Qumran (Hodayot): Texte hébreu, introduction, traduction, commentaire*, Paris, 1962.

PRAISE OF GOD THE CREATOR

1.6 [...You are compassionate] and long suffering in [your]
   judgeme[nts]
(and) righteous in all your deeds.
7 In your wisdom [you established the generations] of eternity,
and before you created them you knew their deeds 8 for all
   eternity.
[For without you nothing] is done,
and nothing known except by your will.
You formed 9 every spirit
and [...] and a law for all their deeds.

You spread out the heavens 10 for your glory,
all [their hosts] you [appointed] according to your will
and the mighty winds according to their decrees
before ever 11 they became [your] messengers of ho[liness.
You entrusted] to the eternal spirits in their dominions
the lights according to their mysteries,
12 the stars according to their paths,
[...] according to their duties,
the thunderbolts and lightnings according to their service,
the (well-)planned storehouses 13 according to their purposes,
[...]according to their mysteries.

You created the earth by your strength,
14 the seas and the deeps wi[th...
All] their [inhabi]tants you established by your wisdom,
and all that is in them 15 you appointed according to your will.
[...] to the spirit of man whom you formed in the world
for all the days of eternity 16 and the everlasting generations
to [...] in their times.
You assigned their service in all their generations
and a law 17 in the appointed times of the domin[ion...] for
   all generations.

And their visitation for reward as well as [18] all their
   chastisements [...],
and you assigned it to all their offspring
for the number of the generations of eternity [19] and for all the
   everlasting years.
[...] and in the wisdom of your knowledge
you determined their fate before ever [20] they existed.
All things [occ]ur in accordance with [your will],
and without you nothing is done.

[21] These things I know through the understanding which
   comes from you,
for you have opened my ears to wonderful mysteries.
And I, a creature of clay and a thing kneaded with water,
[22] a foundation of shame and a spring of impurity,
a furnace of iniquity and an edifice of sin,
a spirit of error, perverted, with no [23] understanding, and
   terrified by (your) righteous judgements –
what shall I say that is not known,
or utter that has not been recounted?
All things [24] are engraved before you on the stela of
   remembrance
for all the everlasting ages
and the circuits of the number of the years of eternity
in all their appointed times;
[25] they are not hidden or missing before you.
And how shall a man give an account of his sin?
And how shall he plead concerning his iniquities?
[26] And how shall the wrongdoer answer to righteous
   judgement?
To you, O God of knowledge, belong all deeds of
   righteousness [27] and the counsel of truth;
but to the sons of men belong the service of iniquity and deeds
   of deceit.

You created [28] breath for the tongue,
and you know its words
and determine the fruit of the lips before ever they exist.
You set words to metre
[29] and the outpouring of the breath of the lips by measure.
You bring forth sounds according to their mysteries
and the outpourings of breath according to their rhythm,
that (men) may make known [30] your glory,
and may recount your wonders in all your deeds of truth and
    your righteous [judgements],
and may praise your name [31] by the mouth of all;
and that they may know you according to their insight,
and may bless you for [all] eternity.

In your compassion [32] and your great kindness
you have strengthened the spirit of man in the face of
    affliction,
and [the perverted spirit] you have cleansed of great iniquity,
[33] that it might recount your wonders before all your
    creatures.
[I will declare...] the judgements by which I was afflicted,
[34] and to the sons of men all the wonders by which you showed
    yourself mighty i[n me...]

Hear, [35] you wise men, you who meditate on knowledge and
    are anxious,
and be of a constant mind!
[You...], increase discernment!
[36] You righteous, put an end to injustice,
and all you perfect of way, hold fast [...!
...] misery, be long-suffering
[37] and do not reject [...!
Those who are stu]pid of heart do not understand [38] these
    things.
[...]

The beginning and end of the first psalm are lost, but it appears that the first psalm ended at the bottom of column I or the very top of column II. This psalm belongs to the literary type known from the Old Testament as the hymn, in which the chief concern is the praise of God for his character and his deeds. In view of its theme, namely God's marvellous creation of the world, this psalm may be compared with Ps. 104; but the psalm has a markedly learned character, and a closer parallel is provided by the hymns in Ecclesiasticus such as 39:12–35 or 42:15–43:33, which are also learned or didactic in character.

The psalm no doubt began with the formula that occurs most frequently in this collection, 'I thank you, O Lord'; for other possibilities see above, p. 157. What has actually survived of the psalm corresponds to the so-called main body of a hymn in the Old Testament, i.e. the part in which God's character and deeds are described as the motive for praising him. The existing material divides up into four main sections. The first (lines 6–20) describes the way in which God marvellously created the world and predetermined everything that would happen in it. In the second (lines 21–27a) a contrast is drawn between man's ignorance and sinfulness and God's knowledge and righteousness; this contrast serves to increase yet further God's status as a being worthy to be praised. In the third section (lines 27b–34a) the composition of poetry and music, and hence of psalms and hymns, is directly attributed to God's activity as creator; in effect man's ability to praise God is presented as being entirely dependent on God. The final section (lines 34b–38) consists of an exhortation to the wise to stand firm and show understanding. Two main themes run through this hymn: the emphasis on the way in which God has predetermined all things, and the contrast between the exalted status of God and the lowly status of man.

1.6. [... *You are compassionate*] *and long-suffering*: cp. the list of God's attributes in such passages as Exod. 34:6–7 or Ps. 103:8.

7–8a. For this clear statement of determinism, which forms an important theme in this psalm as a whole, cp. 1QS III.15b–17a (part of the teaching on the two spirits).

8b–9a. *You formed every spirit*: the reference is probably to the spirits mentioned in line 11 that control various elements in the universe. It is impossible to say with any certainty what stood in the gap after 'every spirit and'. *and a law for all their deeds*: i.e. God has prescribed what they should do; cp. 1QS III.16b–17a.

9b–13a. The creation of the heavens, *You spread out the heavens*: a common expression in Old Testament creation passages; cp. for example Job 9:8; Ps. 104:2; Jer. 10:12. *and the mighty winds according to their decrees*: the decrees prescribed for them by God; for the thought here and in the following lines that the various parts of creation observe a divinely imposed order cp. 1 En. 2: 1–5: 3. *before ever they became [your] messengers of ho[liness*: based on Ps. 104:4, 'who makest the winds thy messengers'; the thought is that God foreordained his marvellous arrangement of the universe. *You entrusted] to the eternal spirits in their dominions*: the restoration makes reasonable sense in the context, the thought being that the various elements in the universe are controlled by spirits or angels; cp. Rev. 7:2; 19:17; Jub. 2:2; 1 En. 60:12–21, especially 16–21. *the lights*: namely the sun and moon; cp. Gen. 1:14–19. *according to their mysteries*: the laws prescribed for the sun and moon by God, which are conceived of as being beyond human comprehension. The thought of the proper order observed by the various parts of the universe ('according to their paths...according to their duties', and so on) continues in the following list. The two gaps will have contained references to other astronomical or meteorological phenomena, such as 'the clouds'. *storehouses*: for the winds, the lightning, etc.; for the idea cp. Job 37:9; 38:22; 2 Esdras 5:37; 1 En. 41:4.

13*b*–15*a*. The creation of the earth.

15*b*–20. The predetermination of man's duties and fate. The extensive gaps, which cannot be restored with any certainty, make it difficult to trace the precise development of thought. *You assigned their service*: I take the 'their' here and in the following lines to refer to man. *And their visitation for reward as well as all their chastisements [...]*: the gap must at least have contained something like 'you established'. For the phrase cp. 1QS III.14*b*–15*a*, 'according to their visitation of chastisement as well as their times of reward', and for what was understood by the phrase cp. 1QS IV.6*b*–8, 11*b*–14. *and you assigned it*: i.e. the visitation [...] *and in the wisdom...nothing is done*: a reiteration of the thought of lines 7–8*a*. *their fate*: literally 'their testimony' (Hebrew *te̔ūdāh*), here in the transferred sense 'their law' or 'their decree' (i.e. the decree about them).

21–27*a*. Man's ignorance and sinfulness are contrasted with the knowledge and righteousness of God, who has predetermined all things. *These things*: all that has been said so far about God and the creation of the world. *a creature of clay and a thing kneaded with water*: the idea is of man formed like a piece of pottery out of wet clay; cp. Gen. 2:7; Job10:9; 33:6. The imagery is used to indicate man's frailty and lowly status; cp. III.23*b*–24*a*. The following lines emphasise his

sinfulness. *All things are engraved before you on the stela of remembrance*:
a vivid expression of God's omniscience. There are links with the idea
of a book in which the deeds of men are recorded; cp. Ps. 56:8; Dan.
7:10; Rev. 20:12; 1 En. 89:61–64. *the stela of remembrance*: cp. Mal.
3:16, 'a book of remembrance' (NEB, 'a record'), although the
thought there is of a book in which names are recorded; see the
comment on CD xx.19. *God of knowledge*: cp. 1 Sam. 2:3 and 1QS
III.15b.

27b–34a. God has given man the power of speech that he might praise
him, and has also strengthened man that he might proclaim God's
wonders to his creatures. *You created breath for the tongue*: cp. 1 En.
14:2. *the fruit of the lips*: cp. Hos. 14:2 (see the NEB footnote). *You
set words to metre*: the thought is of the composition of psalms and
hymns, which is presented as being directly inspired and brought about
by God. *rhythm*: literally 'reckoning'.

34b–38. A concluding exhortation to the wise to stand firm and to
show understanding. Because of the damage to the bottom of column I
and the top of column II it is not clear where exactly the psalm ended,
but it does appear that this exhortation formed part of the conclusion;
the material in II.7–19 is quite different in character and must have
belonged to another psalm. *you wise men*: the fact that this exhortation
is addressed to 'the wise' serves to underline the learned character of
this psalm (see above, p. 162). *and be of a constant mind*: see the comment
on 1QS IV.5. *you perfect of way*: used as a term for the members of the
community in 1QS IV.22a; 1QSa I.28.

A FIGURE OF CONTROVERSY

[...] II.7 [...]
You placed the answer of a tongue upon my unc[ircumcised]
    lips,
and you supported me, giving me strength of loins 8 and
    mighty power;
my foot stood in the realm of wickedness.

I was a trap to the transgressors,
but healing to all 9 those who turn from transgression,
discernment to the simple,
and constancy to all those who are anxious of heart.

You made me an object of insult [10] and derision to the traitors,
but a counsel of truth and understanding to the upright of way.
I was the cause of the iniquity of the wicked,
[11] a source of whispering on the lips of the ruthless;
the scoffers ground their teeth.
I was the target of the mocking-songs of the transgressors;
[12] the assembly of the wicked raged against me
and roared like the stormy seas,
whose raging waves cast up mud [13] and filth.
You made me a standard for the chosen ones of righteousness,
a knowledgeable interpreter of wonderful mysteries,
to test [14] [the men] of truth
and to try those who love instruction.
I was an adversary to the interpreters of error,
but [a master [15] of pea]ce to all those who see the truth.
I became a spirit of jealousy to all those who seek smoo[th
    things],
[16] [and all] the men of deceit roared against me –
like the sound of the roaring of many waters.
[All] their [pl]ans were schemes of Belial,
[17] and they turned towards the pit the life of the man
in whose mouth you had established teaching,
and in whose heart you had placed understanding,
[18] that he might open a spring of knowledge to all those who
    understand.
But they exchanged them for uncircumcised lips
[19] and for the strange tongue of a people without
    understanding
that they might come to grief in their straying.

The beginning of the second psalm is lost, but it probably began within
the first few lines of column II. This psalm belongs to the literary type
known from the Old Testament as the individual song of thanksgiving
in which the main theme is the expression of thanks to God for
deliverance from distress; cp. e.g. Ps. 138; Ecclus. 51:1–12. But the
psalm also shows, as is often the case in the Old Testament, many links
with psalms of lament.

Lines 7b–8a, the first lines where it is possible to make clear sense of what has survived, describe the support received by the psalmist in his distress. The remainder of the material (lines 8b–19) describes, in a series of contrasting statements, the effect of the work and teaching of the psalmist on those who opposed him and on those who accepted his teaching. Two features stand out in this material. The first is the frequent use of traditional imagery derived from the psalms, particularly the psalms of lament. The second is the use of terms for the opponents and followers of the psalmist that are sectarian in character inasmuch as parallels can frequently be found for them in the biblical commentaries and in other Qumran writings. The psalmist presents himself as a teacher, and he appears as a much more distinct personality than the author of the first psalm. Many scholars have assumed that the author of this second psalm was the teacher of righteousness. This is a plausible hypothesis, but it cannot be more than this; and the fact that traditional imagery is used so frequently makes it very difficult to use this psalm to reconstruct details of the life and character of the teacher of righteousness, even assuming he was the author.

II.7b–8a. The psalmist acknowledges the support given him by God in his distress. *You placed the answer of a tongue upon my unc[ircumcised] lips:* as in the case of Moses (Exod. 4:12) or Jeremiah (Jer. 1:9), God gave him the words to speak; we are not told the precise circumstances, but in the light of what follows we should no doubt think of some form of teaching ministry (cp. particularly line 17). *my unc[ircumcised] lips:* for the language cp. Exod. 6:12, 30. *the realm of wickedness:* the Jewish world outside the community; cp. III.24b and Mal. 1:4.

8b–19. The contrasting effects of the work and teaching of the psalmist on his opponents and his followers.

8b–9a. *a trap:* i.e a cause of sin. *all those who turn from transgression:* taken from Isa. 59:20, also used in CD II.5; XX.17b; see the comment on CD II.5. *the simple:* used as a term for the members of the community in 1QpHab XII.4. *constancy:* literally 'a constant mind'; see on 1QS IV.5. *all those who are anxious of heart:* cp. 1.35.

9b–10a. *an object of insult and derision:* traditional language used in psalms of lament, cp. Ps. 44:13; 79:4; Jer. 20:8; see also lines 33b–34a. *the traitors:* used of apostates in CD I.12; 1QpHab II.1, 3, 5, but with a more general sense in CD VIII.5 = XIX.17. *the upright of way:* 'the upright' occurs as a term for the members of the community in 1QS III.1; IV.22a; CD XX.2.

10b–11a. *a source of whispering:* again traditional language in psalms of lament, cp. Ps. 31:13; Jer. 20:10. *the ruthless*: 'those who act ruthlessly against the covenant' is used as a technical term for opponents in 1QpHab 11.6; 4QpPs^a 1–10 11.14; 111.12; 1v.1. *the scoffers*: cp. the references to 'the scoffers' in CD xx.11; 4QpIsa^b 11.6, 10, and 'the scoffer' in CD 1.14 (in all cases the Hebrew expression is slightly different from that used in the Hymns). *ground their teeth*: i.e. at the psalmist as a sign of hostility. The expression is used in psalms of lament, cp. Ps. 35:16; Lam. 2:16.

11b–13a. *the target of the mocking songs*: a further expression taken from psalms of lament, cp. Ps. 69:12; Lam. 3:14. *the assembly of the wicked*: the use of 'assembly' suggests a particular group is in mind. *whose raging waves cast up mud and filth*: based on Isa. 57:20.

13b–14a. *a standard*: i.e. a rallying point for members of the community. *the chosen ones of righteousness*: 'chosen ones' is a term used several times for members of the community; cp. e.g. 1QpHab v.4; 1x.12a; 4QpPs^a 1–10 11.5a; also 1QS v111.6b; 1x.14c. *a knowledgeable interpreter of wonderful mysteries*: the 'wonderful mysteries' are probably the secrets contained within scripture; the psalmist presents himself as a teacher who knows the true meaning of the Old Testament writings. For the concept of revelation involved here see 1QpHab v11.1–5a, where the teacher of righteousness is the one 'to whom God made known all the mysteries of the words of his servants the prophets'. For the expression 'knowledgeable interpreter' (literally 'interpreter of knowledge') cp. 4QpPs^a 1–10 1.27. *to test [the men] of truth and to try those who love instruction*: the psalmist sees his task as being to examine the members of the community – with regard, the context suggests, to their understanding of the true meaning of scripture.

15b–16a. *all those who seek smoo[th things]*: in the biblical commentaries 'the seekers after smooth things' is a regular designation of a distinct group of opponents; cp. 4QpIsa^c 23 11.10 and particularly the Commentary on Nahum (4QpNah), where it is clear that 'the seekers after smooth things' are the Pharisees. The present passage, referring to 'those who see the truth' and 'those who seek smooth things', is apparently based on Isa. 30:10.

16b–18a. *they turned towards the pit*: i.e. to Sheol. Although the expression used here does not occur in the Psalms, the thought that the man in distress already belongs in the realm of death is common-place; cp. e.g. Ps. 86:13; 88:3–6 (both psalms of lament). The psalmist is thus using a traditional concept, and for this reason it is difficult to know what exactly lies behind his words; it is by no means clear that the language used indicates a physical attack. *the man in whose mouth...those who understand*: here, above all, the psalmist presents himself as a teacher.

18*b*–19. *But they exchanged them*: the teaching and understanding. *for uncircumcised lips*: the same image as in line 7, but whereas there it suggested hesitancy, here the image is used with a definitely negative meaning (cp. Acts 7:51). *and for the strange tongue*: taken from Isa. 28:11. 'Uncircumcised lips' and 'the strange tongue' are both images for the false teaching of the opponents of the psalmist. *of a people without understanding that they might come to grief*: based on Hos. 4:14; cp. Isa. 27:11.

THANKSGIVING FOR DELIVERANCE FROM ATTACK

II.20 I thank you, O Lord,
because you have placed me in the bundle of life,
21 and have hedged me round against all the snares of the pit.
[For] ruthless men sought my life
when I held fast 22 to your covenant.
But they, an assembly of vanity and a congregation of Belial,
do not know that it is through you that I maintain my
    position,
23 and that in your mercy you will save my life;
for it is from you that my steps proceed.
And it is on account of you that they attack 24 me,
that you might be glorified by the judgement of the wicked,
and show your might in me before the sons 25 of men;
for it is through your mercy that I stand.

And I said, Mighty men have encamped against me,
they have surrounded me 26 with all their weapons of war.
They have let fly arrows against which there is no cure,
and the flash of (their) spear is like a fire devouring trees.
27 The clamour of their voice is like the roaring of many
    waters,
(like) a violent storm which destroys many;
up to the stars burst 28 nothing and vanity

when their waves rear up.
But although my heart melted like water,
I held fast to your covenant.
²⁹ The net which they spread for me caught their own foot,
and the traps which they hid for me they fell into themselves.
My foot stands on level ground;
³⁰ far from their assembly I will bless your name.

This psalm consists of the thanksgiving of an individual for deliverance from attack by enemies; their downfall is depicted in line 29a. Apart from an introduction (20–21a) and a concluding vow (29b–30), the contents divide into two parts (21b–25a, 25b–29a). In the first there is a noticeable emphasis on the thought that the psalmist was utterly dependent on God, and that all his experiences were part of God's purpose. The second part largely consists of a description of the attacks suffered by the psalmist in which a variety of images is used.

The character of this psalm is in some ways similar to that of the preceding one: it is an individual song of thanksgiving, but its literary form also shows affinities with that of the individual lament. And the language and imagery are frequently derived from the Old Testament, particularly from psalms of lament and thanksgiving. But there the similarity with the preceding psalm ceases. Thus although parallels can often be observed with the language and thought of other psalms in this collection, there is little that is distinctively sectarian about the language used. Further, the author does not stand out as a distinct personality in the way that the author of the preceding psalm does, and the precise nature of the attack he suffered is unclear. Like many psalms in the Old Testament, this psalm was no doubt capable of being used by members of the Qumran community in a variety of circumstances.

II.20–21a. Introduction. *I thank you, O Lord*: this formula is used at the beginning of the psalms in this collection in the majority of cases where the beginning has survived (see above, p. 157). The same formula – or one in which the divine name *Yahweh* (represented in the RSV and NEB as 'Lord') is used instead of *ʾadōnāy* (= 'Lord') – occurs frequently in the Old Testament. It is found at the beginning of an individual song of thanksgiving in the case of Ps. 138, 'I give thee thanks, O Lord' (RSV). Cp. Isa. 12:1; also Ps. 57:9; 86:12 for the use of *ʾadōnāy*. *because you have placed me in the bundle of life*: the image is taken from 1 Sam. 25:29. *all the snares of the pit*: i.e. of Sheol; cp. Ps. 18:5 = 2 Sam. 22:6, 'the snares of death'.

21*b*–25*a*. The psalmist acknowledges his dependence on God, and that all his experiences were part of God's purposes.

21*b*–22*a*. *ruthless men sought my life*: quoted from Ps. 54:3; 86:14 (both psalms of lament); for 'ruthless men' see also the comment on lines 10*b*–11*a*.

22*b*–23*a*. *But they…do not know…for it is from you that my steps proceed*: cp. line 33*b*.

23*b*–25*a*. *show your might in me*: cp. 1.34*a*.

25*b*–28*a*. *And I said*: this phrase is used in the Old Testament in psalms of thanksgiving and lament to introduce the narrative section, i.e. the description of distress; cp. Ps. 30:6; 31:22; 41:4; Jonah 2:4. *like a fire devouring trees*: for the imagery cp. III.29. *like the roaring of many waters*: cp. line 16*a*. *up to the stars burst nothing and vanity when their waves rear up*: the translation of this passage is uncertain, but the one adopted here seems to fit the context best. The passage draws on the language of Isa. 59:5 (more obvious in the Hebrew), but the sense is different. The imagery of a violent storm is continued, and 'nothing' and 'vanity' are terms used to describe the evil character of the actions of the psalmist's enemies. The word translated 'nothing' has the same form as that translated 'the viper' (i.e. the personification of the forces of evil) in III.12*b*, 17, 18; the meaning of the word 'vanity' is indicated by the fact that it stands parallel to 'Belial' in line 22*b* above. Both words have far greater undertones of evil than their English translations suggest.

28*b*–29*a*. *my heart melted like water*: a frequent image in the Old Testament; cp. e.g. Josh. 7:5; Ps. 22:14. *The net…they fell into themselves*: for the thought and language cp. Ps. 9:15; 35:7–8 (both psalms of lament).

29*b*–30. A concluding vow. *My foot stands on level ground; far from their assembly I will bless your name*: a quotation of Ps. 26:12 (a psalm of lament), but with two significant changes: instead of being 'in the full assembly' (NEB) the psalmist is now 'far from their assembly', i.e. the assembly of his enemies; and 'your name' has been substituted for 'Yahweh' (NEB, 'the LORD') out of a reverential desire to avoid pronouncing or even writing the divine name (see above, p. 134).

ANOTHER THANKSGIVING FOR DELIVERANCE FROM ATTACK

11.31 I thank you, O Lord,
    because your eye wa[tches] over me

and you have saved me from the jealousy of the interpreters of
    lies
32 and from the congregation of the seekers after smooth
    things.
You have redeemed the life of the poor one whom they
    planned to destroy,
pouring out his blood 33 because he served you.
But they [did not kno]w that my steps proceed from you,
and they made me an object of contempt 34 and insult in the
    mouth of all those who seek deceit.
But you, O my God, have protected the life of the poor and
    needy one 35 from one stronger than he.
You have redeemed my life from the hand of the mighty,
and you have not allowed me to be dismayed by their taunts
36 so that I forsook your service out of fear of the threats of
    the w[icke]d
or exchanged for folly the constancy which 37 [...]

This individual song of thanksgiving reveals similarities with both of
the immediately preceding psalms. It is the thanksgiving of an
individual whose life has been threatened – although it is not clear how
far this should be taken literally – and in a number of respects can be
seen to be very similar to the psalm in lines 20–30. But, in contrast
to that psalm, the terms used here to describe the psalmist's enemies,
particularly 'the seekers after smooth things' (32a), suggest that the
activities of a distinct rival group of opponents are in mind, even
though the precise circumstances are unclear. It has often been assumed
that this psalm reflects the experiences of the teacher of righteousness,
but again it has to be said that although this is a plausible hypothesis,
it cannot be more than this. However, inasmuch as the psalm has this
character, it can be seen to be similar to the material in lines 7–19.

    Too little has survived of the last few lines of column II and the
opening lines of column III for it to be possible to say where this psalm
ended. But the material in the upper half of column III is of such a
different character that it is commonly assumed that a new psalm began
somewhere at the top of column III.

    II.31–32a. *I thank you, O Lord*: see the comment on line 20. *the
interpreters of lies*: the same title is used in IV.9b–10a and is synonymous

with 'the interpreters of error' (above, line 14*b*). The use of this title suggests that the major point at issue between the psalmist and his enemies was false teaching. *the seekers after smooth things*: see the comment on lines 15*b*–16*a* for the use of this title in the biblical commentaries to refer to the Pharisees.

32*b*–33*a*. *the poor one*: the psalmist himself. In the biblical commentaries 'the poor' is a term used for the members of the community; cp. e.g. 1QpHab XII.3, 6*a*, 10*a*; also 1QM XI.9, 13; XIII.14.

33*b*–34*a*. *But they [did not kno]w that my steps proceed from you*: cp. lines 22*b*–23*a*. *and they made me an object of contempt and insult*: cp. lines 9*b*–10*a*, where it is God who is said to have made the psalmist 'an object of insult and derision'. *all those who seek deceit*: 'deceit' is a word often used with reference to opponents of the community; cp. 'the men of deceit' (II.16*a*; XIV.14; 1QS IX.8); 'the interpreters of deceit' (1QH IV.7); 'the seers of deceit' (IV.10).

34*b*–35*a*. *the poor and needy one*: i.e. the psalmist, as in the reference to 'the poor one' (not the same Hebrew word as here) in line 32*b*. The same two Hebrew words 'poor and needy' are used in combination in Ps. 82:3 (NEB, 'the destitute and downtrodden').

35*b*–36. *folly*: i.e. false doctrine. *the constancy*: literally 'the constant mind'; see on 1QS IV.5.

THE BIRTH-PANGS OF THE MESSIAH

[...] III.6 [...]

They caused me to be like a ship on the depths of the sea,
⁷ and like a fortified city before [the enemy].
I was in distress like a woman in labour bearing her first child,
when pains and grievous pangs come ⁸ upon the mouth of her
    womb,
causing writhing-pain in the womb of her that is pregnant.
For children have come to the mouth of the womb of death,
⁹ and she that is pregnant with the man is in anguish because of
    her birth pangs.
For amid the waves of death she will give birth to a son,
and amid the pangs of Sheol there will burst ¹⁰ from the womb
    of her that is pregnant
a wonderful counsellor with his might;
and the man will be delivered from the waves.

At his conception all wombs will feel pain,
[11] and there will be grievous pangs at the time of their giving
    birth,
and horror will seize those who are pregnant.
At his birth every pain will come [12] upon the womb of her
    that is pregnant.
And she that is pregnant with the viper will be subject to
    grievous pangs,
and the mouth of the womb of the pit (will open) for all the
    works of horror.
The foundations of the wall will rock [13] like a ship on the face
    of the waters,
and the skies will thunder with a resounding crack.
Those who dwell in the dust [14] like those who go to sea will
    be terrified by the roar of the waters,
and their wise men will be like sailors on the depths,
for all their wisdom will be swallowed up [15] in the roaring of
    the seas.
As the deeps boil above the springs of the waters,
the waves and billows will rage and rear up [16] with their
    roaring noise.
And as they rage, Sh[eo]l [and Abaddon] will open,
and all the flying arrows of the pit [17] will send out their sound
    to the deep.
The gates [of Sheol] will open [for all] the works of the viper.
[18] But the doors of the pit will shut on her that is pregnant
    with injustice,
and the bars of eternity on all the spirits of the viper.

This psalm raises a considerable number of problems, and opinions as
to its meaning have varied widely. The problems stem partly from the
fact that the beginning is lost and several lines are damaged, partly from
the difficulties of translation that are only touched on to a limited extent
in the notes below, and partly from the ambiguity of much of the
material.
    The psalm no doubt began like others in this collection, 'I thank
you, O Lord', that is as the thanksgiving of an individual. But

thanksgiving and lament are closely related, and this psalm is essentially a lament. Only fragments of the first few lines of the column have survived, but when it begins to be possible to make sense of the material (line 6), the psalmist is describing his distress by means of three images: a ship on the sea, a besieged city, and a woman in labour. The last of these images is, however, developed at such great length that it seems difficult to think of mere illustration. In fact it appears that the thought of the distress accompanying childbirth leads the psalmist to describe the birth of a particular individual, the messiah, and the distress that was expected to accompany his appearance, the so-called birth-pangs of the messiah (lines 8b–12a). By this means the psalmist is able to link his own sufferings to those that would inaugurate the new age. The birth of the messiah is contrasted with the birth of 'the viper', the personification of the forces of evil. The birth of this evil figure marks the beginning of an era of chaos and terror and is accompanied by the release from Sheol of all the forces of evil (lines 12b–17). The psalm ends, almost abruptly, with an expression of confidence that the forces of evil will be shut up once more in Sheol (line 18). Understood in this way the psalm may be seen to offer an answer to the sufferings of the psalmist both by linking them to the sufferings that would inaugurate the new age and by providing an assurance that the forces of evil would ultimately be defeated.

Support for an interpretation of this kind may be found in the use in Rev. 12 of what appears to be a similar tradition about the birth of the messiah, and the psalm may be regarded as messianic in content. It is not clear, however, how the ideas present in this psalm relate to the messianic conceptions of other Qumran writings, particularly the belief in two messiahs. It is also the case that nothing is said in the psalm about the character and functions of the messiah; the concern is entirely with the woes that would inaugurate the messianic age.

The kind of approach suggested here is not without difficulties, and many scholars have rejected a messianic interpretation altogether. Thus, for example, it has been suggested that the picture of the woman bearing a child (lines 7–12) is an extended simile intended to portray the sudden onrush of a crisis. Or it has been suggested that the mother represents the teacher of righteousness and the child the community; the psalm depicts the difficulties experienced by the teacher in bringing the community to birth. It should be noted that interpretations like these are linked to translations which in a number of respects differ significantly from the one offered here. In complete contrast some scholars who adopt a messianic interpretation have sought to identify the mother of the man (line 9) with the community and the mother of the viper (line 12) with its opponents; on this view the messiah is born from the community.

It is impossible here to discuss these views, or the many others that have been put forward, in any detail; all that is possible is to present the view which seems to make the best sense of the evidence. One comment should be made, however. It is right to think that the psalm ultimately reflects the sufferings experienced by the author and the group which he represents, but it is misleading to try to make a close connection between the contents of the psalm and the author and his community. Thus attempts to identify the two mothers seem not very helpful. The mothers are incidental to the main theme, namely the birth of the messiah and the depiction of the woes that would accompany his birth. It is as misleading to try to identify the mothers as it is to press the interpretation of some other details in the psalm.

It has been suggested that the author was the teacher of righteousness, but there is no way of knowing whether this is so or not.

III.6–8a. The psalmist uses a series of three images to describe his distress. *like a woman in labour*: the same Hebrew phrase that occurs in Jer. 13:21. *bearing her first child*: cp. Jer. 4:31. *when pains and grievous pangs come upon the mouth of her womb*: cp. 1 Sam. 4:19, 'for her pains came upon her' (RSV). 'The mouth of the womb' represents one word in the Hebrew, the plural of *mašbēr* (used e.g. in 2 Kings 19:3); but it could be understood differently, as the plural of *mišbār*, to mean 'the waves' (cp. e.g. 2 Sam. 22:5). There is a deliberate play on these two meanings in the following lines, but here the sense 'the mouth of the womb' is clear. The plural is apparently used throughout because of the two meanings. *in the womb*: literally 'in the furnace', but the Hebrew word (*kūr*) is apparently used here, and in lines 10 ('from the womb') and 12 ('upon the womb'), with the sense 'womb'. The pain accompanying childbirth often serves in the Old Testament as an image of suffering; cp. for instance Isa. 13:8.

8b–12a. The thought of the pain accompanying childbirth leads the author to consider the birth of a particular individual, the messiah, and the distress that was expected to accompany his appearance – the so-called birth-pangs of the messiah (cp. Matt. 24:8; Mark 13:8). The sufferings of the psalmist are thereby brought into relationship with, and seen as part of, the sufferings that would inaugurate the new age.

8b–9a. *For children have come to the mouth of the womb of death*: 'the mouth of the womb' seems right here, but the word could also be understood as 'the waves' (see above). Part of 2 Kings 19:3 = Isa. 37:3 (literally, 'For children have come to the mouth of the womb') is here quoted in a form influenced by 2 Sam. 22:5 (NEB, 'When the waves of death swept round me'). The thought that the moment of birth marks entry into a realm of danger and death introduces the picture of the sufferings that would accompany the birth of the messiah. *and she that is pregnant with the man*: or 'with a man'. But in either case it seems most likely in the light of line 10*a* ('a wonderful counsellor with his might') that we have to do with a messianic figure. For the birth of the messiah cp. Isa. 7:14; 9:6; Micah 5:2–4; Rev. 12.

9*b*–10*a*. *For amid the waves of death*: or 'at the mouth of the womb of death'. Here, and in line 10 ('from the waves') there is very clearly a play on the two possible meanings; for the translation 'the waves of death' cp. 2 Sam. 22:5. *she will give birth to a son*: possibly an allusion to Isa. 66:7. *and amid the pangs of Sheol*: the horrendous character of the pains is indicated by the fact that they stem from the realm of death. But there may be a play on words here in that the translation 'and amid the bonds of Sheol' (with an allusion to 2 Sam. 22:6) would also be possible. *from the womb*: literally 'from the furnace' (see above). *a wonderful counsellor with his might*: a clear allusion to Isa. 9:6, 'and his name will be called "Wonderful Counselor, Mighty God, Everlasting Father, Prince of Peace"' (RSV). In Jewish tradition the title 'Wonderful Counselor' was not understood in a messianic sense (e.g. the Targum of Jonathan takes this title to refer to God, not the messiah; but that seems no reason to exclude a messianic interpretation here of 'a wonderful counsellor with his might'. *and the man*: or 'and a man' (see above).

10*b*–12*a*. These lines apparently describe the effect of the conception and birth of the messiah upon those who are pregnant at the time; cp. (although the parallel is not exact) Mark 13:17 and parallels. *all wombs*: the same word in the plural that is translated elsewhere in this psalm as either 'the mouth of the womb' or 'the waves'. *upon the womb*: literally 'upon the furnace' (see above).

12*b*–17. The birth of the messiah is contrasted with the birth of 'the viper', the personification of the forces of evil. The birth of this evil figure will cause chaos in the world and utter terror amongst its inhabitants, and will be accompanied by the release from Sheol of all the forces of evil.

12*b*. *she that is pregnant with the viper*: a deliberate contrast is intended with line 9, 'she that is pregnant with the man'. *the viper*: this word occurs in Isa. 30:6; 59:5; Job 20:16. It has the same form as the word translated as 'nothing' in II.28a, and a translation such as 'she that is pregnant with worthlessness' would be possible here (cp. line 18). But this seems too weak because a real contrast does appear to be intended between two figures, 'the man' and 'the viper'. In the background lies the mythology connected with the monster of chaos (cp. e.g. Ps. 74:12–17). *and the mouth of the womb of the pit (will open) for all the works of horror*: 'the pit' is Sheol; cp. II.21a. The passage could also be translated 'and the waves of the pit (will be unleashed) for all the works of horror'.

12c–13a. *The foundations of the wall will rock*: the thought is of an earthquake; cp Mark 13:8 and parallels. *like a ship on the face of the waters*: note the reuse here, and in the following line, of the imagery of line 6.

13b–16a. *those who go to sea*: cp. Ps. 107:23. *will be terrified by the roar of the waters*: cp. Luke 21:25. The thought is of flooding and a violent storm. Traditional mythology lies in the background: the waters represent the forces of chaos that were thought to have been subdued by God at the time of creation; what is depicted is the unleashing of these chaotic forces. *for all their wisdom will be swallowed up*: perhaps borrowed from Ps. 107:27 (more obvious in the Hebrew). *the waves*: Hebrew *gallīm*. *and billows*: literally 'and the waves (from Hebrew mišbār, cp. the comment on lines 6–8a) of the sea'.

16b–17. The release of the forces of evil from Sheol. *Sh[eo]l [and Abaddon]*: cp. Job 26:6; Prov. 15:11. *and all the flying arrows of the pit*: the words symbolise demonic forces; cp. Ps. 91:5 and line 27 below. *will send out their sound to the deep*: apparently an allusion to the hissing sound of the arrows.

18. The psalm ends with an expression of confidence: the forces of evil will be shut up once more in Sheol. The thought of the ultimate defeat of the forces of evil represents an answer to the lament of the psalmist. For an expression of confidence at the end of an individual lament cp. for example Ps. 6:8–10, especially verse 10. *her that is pregnant with injustice*: cp. line 12b.

THE TORRENTS OF BELIAL

III.19 I thank you, O Lord,
    because you have redeemed me from the pit,
    and from Sheol of Abaddon 20 you have raised me up to
      eternal heights.

I walk on unending level ground,
and I know that there is hope for the one whom [21] you
    formed from dust for an eternal fellowship.
You have cleansed a perverted spirit of great transgression
that it might take its place with [22] the host of the holy ones,
and might enter into community with the congregation of the
    sons of heaven.
And you have allotted to the man an eternal place with the
    spirits [23] of knowledge
that he might praise your name in common rejoicing,
and might recount your wonders before all your creatures.
But I, a creature [24] of clay, what am I?
A thing kneaded with water, what am I worth, and what is
    my strength?
For I stood in the realm of wickedness,
[25] and with the wretched was my lot.
The soul of the poor one sojourned amid great troubles
and overwhelming destruction accompanied my steps
[26] when all the traps of the pit were opened,
and all the snares of wickedness were spread,
and the nets for the wretched (were spread) on the water;
[27] when all the arrows of the pit flew without turning back,
and were let fly leaving no hope;
when the plumb-line fell for judgement,
and a destiny of anger (fell) [28] upon the abandoned,
and an outpouring of fury upon the hypocrites.
It was a time of wrath of all Belial.
The bonds of death tightened leaving no escape,
[29] and the torrents of Belial overflowed all the high banks
like a fire devouring all their shores,
destroying every tree, both green [30] and dry, from their
    channels.
It sweeps on with whirling flames,
wiping out all that drink there.
It devours the foundations of clay [31] and the expanse of the
    dry land;

the foundations of the mountains are turned into fire,
and the roots of the granite rock into torrents of pitch.
It devours as far as the great deep;
32 the torrents of Belial burst into Abaddon,
and the recesses of the deep roar with the roaring of (the
    waves) stirring up the mud.
And the earth 33 will cry out because of the destruction which
    has come upon the world,
and all its recesses will howl;
all those upon it will go mad
34 and will reel because of the great destruction.
For God will thunder with his mighty roar,
and his holy habitation will roar with his glorious truth.
35 The heavenly host will give voice,
and the eternal foundations will reel and shake.
The war of the heavenly warriors 36 will sweep through the
    world
and will not stop before the decreed destruction,
which will be for ever, with nothing like it.

This psalm has survived virtually intact; the few small gaps in the
manuscript can easily be restored, and a new psalm clearly begins in
line 37. It is an individual song of thanksgiving and begins in a
straightforward enough fashion with an expression of thanks to God
for delivering the psalmist from distress and for giving him security
within the community (lines 19–23a). In the main body of the psalm
the author gives an account of his sufferings, which he sees as being
caused by the forces of evil; but almost imperceptibly the account of his
own distress becomes an account of the distress that will be caused by
the last great assault of the forces of evil, here represented by the
inundation of the earth by 'the torrents of Belial' (lines 23b–32a). The
earth cries out in horror, and the psalm ends with a description of the
intervention of God, who, supported by the angels, defeats the forces
of evil in battle (lines 32b–36).

We do not know who the author of this psalm was, and because
of the frequent use of traditional language and imagery drawn from
the Old Testament – a feature that we have seen to be characteristic
of these psalms – it is impossible to say what was the nature of his
distress. The psalm was no doubt capable of being used in, and adapted

to, a variety of circumstances. There is a certain reflective element in the psalm, marked by the occurrence of a number of parallels with column I. Its real importance lies in the beliefs about the future which it contains.

III.19–23a. The psalmist thanks God for deliverance from distress and for the security that he has found by being brought into the community.

19–21a. *I thank you, O Lord*: see the comment on II.20. *the pit...Sheol of Abaddon*: as in the Old Testament the individual who is sick, or otherwise in distress, is thought of as being already in Sheol, the realm of death (cp. e.g. Ps. 30:3; 86:13), so here 'the pit' and 'Sheol of Abaddon' are used as metaphorical expressions for distress. *you have raised me up to eternal heights. I walk on unending level ground*: metaphorical expressions for the deliverance of the psalmist and the security enjoyed by him within the community. *the one whom you formed from dust*: cp. Gen. 2:7. The psalmist is referring to himself. *for an eternal fellowship*: a title for the community, cp. 1QS II.25a, 'members of an eternal fellowship'. The background to the use of this title can be found in the belief of the community that its members were companions of the angels (cp. 1QS XI.7b–9a; 1QSa II.8b–9a), and already shared in their life (cp. lines 21b–23a below); as such they could be thought of as already forming a part of God's heavenly 'council' or 'fellowship' (Jer. 23:18, 22).

21b–22a. *You have cleansed a perverted spirit of great transgression*: cp. 1.32, and for 'a perverted spirit' also I. 22. *the host of the holy ones...the congregation of the sons of heaven*: i.e. the angels; for the former term cp. X.35; Ps. 89:5, 7; for the latter 1QS IV.22a; XI.8; I En. 6:2; 13:8. Within the community the members share in the life of the angels.

22b–23a. *allotted to the man an eternal place*: literally 'cast for the man an eternal lot'; cp. 1QS II.17b. By 'the man' the psalmist again means himself. *with the spirits of knowledge*: i.e. heavenly beings, angels. *that he might praise your name*: cp. 1.30b–31a. *and might recount your wonders before all your creatures*: cp. 1.30, 33.

23b–28a. After a short reflective section the psalmist begins to describe the distress he experienced before entry into the community. For his account the author used a number of traditional images drawn from the Old Testament, and it is impossible to say what the nature of his distress was, only that it was caused by the forces of evil.

23b–24a. *a creature of clay...a thing kneaded with water*: cp. 1.21b and the comment there. The thought is of the frailty and insignificance of man.

24b–25a. *the realm of wickedness*: the Jewish world outside the community; cp. II.8a and Mal. 1:4.

25b–28a. The soul of the poor one: the psalmist himself; see the comment on II.32b. *when all the traps of the pit were opened*: the pit is Sheol; for the imagery cp. e.g. Ps. 140:5; Isa. 24:17–18. *and all the snares of wickedness were spread*: for the imagery cp. Ezek. 12:13; 17:20. *and the nets for the wretched (were spread) on the water*: cp. Isa. 19:8. *all the arrows of the pit*: a metaphorical expression for demonic forces, cp. Ps. 91:5 and line 16b above. *when the plumb-line fell for judgement*: the plumb-line is mentioned in several passages in the Old Testament referring to destruction; cp. e.g. 2 Kings 21:13; Lam. 2:8. *a destiny*: literally 'a lot'; cp. 1QS II.17b. *the abandoned...the hypocrites*: the psalmist is describing his circumstances before entry into the community, and so he links his fate at that time to that of those outside the community, whom he describes in negative terms. Earlier (lines 25, 26) he had referred to 'the wretched'. The word used for 'hypocrites' occurs in Ps. 26:4; 'abandoned' means abandoned by God.

28b–32a. Almost imperceptibly the psalmist's account of his own distress becomes an account of the distress caused by the last great assault of the forces of evil, here represented by the inundation of the earth by 'the torrents of Belial'. The sufferings of the psalmist are thus brought into relationship with those of the last age and were perhaps seen as marking the beginning of the final battle between the forces of good and evil.

28b–30a. It was a time of wrath of all Belial: in the sense that it was caused by the forces of evil. *The bonds of death tightened leaving no escape, and the torrents of Belial overflowed*: based on Ps. 18:4 (cp. 2 Sam. 22:5):

When the bonds of death held me fast,
destructive torrents (or 'torrents of Belial') overtook me.

'The torrents of Belial', a symbol of the forces of evil, are depicted as a river of fire which sweeps through the entire world and destroys everything in its path. *like a fire devouring*: cp. II.26. *destroying every tree, both green and dry*: cp. Ezek. 20:47.

30b–32a. Nothing escapes destruction. *It devours as far as the great deep*: or 'the great abyss'; cp. Amos 7:4. 'The great deep' is the subterranean cosmic ocean, on which the earth was believed to rest; cp. Gen. 7:11; Ps. 24:2. *the torrents of Belial burst into Abaddon*: cp. Job 31:12 (see the RSV). Not even the realm of the dead, which was thought to lie under the earth, was safe from this river of destruction. *with the roaring of (the waves) stirring up the mud*: cp. II.12b–13a and Isa. 57:20.

32b–36. The assault of the forces of evil will cause terror and horror in the world, but God will intervene and with his heavenly warriors will defeat the forces of evil in battle. The theme of the final war against the forces of evil is treated at length in the War Scroll.

34b. *For God will thunder*: cp. Ps. 18:13; 29:3. The underlying thought is of God manifesting himself in a thunderstorm. *and his holy habitation*: for the expression cp. Isa. 63:15.

35–6. *The heavenly host…the heavenly warriors*: the angels, who take part with God in the eschatological war. *the eternal foundations*: i.e. of the earth. *the decreed destruction*: the Hebrew expression occurs in Isa. 10:23; 28:22; Dan. 9:27.

The Genesis Apocryphon

The crucial importance of the Hebrew Bible within the Qumran community can hardly be overstated. Manuscripts of the books of the Old Testament form a major part of the manuscripts found at Qumran. Study and observance of the law represented one of the basic aims of the community, as we have noticed several times. The sectarian writings, such as the Damascus Document or the Community Rule, were profoundly influenced by the Hebrew Bible and quote from it, or allude to it, in practically every line of text. In these circumstances it is perhaps hardly surprising that the Qumran writings should include a number of works that may be described as exegetical. These vary considerably in character. Some represent a reworking or elaboration of biblical material, as for example the Words of Moses (1Q22, also known as 1QDM), a farewell speech inspired by various passages in Deuteronomy, or the New Jerusalem (found in several fragmentary manuscripts, particularly 5Q15 (5QJN ar)), a description in Aramaic of the Jerusalem of the eschatological period that draws its inspiration from Ezek. 40–8. One of the most important writings of this kind is the work in Aramaic known as the Genesis Apocryphon, a reworking of material in the book of Genesis.

The Genesis Apocryphon (1QapGen) is one of the seven major manuscripts that were found in Qumran Cave 1 in 1947 and was thus one of the first of the scrolls to be discovered. It was in a very poor state of preservation, and only the three innermost columns (xx–xxii) survived in reasonable condition. Apart from these columns it proved possible to decipher only column ii and column xix, and even these are poorly preserved. Of the remaining columns only odd words and phrases have been deciphered. Our knowledge of the Genesis Apocryphon is thus largely confined to columns ii and xix–xxii, and these columns alone are translated here. It is clear that column i was not the first column of the manuscript, and that column xxii was not the last (see below, p. 202). The manuscript dates from the end of the first century BC or the first half of the first century AD, but the work itself may have been composed a little before this.

As we have noted, the Genesis Apocryphon represents a reworking in Aramaic of the narrative of Genesis. The material that has survived covers the story of the birth of Noah (column II, cp. Gen. 5:28–9) and the early part of the story of Abraham (columns XIX–XXII, cp. Gen. 12:8–15:4). The author's approach to the biblical material varies. Sometimes he stays close to the biblical text and in places provides a literal translation of Genesis (see particularly the material corresponding to Gen. 14). Elsewhere the author paraphrases the text and introduces significant additions to the story. The narrative is cast in the first person down as far as XXI.22. Thereafter, from the point where the material corresponding to Gen. 14 begins, the narrative changes from the first person to the third person.

The literary genre of the Genesis Apocryphon is closest to that of the book of Jubilees, itself a reworking of Gen. 1:1–Exod. 15:22, and to the narrative portions of 1 Enoch and of the Testaments of the Twelve Patriarchs; for these three writings see in this series *Outside the Old Testament*, pp. 111–44, 26–55, and 71–91. Close parallels to the material that has survived of the Genesis Apocryphon can be found in 1 En. 106–7 (the birth of Noah) and in Jub. 13:1–14:3 (the story of Abraham). But the Genesis Apocryphon needs to be read in a wider context than this.

Inasmuch as the Genesis Apocryphon contains passages of literal or almost literal translation it can be seen to represent an early stage in the development of the targums. The targums are Aramaic translations of the Old Testament, and for the Pentateuch three complete targums are known: Targum Onqelos, Targum Pseudo-Jonathan, and Targum Neofiti I. A number of targums were found among the Qumran scrolls, particularly the Targum of Job from Cave 11 (11QtgJob), but despite the fact that the literary genre of the Genesis Apocryphon is in some respects similar to that of the targums, it is not itself a targum.

Inasmuch as the Genesis Apocryphon is a reworking of Genesis and contains significant elaborations of the biblical narrative it can also – like Jubilees – be seen to represent an early stage in the development of the midrashim. The Hebrew word 'midrashim' is the plural form of 'midrash' (literally 'study'). This word is used to refer to a piece of biblical exposition or interpretation (cp. e.g. the use of the title 'the Amos–Numbers midrash' for CD VII.13*b*–VIII.1*a*; see above, pp. 60–1), and then to a literary work of biblical exposition. Within the rabbinic literature several different types of writing are embraced under the term 'midrashim', but particularly relevant here are the homiletic midrashim, and notably Genesis Rabbah, a homiletic exposition of Genesis. As a pious elaboration of the biblical narrative the Genesis Apocryphon may be regarded as an early form of midrash, but it differs considerably in form from the later rabbinic midrashim.

Quite apart from the question of the literary genre, the way in which the story of Abraham is handled in the Genesis Apocryphon deserves to be compared with the treatment of this story in other ancient sources. Reference has already been made to Jubilees, the targums, and Genesis Rabbah. In addition reference should be made to the treatment of Abraham in the writings of hellenistic Jewish authors: the fragments of Pseudo-Eupolemus, as preserved in Eusebius, Praeparatio Evangelica 9.17.1–9; 9.18.2; Philo, De Abrahamo 60–244; Josephus, War v.9.4 (380–1); Ant. 1.7.1–10.3 (154–85).

Although the Genesis Apocryphon was found amongst the Qumran writings, there is nothing sectarian about its contents. It may be of Essene authorship, but this cannot be proved or disproved.

Bibliography

N. Avigad and Y. Yadin, *A Genesis Apocryphon: A Scroll from the Wilderness of Judaea*, Jerusalem, 1956.

J. A. Fitzmyer, *The Genesis Apocryphon of Qumran Cave 1: A Commentary* (Biblica et Orientalia, 18A), second, revised edition, Rome, 1971.

B. Jongeling, C. J. Labuschagne and A. S. van der Woude (eds.), *Aramaic Texts from Qumran with Translations and Annotations* (Semitic Study Series, New Series, 4), Leiden, 1976, 75–119.

For information about the targums and the midrashim see J. Bowker, *The Targums and Rabbinic Literature: An Introduction to Jewish Interpretations of Scripture*, Cambridge, 1969. A French translation of Targum Neofiti I and Targum Pseudo-Jonathan is available in R. Le Déaut and J. Robert, *Targum du Pentateuque: Traduction des deux recensions palestiniennes complètes avec introduction, parallèles, notes et index*. Tome I: *Genèse* (Sources Chrétiennes, 245), Paris, 1978. Bowker himself provides in the second part of his book extracts from Targum Pseudo-Jonathan on Genesis and information about Jewish interpretation of Genesis; for material relevant to the Genesis Apocryphon see pp. 190–203. For Genesis Rabbah see H. Freedman, *Midrash Rabbah: Genesis*, 2 volumes, London, 1939.

For the fragments of Pseudo-Eupolemus see C. R. Holladay, *Fragments from Hellenistic Jewish Authors*, volume I: *Historians* (Society of Biblical Literature, Texts and Translations, 20, Pseudepigrapha Series, 10), Chico, California, 1983, 157–87.

THE BIRTH OF NOAH

ii.1 So then I thought in my mind that the conception was due to the watchers, or that it w[a]s due to the holy ones, or to the Nephil[im...] 2 and my mind was disturbed because of this child.

3 Then I, Lamech, went in haste to Bitenosh [my] wi[fe, and I said, '...] 4 [...]...by the Most High, by the Great Lord, by the King of all A[ges...] 5 [...] the sons of heaven, that you tell me everything truthfully, whether [...] 6 you must tell me [truthfully] and without lies, whether this .[...] 7 by the King of all Ages that you speak to me truthfully and without lies [...]'

8 Then Bitenosh my wife spoke to me with great violence and [...] 9 and said, 'O my brother, O my lord, remember my sexual pleasure .[...] 10 [...]. the time and my panting breath within me. I [will tell you] everything truthfully [...].' 11 [...]... But my mind was still greatly disturbed.

12 When Bitenosh my wife saw that my face was disturbed [...] 13 then she suppressed her feelings as she spoke to me and said, 'O my lord, [O my brother, remember...] 14 my sexual pleasure. I swear to you by the Great Holy One, by the King of H[eaven...] 15 that this offspring is yours, this conception is from you, from you the planting of [this] fruit [...] 16 and not from any stranger, or from any of the watchers, or from any of the sons of hea[ven... Why] 17 is your expression disturbed and distorted like this, and (why) is your spirit depressed like this? [...For I] 18 am speaking the truth to you.'

19 Then I, Lamech, ran to Methuselah my father, and [I told] him everything. [And I asked him to go to Enoch] 20 his father and learn everything from him with certainty, for he is beloved ..[...and with the holy ones] 21 his lot has been assigned, and they tell him everything. And when Methusela[h] heard [these things...] 22 [he ran] to Enoch his father to learn the truth about everything [...] 23 his will. And he went through the length of the land of Parvaim, and there he found [Enoch his father...] 24 [And] he said to Enoch his father, 'O my father, O my lord, to whom I [...] 25 [...] and I am telling you so that you will not be angry with me, because I have come here to [you...]'

The story of the birth of Noah represents a considerable elaboration
of the brief statement in Gen. 5:28–9. Column II begins in the middle
of the story, but we are able to follow the narrative because we have
a close parallel to it in 1 En. 106–7, and from this we can see that the
Genesis Apocryphon has elaborated the statement of Genesis in the light
of a tradition like that preserved in 1 Enoch. At the beginning of
column II Noah has already been born. His father Lamech is disturbed
by his remarkable appearance (cp. the description in 1 En. 106:2–3,
5, 10–11) and suspects that the father is one of the angels. He compels
his wife Bitenosh to swear that he, Lamech, is the father; but he is still
not satisfied and asks his father Methuselah to go to Enoch to find out
the truth. Here column II ends. In 1 Enoch the narrative goes on to
tell how Enoch reassured Methuselah that Lamech was indeed the father
of Noah, and how Enoch announced the flood and the survival of Noah
and his family. From what survives of columns III–V it seems clear that
the Genesis Apocryphon continued in much the same way.

II.1. *the conception was due to the watchers, or...to the holy ones*: i.e.
to the angels. There is here a link with the tradition of the descent of
the watchers to earth because of their lust for the daughters of men;
see 1 En. 6–11, itself an elaboration of Gen. 6:1–4 (cp. in this series
Outside the Old Testament, pp. 29–38). For 'watchers' and 'holy ones'
as terms for angels cp. Dan. 4:13, 17, 23; 1 En. 9:3; 10:7; 12:2. *the
Nephilim*: giants (cp. Num. 13:33) who, by implication in Gen. 6:4,
but explicitly in Jub. 5:1–2; 1 En. 7:2, were the offspring of the
intercourse between the angels and the daughters of men.

3. *Bitenosh*: not mentioned in Gen. 5:28–9; in Jub. 4:28 she is
described as his cousin.

4. *the Most High*: for this title for God cp. Dan. 4:17, 24, 25, etc.
the Great Lord: cp. 1 En. 12:3; 81:3. *the King of all A[ges*: cp. 1 En.
9:4; 12:3, where the Greek version has 'King of the Ages'.

5. *the sons of heaven*: 'heaven' is a substitute for 'God', and the
expression is the equivalent of 'the sons of God', i.e. angels; cp. Gen.
6:2; 1 En. 6:2; 14:3. The end of line 4 probably contained a demand
that Bitenosh swear that she had not had intercourse with 'the sons
of heaven'.

9. *O my brother*: a polite form of address, not literally her brother.

10. *the time*: the word perhaps means 'intercourse'.

14. *I swear...by the Great Holy One*: cp. 1 En. 98:6, and for the title
cp. also 1 En. 1:3; 10:1, etc. *the King of H[eaven*: cp. Dan. 4:37.

19–21a. Cp. 1 En. 106:4, 5a, 7. *and with the holy ones] his lot
has been assigned*: cp. 1 En. 106:7, 'for his dwelling is with the angels';

12:2; and for the idea that Enoch's knowledge derives from his association with the angels see Jub. 4:21; 1 En. 1:2.

21*b*–23. Cp. 1 En. 106:8. *Parvaim*: an unknown place, mentioned in 2 Chron. 3:6 as being famous for its gold. In 1 En. 106:8 Enoch is said to be 'at the ends of the earth', and correspondingly 'Parvaim' is used in the Genesis Apocryphon to denote a mysterious and far-away place.

Column II breaks off at this point. Columns III–XVII continued the story of the birth of Noah and then recounted the story of the flood and its aftermath, but only a few small fragments of this have been deciphered. The story of Abram began in column XVIII, but nothing of this can be deciphered. With column XIX we pick up the story of Abram in Canaan and the journey to Egypt (Gen. 12).

ABRAM IN CANAAN

XIX.7 [...and I built there an alta]r, [and I called] ther[e on the name of G]o[d], and I said, 'You are ⁸ [my G]o[d, G]o[d et]er[nal...].' Up till then I had not reached the holy mountain, so I set out ⁹ for [...] and I journeyed towards the south [...] until I reached Hebron; at [that time] Hebron was built, and I dwelt ¹⁰ [there for two ye]ars.

The immediately preceding material will have begun the story of Abram's journey from Harran to Canaan (Gen. 12:1–9; cp. Jub. 13:1–10); line 7 apparently corresponds to Gen. 12:8.

XIX.7–8*a*. [*my G*]o[*d, G*]o[*d et*]er[*nal*: possible restoration, cp. Jub. 13:8.

8*b*–10*a*. Cp. Gen. 12:9 (which only mentions journeying to the south); Jub. 13:10. *the holy mountain*: possibly the temple mount is meant; cp. the identification of the mountain in the land of Moriah (Gen. 22:2) as the site of the temple in 2 Chron. 3:1. *so I set out*: i.e. from near Bethel (Gen. 12:8). *until I reached Hebron...and I dwelt [there for two ye]ars*: cp. XXII.28; Jub. 13:10. The tradition of a two-year stay at Hebron is found only in the Genesis Apocryphon and Jubilees.

ABRAM IN EGYPT

This section (1QapGen XIX.10*b*–XX.32) covers Gen. 12:10–20, the first narrative about the jeopardising of the ancestress of the nation. It provides a good illustration of the author's technique. The author has preserved the main points of the biblical narrative, which he sometimes translates fairly literally. But he has mostly paraphrased the narrative, and he has introduced several major additions to the story. He has also interwoven elements taken from Gen. 20, the story of Abraham and Abimelech, the second account of the jeopardising of the ancestress of the nation.

THE JOURNEY TO EGYPT AND ABRAM'S DREAM

XIX.10 Now there was a famine in all this land, but I heard that [there was] gr[ai]n in Egypt. I set out ¹¹ to [enter] the land of Egypt [...] I [reached] the river Karmon, one of ¹² the branches of the River [...] At that time we [...] our land [and] I [cro]ssed the seven branches of this river, which ¹³ [...] At that time we crossed (the border of) our land and entered the land of the sons of Ham, the land of Egypt.

¹⁴ And in the night that I entered the land of Egypt I, Abram, had a dream, and in my dream I saw a cedar and a palm-tree ¹⁵ [...] and men came and sought to cut down and uproot the cedar, but to leave the palm-tree on its own. ¹⁶ But the palm-tree cried out and said, 'Do not cut down the cedar, for we are both from [...].' And the cedar was spared with the help of the palm-tree ¹⁷ and [was] not [cut down].

And in the night I awoke from my sleep and said to Sarai my wife, 'I have had a dream, ¹⁸ [and I] am frightened [because of] this dream.' She said to me, 'Tell me your dream that I may know it.' So I began to tell her this dream ¹⁹ [and I made known] to [her the interpretation of this] dream, and I s[aid, '...who will seek to kill me and to spare you [on]ly. This is the only kindness ²⁰ [that you must do for me]: at every [place wh]ere [we shall be, say] of me, "He is my brother"; and I will live with your help, and my life will be saved because of you. ²¹ [...they will seek] to ta[ke] you away from me and to kill me.' And Sarai wept that night because of my words ²² [...]. and the Pharaoh of Zo[an...] Sarai to go to Zoan ²³ [...]...in her soul that no [one] should see her [...]

XIX.10*b*–11*a*. Cp. Gen. 12:10; Jub. 13:11. *Now there was a famine in all this land*: an example of (almost) literal translation. *but I heard that [there was] gr[ai]n in Egypt*: cp. Gen. 42:2.

11b–12a. the river Karmon, one of the branches of the River: 'the River' is the Nile (cp. the absolute use of Hebrew *y^eōr* to mean 'the Nile', for instance in Gen. 41:1), and Karmon is probably meant as the eastern branch of the Nile Delta.

13b. the land of the sons of Ham: cp. Gen. 10:6.

14–23a. Abram's dream. This story represents a significant addition to the Genesis narrative. It is not said that the dream comes from God, but that is the clear implication. The dream is intended to explain why Abram passed off Sarai as his sister and serves to some extent to justify his action, which the biblical narrative does not attempt to do. The brief account in Jubilees gets over the difficulty by cutting out the deception: Jub. 13:11–13 merely refers to Pharaoh seizing Sarai.

14. a cedar and a palm-tree: the elements of the dream were perhaps drawn from Ps. 92:12, which in rabbinic literature was related to the story of Abram and Sarai (cp. e.g. Genesis Rabbah XLI.1).

19b–21. The narrative links up again with Gen. 12 (see verses 12–13). *who will seek to kill me and to spare you [on]ly*: cp. Gen. 12:12b. *This is the only kindness... "He is my brother"*: the author here draws on Gen. 20:13, part of the second narrative about the jeopardising of the ancestress of the nation, not on Gen. 12. *[that you must do for me]*: for the restoration cp. Gen. 20:13. *and my life will be saved because of you*: another example of fairly literal translation: cp. Gen. 12:13b.

22. the Pharaoh of Zo[an: the Pharaoh is named after the capital city in which he resided. Zoan (in Greek, Tanis) is the name of the city earlier called Avaris, the Rameses of Exod. 1:11; 12:37. Zoan may have been mentioned here because of the tradition linking its building to that of Hebron (Num. 13:22; Jub. 13:12). The end of the line was probably a statement to the effect that Sarai did not wish to go to Zoan.

23a. Probably a statement that Sarai attempted to conceal herself.

SARAI'S BEAUTY AND HER MARRIAGE TO THE PHARAOH

XIX.23 And after those five years ²⁴ three men from among the princes of Egypt [came...] of the Phara[oh] of Zoa[n] to inquire after [my] business and after my wife. And they gave ²⁵ [...] goodness, wisdom, and truth. And I read before them the [book] of the words of Enoch ²⁶ [...] during the famine which [...] and they came to the place in order to [...] the words of ²⁷ [...] with much eating and drinking [...] the wine ²⁸⁻³⁴ [...] XX.1 [...] ² ['...] how splen[did] and beautiful is her expression, and how ³ [...and] h[ow] fine the hair of

her head! How lovely are her eyes, and how desirable her nose, and all
the radiance [4] of her face [...]! How lovely are her breasts, and how
beautiful all her whiteness! How beautiful are her arms, and how
perfect her hands, [5] and (how) [desirable] the whole appearance of her
hands! How lovely are her palms, and how long and slender all the
fingers of her hands! How beautiful are her feet, [6] and how perfect her
legs! No virgin or bride who enters the bridal chamber is more
beautiful than she. She is more beautiful than all other [7] women,
and her beauty surpasses all of them. Yet with all this beauty she
possesses much wisdom, and whatever she has [8] is lovely.'

When the king heard the words of Horqanosh and the words of his
two companions, for the three of them spoke with one voice, he desired
her greatly and sent [9] immediately and had her brought. And when
he saw her, he was amazed by all her beauty and took her as his wife.
He sought to kill me, but Sarai said [10] to the king, 'He is my brother',
that I might benefit on account of her. And I, Abram, was spared
because of her and was not killed. And I, Abram, wept [11] bitterly – I
and my nephew Lot with me – on the night when Sarai was taken from
me by force.

Evidently Sarai was able to conceal her beauty from the Egyptians for
five years until three courtiers came to visit Abram.

XIX.23*b*–24*a*. *And after those five years*: Jub. 13:11 also refers to a
five-year residence in Egypt before Sarai was taken from Abram. The
five years in Egypt plus the two years in Hebron (XIX.9*b*–10*a*) are
probably linked to the tradition that Hebron was built seven years
before Zoan (Num. 13:22; Jub. 13:12). *the princes*: cp. Gen. 12:15.

24*b*–25. The courtiers apparently gave gifts to Abram and in return
sought wisdom from him. *And I read before them the* [*book*] *of the words
of Enoch*: Enoch has become in the tradition the archetypal wise man,
the one who possesses all knowledge, and so it is perhaps not surprising
that appeal should be made here to his writings. In a similar way
reference is made to his writings in Jub. 21:10 (in relation to the law)
and frequently in the Testaments of the Twelve Patriarchs (in relation
to the future, for instance in T. Levi 10:5; 14:1; 16:1), but it would
be misleading to try to tie any of these passages to the actual books
of Enoch that we possess. According to Pseudo-Eupolemus (as preserved
in Eusebius, Praeparatio Evangelica 9.17.8) Abraham taught the

Egyptians 'astrology and other such things', the discovery of which he traced back to Enoch.

27. Abram apparently provides a feast for the courtiers. The bottom of the column, which has not survived, must have told how the courtiers in some way saw Sarai and went to the Pharaoh to report.

XX.2–8a. The account of Sarai's beauty has been built up on the basis of the brief note in Gen. 12:14–15a and represents another major expansion of the Genesis narrative. But it serves no real purpose in the Genesis Apocryphon other than to add liveliness to the story. The description is to some extent reminiscent of the description of the bride in the Song of Songs (e.g. 4:1–7; 6:4–10; 7:1–9).

8b–9a. Gen. 12:15b merely states that she was taken into Pharaoh's house. *Horqanosh*: one of the Egyptian courtiers.

9b–10a. In contrast Gen. 12:16 states that Abram was well treated by Pharaoh because of Sarai.

ABRAM'S PRAYER AND THE AFFLICTION OF THE PHARAOH

XX.12 That night I prayed and entreated and made supplication, and I said in sorrow, as my tears ran down, 'Blessed are you, O God Most High, my Lord, for all [13] ages! For you are lord and sovereign over all, and you have power to judge all the kings of the earth. And now [14] I make my complaint before you, my Lord, against the Pharaoh of Zoan, the king of Egypt, because my wife has been taken from me by force. Judge him for me and show forth your great hand [15] against him and against all his house. May he not be able tonight to make my wife unclean to me, that it may be known of you, my Lord, that you are lord of all the kings [16] of the earth.' And I wept and suffered.

That night God Most High sent a pestilential spirit to afflict him and all the men of his house, an evil spirit [17] that kept on afflicting him and all the men of his house. He was unable to approach her, and he did not have intercourse with her, although he was with her [18] for two years.

At the end of two years the afflictions and punishments grew more grievous and severe for him and for all the men of his house, so he sent [19] for all the [wise men] of Egypt, for all the exorcists and all the physicians of Egypt, (to see) whether they could cure him and the men of his house of this affliction. [20] But not one of the physicians or exorcists or wise men was able to cure him, for the spirit afflicted them all, ²¹ and they fled.

xx.12–16*a*. Abram's prayer. Another addition to the Genesis narrative. There is no reference to a prayer in Jubilees, but a prayer is mentioned in later versions of the story (e.g. Josephus, *War* v.9.4 (380)). *God Most High*: the expression used here (and frequently in the remainder of the narrative) corresponds to the Hebrew *'el 'elyôn* (e.g. Gen. 14:18).

16*b*–18*a*. The affliction of the Pharaoh. Cp. Gen. 12:17; Jub. 13:13. *a pestilential spirit*: for spirits as the source of illness cp. Jub. 10:9–13; Luke 13:11. *for two years*: Jub. 13:16 likewise presupposes that Sarai was with the Pharaoh for two years.

18*b*–21*a*. The failure of the Egyptian wise men to heal the Pharaoh is reminiscent of the failure of the Egyptian magicians to interpret Pharaoh's dream (Gen. 41:8), and of the similar failure of the Babylonian wise men in the narratives about Daniel (Dan. 2:2–13; 4:6–7; 5:7–9); but cp. also Exod. 8:18–19. [*wise men*]...*exorcists*: for the mention of the two together cp. for example Dan. 2:27; 5:15.

SARAI RESTORED TO ABRAM

xx.21 Then Horqanosh came to me and asked me to come and pray for ²² the king and to lay my hands upon him that he might recover, for [he had seen me] in a dream. But Lot said to him, 'Abram my uncle cannot pray for ²³ the king while Sarai his wife is with him. Now go and tell the king that he should send Abram's wife back to her husband; then he will pray for him that he might recover.'

²⁴ When Horqanosh heard the words of Lot, he went and said to the king, 'All these afflictions and punishments ²⁵ with which my lord the king is afflicted and punished are because of Sarai the wife of Abram. Let Sarai be returned to Abram her husband, ²⁶ and this affliction and the spirit of purulence will depart from you.'

So he summoned me to him and said to me, 'What have you done to me because of Sar[ai]? You said ²⁷ to me, "She is my sister", whereas she is your wife; and I took her as my wife. Here is your wife; take her, and go and get out of ²⁸ all the provinces of Egypt. But now pray for me and for my house, that this evil spirit may be rebuked (and come out) from us.'

So I prayed [that] he [be] cured, ²⁹ and I laid my hands upon his [he]ad; the affliction was removed from him, and the evil [spirit] was rebuked (and came out) [from him], and he recovered. And the king rose and [to]ld ³⁰ me [...] and the king swore an oath to me that [he had] not [...] ³¹ Sarai to [me]. And the king gave her [mu]ch [silver and go]ld, and many garments of fine linen and purple [...] ³² before her, and also Hagar. He [ha]nded her over to me and appointed men to escort [me] out [of Egypt...]

xx.21b–22a. *and to lay my hands upon him that he might recover*: for the laying on of hands in acts of exorcism and healing cp. for instance Mark 5:23; 6:5; Luke 4:40–1. *for [he had seen me] in a dream*: the motif of the dream was probably derived from Gen. 20:3, one of several elements here taken from Gen. 20, the second narrative about the jeopardising of the ancestress of the nation.

23b. *Abram's wife*: literally 'his wife'.

26b–28a. These lines are closely dependent on Gen. 12:18–19, with some pieces of literal translation.

28b. *But now pray for me*: cp. Gen. 20:7. *that this evil spirit may be rebuked (and come out) from us*: cp. Mark 1:25; 9:25; Luke 4:39.

28c–29a. Cp. Gen. 20:17.

30b–31a. The restoration of Sarai to Abram was mentioned at this point, but the text cannot be read with certainty.

31b–32a. Cp. Gen. 20:14–16, where Abimelech gives the gifts to Abraham, not to Sarah. *Hagar*: she is described in Gen. 16:1 as an Egyptian maid and so it came to be thought in later tradition that she was given by the Pharaoh to Sarai. According to Genesis Rabbah xlv.1 Hagar was the daughter of the Pharaoh.

32b. Cp. Gen. 12:20; Jub. 13:15a.

ABRAM VIEWS THE PROMISED LAND

^{xx.33} And I, Abram, set off with very many flocks, and with silver and gold also, and I went up from [Egyp]t, [and Lot] ³⁴ my nephew (was) with me. Lot also had acquired many flocks, and he had taken a wife for himself from the daughters [of Egypt. And I camped with him] ^{xxi.1} [at] every place where I had camped (before), until I reached Bethel, the place where I had built an altar. I built it again ² [and] offered upon it whole-offerings and a grain-offering to God Most High.

And there I invoked the name of the Lord of the ages, and I praised the name of God, and I blessed ³ God. And there I gave thanks before God for all the flocks and the good things which he had given to me, and because he had shown kindness to me and had brought me safely back ⁴ to this land.

⁵ After this day Lot parted from me because of the deeds of our shepherds, and he went and settled in the valley of the Jordan, (taking) all his flocks ⁶ with him; and I too added much to what he had. He pastured his flocks and came to Sodom. He bought himself a house in Sodom ⁷ and dwelt in it. But I was dwelling on the mountain of Bethel, and it grieved me that my nephew Lot had parted from me.

⁸ And God appeared to me in a vision by night and said to me, 'Go up to Ramath-hazor, which is to the north ⁹ of Bethel, the place where you are dwelling; and lift up your eyes and look to the east, the west, the south, and the north, and see all ¹⁰ this land which I am giving to you and to your descendants for ever.' The next day I went up to Ramath-hazor, and from this height I looked at the land, ¹¹ from the River of Egypt to Lebanon and Senir, and from the Great Sea to Hauran, and all the land of Gebal as far as Kadesh, and all the Great Desert ¹² which is to the east of Hauran and Senir as far as the Euphrates. And he said to me, 'I will give all this land to your descendants, and they will possess it for ever. ¹³ I will multiply your descendants like the dust of the earth which no man can number; and neither will your descendants be numbered. Arise, walk about! Go ¹⁴ and see how great is its length and breadth. For I will give it to you and to your descendants after you for ever.'

¹⁵ And I, Abram, set off to travel around and see the land. I began travelling around from the river Gihon, and I went along the coast of the Sea until ¹⁶ I reached the Mountain of the Ox. I travelled from [the coast] of this Great Salt Sea, and I went towards the east by the Mountain of the Ox, through the breadth of the land, ¹⁷ until I reached the river Euphrates. I travelled along the Euphrates until I reached the Red Sea in the east. I went along the coast ¹⁸ of the Red Sea until I reached the tongue of the Sea of Reeds, which flows out of the Red Sea. I travelled towards the south until I reached the river Gihon, ¹⁹ and

then I returned, came safely back to my house and found all my men
safe. And I went and dwelt by the oaks of Mamre which are at
Hebron, 20 to the north-east of Hebron. There I built an altar and
offered on it a whole-offering and a grain-offering to God Most High.
I ate and drank there, 21 I and all the men of my house, and I sent for
Mamre, Arnem, and Eshcol, the three Amorite brothers, my friends,
and they ate 22 and drank with me.

This section covers Gen. 13.

xx.33–xxi.4. Cp. Gen. 13:1–4; Jub. 13:14–16. The author of the
Genesis Apocryphon has paraphrased and reordered the biblical
material, but there are some pieces of almost literal translation.

xx.34. *a wife...from the daughters* [*of Egypt*: this detail is not found
in the Old Testament or in Jubilees.

xxi.5–7. Cp. Gen. 13:5–13; Jub. 13:17–18. Here the author has
considerably abbreviated the biblical material.

8–22. Cp. Gen. 13:14–18; Jub. 13:19–21. Whereas Jubilees stays
fairly close to the biblical narrative, the author of the Genesis
Apocryphon has again expanded the material, probably because of the
importance attached to the promise of the land and of descendants.
Thus (1) God appears to Abram in a vision (in Genesis he merely
speaks); (2) Abram has to ascend a mountain and view the land (in
Gen. 13:14 he is merely told to look from where he is); (3) the promise
of Gen. 13:15–16 is given to Abram on the mountain; (4) the
fulfilment of the command to walk through the land (Gen. 13:17) is
described in detail (it is not described at all in Genesis). These changes
were no doubt intended to heighten the solemnity and importance of
the occasion.

8–10a. Cp. Gen. 13:14–15. *Ramath-hazor*: this height is identified
with Baal-hazor (2 Sam. 13:23), which is about five miles north-east
of Bethel and is the highest point in the region. For the motif of
climbing the mountain to view the land cp. Deut. 34:1–4. *and lift up
your eyes...for ever*: here the author follows the biblical text quite
closely.

10b–12a. The description of the boundaries of the land does not
occur in Gen. 13, but the author is perhaps building on the description
of the land in Gen. 15:18 as being 'from the River of Egypt to the Great
River, the river Euphrates'. The boundaries of the promised land given
here represent an ideal that was based on the extent of the Davidic
empire; cp. Deut. 11:24 for a similar description. *from the River of Egypt
to Lebanon and Senir*: Abram first looks from south to north. From the

reference to Gihon in line 15 it is clear that by 'the River of Egypt' (Gen. 15:18) the author understood the Nile itself, and not the 'Brook' or 'Torrent' of Egypt (Wadi el-'Arîs), which is sometimes mentioned as the southern border of the land (e.g. Num. 34:5). 'Lebanon' and 'Senir' are the Lebanon and Anti-Lebanon ranges of mountains (cp. Ezek. 27:5), but for the latter contrast the more specific identification in Deut. 3:9. *and from the Great Sea to Hauran*: Abram now looks from west to east. 'The Great Sea' is the Mediterranean (cp. Num. 34:6). 'Hauran' is the high plateau south of Damascus (Ezek. 47:16, 18); it serves here to represent the east. *and all the land of Gebal as far as Kadesh*: Abram, having looked in all four directions, turns to the south-east and the north-east. 'Gebal' is mentioned in Ps. 83:7; from the reference to it in line 29, for which see Gen. 14:6, it is clear that it is the region more commonly known as Seir, the territory of the Edomites in the south-east (cp. Gen. 32:3). 'Kadesh' is probably the Kadesh-barnea of the Old Testament (cp. e.g. Deut. 1:2). *and all the Great Desert which is to the east of Hauran and Senir as far as the Euphrates*: the Syrian desert in the north-east of the land.

12*b*–13*a*. The wording of the promise of land and descendants is close to that of the biblical text (Gen. 13:15–16).

13*b*–14*a*. Cp. Gen. 13:17.

15–19*a*. In fulfilment of the command of Gen. 13:17 Abram travels round the borders of the land, rather as if he were the new owner of a property; the journey around the borders represents the symbolic taking possession of the promised land. This element in the story does not occur in Genesis or Jubilees.

15–16*a*. Abram begins his journey in the south-west, by the river Nile. *Gihon*: mentioned in Gen. 2:13 as one of the four rivers of Eden, Gihon was identified in later tradition as the Nile (cp. the Septuagint of Jer. 2:18, where 'the Shihor' (i.e. the Nile) is rendered as 'Gihon'; Jub. 8:15). *the Sea*: the Mediterranean. *the Mountain of the Ox*: that part of the Taurus mountain range which was known as Mount Amanus. In later rabbinic tradition (e.g. Mishnah Šeb. 6:1) Amanus was likewise regarded as the northern border of the land.

16*b*–17*a*. *this Great Salt Sea*: the Mediterranean, although in the Old Testament 'the Salt Sea' is the Dead Sea (e.g. Num. 34:12).

17*b*. *the Red Sea*: the Persian Gulf and the Indian Ocean, not what is today known as the Red Sea; for the usage in the Genesis Apocryphon cp. e.g. 1 En. 32:2.

17*c*–18*a*. *the tongue of the Sea of Reeds*: the Gulf of Suez at the upper end of the modern Red Sea; cp. Jub. 8:14.

18*b*–19*a*. *I travelled towards the south until I reached the river Gihon*:

from the mouth of the Euphrates (line 17*b*) Abram has journeyed all round the Arabian Peninsula as far as the Gulf of Suez (line 18*a*). He now goes to the Gihon (the Nile). The fact that he is said to travel south rather than west reflects a Palestinian viewpoint.

19*b*–20*a*. The narrative rejoins Genesis; the wording is fairly close to that of Gen. 13:18. *the oaks of Mamre*: apparently understood in the Genesis Apocryphon as the oaks belonging to Mamre, although in Gen. 13:18 'Mamre' is normally assumed to be a place-name.

20*b*–22. Not in Genesis, but the introduction of *Mamre, Arnem, and Eshcol* (cp. Gen. 14:13, 24) serves to link 'the oaks of Mamre' with Mamre and his two brothers and prepares the way for the mention of the three of them in the narrative which follows. *Arnem*: the 'Aner' of the biblical text.

THE WAR WITH KEDORLAOMER

XXI.23 Before those days Kedorlaomer king of Elam, Amraphel king of Babylon, Arioch king of Cappadocia, and Tidal king of Goyim, which lies between the two rivers, had come 24 and made war on Bera king of Sodom, Birsha king of Gomorrah, Shinab king of Admah, 25 Shemiabad king of Zeboyim, and the king of Bela. All these had joined together for battle in the valley of Siddim, but the king of Elam and the kings who were with him had prevailed 26 over the king of Sodom and all his allies. They had imposed tribute on them. For twelve years they kept paying 27 their tribute to the king of Elam, but in the thirteenth year they rebelled against him.

In the fourteenth year the king of Elam led (out) all 28 his allies and went up by the way of the desert; and they were destroying and plundering from the river Euphrates (onward). They defeated the Rephaim who were in Ashteroth- 29 karnaim, the Zumzammim, who were in Ammon, the Emim, [who were in] Shaveh-hakerioth, and the Horites, who were in the mountains of Gebal, until they reached El- 30 Paran, which is in the desert. Then they turned back and defeated [...] in Hazazon-tamar.

31 The king of Sodom went out to meet them, together with the king of [Gomorrah], the king of Admah, the king of Zeboyim, and the king of Bela, [and they fought] a battle 32 in the valley of [Siddim] against Kedorla[omer king of Elam and the kings] who were with

him. But the king of Sodom was defeated and fled, and the king of Gomorrah [33] fell into pits [of bitumen...] And the king of Elam plundered all the property of Sodom and [34] [Gomorrah...] And they carried off Lot, the nephew [XXII.1] of Abram, who dwelt in Sodom, together with them – and all his possessions.

But one of the shepherds [2] of the flock which Abram had given to Lot escaped from captivity and came to Abram; at that time Abram was [3] dwelling in Hebron. He told him that Lot his nephew had been carried off, together with all his possessions, but that he had not been killed, and that [4] the kings had set out by the way ⟨of⟩ the Great Valley towards their province, taking captives, plundering, destroying, and killing, while making their way [5] towards the province of Damascus.

Abram wept over Lot his nephew. Then Abram recovered himself; he rose up [6] and chose from his servants three hundred and eighteen picked men, and Arnem [7] and Eshcol and Mamre set out with him. He pursued them until he reached Dan and found them [8] encamped in the valley of Dan. He fell upon them by night from (all) four sides. He killed [9] some of them during the night, defeated them and pursued them, and all of them fled before him [10] until they reached Helbon which is situated to the north of Damascus. He rescued from them all that they had captured [11] and all that they had plundered – and all their own goods. He also saved Lot his nephew, together with all his possessions, and he brought back all [12] the captives which they had taken.

The king of Sodom heard that Abram had brought back all the captives [13] and all the plunder, and he went up to meet him. He came to Salem, that is Jerusalem, while Abram was camped in the valley of [14] Shaveh, that is the King's Valley, the valley of Beth-hakkerem. Then Melchizedek king of Salem brought out [15] food and drink for Abram and for all the men who were with him. He was the priest of God most High, and he blessed [16] Abram and said, 'Blessed be Abram by God Most High, lord of heaven and earth! And blessed be God Most High [17] who has delivered your enemies into your hand!' And he gave him a tithe of all the property of the king of Elam and his allies.

[18] Then the king of Sodom approached and said to Abram, 'My lord Abram, [19] give me the people who are mine, who are captives

with you, whom you have rescued from the king of Elam; but all the property ²⁰ (shall be) left for you.'

Then Abram said to the king of Sodom, 'I raise ²¹ my hand this day to God Most High, the lord of heaven and earth. Not a thread or a sandal-strap ²² will I take from anything that is yours, lest you say, "Abram's wealth (comes) from my property!" ²³ (I will take nothing) except for what my young men who are with me have already eaten, and except for the portion of the three men who ²⁴ went out with me; they will decide whether to give you their portion.' And Abram returned all the property and all ²⁵ the captives and gave (them) to the king of Sodom; he set free all the captives who were with him from this land ²⁶ and sent them all away.

This section covers Gen. 14. Here the author has stayed fairly close to the biblical story, and the narrative consists mostly of literal translation or of paraphrase of the Old Testament text. The narrative changes now from the first person to the third person and remains in the third person to the end of column XXII. The parallel narrative in Jub. 13:22–9 considerably abbreviates the story and builds on Gen. 14:20b to introduce the law of tithing.

XXI.23–30. Cp. Gen. 14:1–7.

23–25a. *Kedorlaomer*: placed first because he is the leader of the group (cp. Gen. 14:4–5a; lines 26b–28a); in Gen. 14:1 he is mentioned third. *Babylon*: the contemporary name of the Old Testament 'Shinar'. *Cappadocia*: 'Ellasar' of the Old Testament is here identified with a region of Asia Minor. *the two rivers*: the Tigris and the Euphrates. *Shemiabad*: in the Massoretic text the name is Shemeber, but the form in the Samaritan version is similar to that of the Genesis Apocryphon.

25b–26a. The author has adapted and expanded the story by explicitly introducing the initial campaign in which the five kings were subjugated; cp. also 'Before those days' in line 23. Gen. 14 refers only to the campaign in the fourteenth year after the five kings had rebelled.

27b–30. *the Zumzammim who were in Ammon*: Gen. 14:5 has 'the Zuzim in Ham'; the text of the Genesis Apocryphon has been influenced by Deut. 2:20 (where the name is spelt 'Zamzummim'). *Gebal*: Gen. 14:6 has 'Seir'; see the comment on line 11.

XXI.31–XXII.1a. Cp. Gen. 14:8–12.

XXI.32b–33a. *the king of Sodom...fled, and the king of Gomorrah fell into pits [of bitumen*: in Gen. 14:10 both kings fall into the pits. The author was no doubt concerned to deal with the fact that the king of

Sodom reappears later in the narrative (Gen. 14:17; cp. XXII.12*b*); in a similar way Jub. 13:22 says that the king of Gomorrah was killed, and the king of Sodom fled.

XXII.1*b–12a*. Cp. Gen. 14:13–16.

3*b–5a*. *the Great Valley*: the Jordan valley.

5*b–7a*. *Arnem and Eshcol and Mamre*: cp. XXI.20*b*–22.

8*b–10a*. *Helbon*: Gen. 14:15 has 'Hobah'. 'Helbon', mentioned in Ezek. 27:18, is identified with the modern Ḥalbûn, which is about fifteen miles north-west of Damascus. The reason for the change is not apparent.

12*b–17*. Cp. Gen. 14:17–20.

12*b–14a*. The narrative has been slightly expanded to overcome the abruptness of the biblical text. *Salem, that is Jerusalem*: the explicit identification made here occurs already in Ps. 76:2 (cp. 110:2, 4); in Gen. 14:18–20 the identification is only implicit. *the valley of Shaveh, that is the King's Valley, the valley of Beth-hakkerem*: the third element, 'the valley of Beth-hakkerem' (cp. Neh. 3:14; Jer. 6:1), is not mentioned in Gen. 14:17 and is meant to locate 'the valley of Shaveh, that is the King's Valley'. The place is identified with the site of Ramat Rahel between Jerusalem and Bethlehem.

14*b–17*. For Melchizedek see, in addition to the Jewish sources mentioned above (p. 185), the Christian use of this tradition in Heb. 7. In the scrolls reference may be made to the Melchizedek Document (11QMelch), in which Melchizedek is presented as a heavenly figure and as a saviour. *And he gave him a tithe*: it is clear from the context that Abram gives Melchizedek the tithe; in Gen. 14:20 it is not clear who pays the tithe (RSV and NEB have supplied 'Abram' as the subject).

18–26. Cp. Gen. 14:21–4.

20*b–21a*. *I raise my hand…to*: i.e. 'I swear by', the same idiom that is used in Gen. 14:22; cp. Dan. 12:7.

THE PROMISE OF AN HEIR

XXII.27 After these things God appeared to Abram in a vision and said to him, 'Look, ten years ²⁸ have passed since the day that you set out from Harran; you spent two (years) here, seven in Egypt, and one ²⁹ since you returned from Egypt. And now examine and count all that you have; see how it has grown to be double ³⁰ all that came out with you on the day that you set out from Harran. And now do not

be afraid, I am with you; I will be your ³¹ support and strength. I (will
be) a shield over you and a buckler for you against the one who is
stronger than you. Your wealth and your flocks ³² will increase greatly.'
But Abram said, 'My Lord God, my wealth and flocks are great, but
what use are all these things to me? ³³ For when I die, I will go hence
childless (and) without sons. One of my household servants will be my
heir, ³⁴ Eliezer, the son of […] … ' But he said to him, 'This (man) shall
not be your heir, but the one who shall come forth

This section covers Gen. 15:1–4 (cp. Jub. 14:1–3) and forms the last
part of the Genesis Apocryphon that we have, but it was manifestly
not the original end of the document. Column XXII was the last (the
innermost) column of the scroll when it was rolled up in antiquity,
but it is clear from remains of sewing that another piece of leather had
originally been attached to the scroll after column XXII, and column
XXII ends in the middle of a sentence.

   XXII.27–29a. *here*: Abram is at Hebron (cp. XXI.19b–20a and
XXII.2b–3a). For the original two years spent in Hebron see XIX.9b–10a,
and for the seven years in Egypt see XIX.23b–24a and XX.18. The same
chronology is presupposed in Jub.13:8–14:3.

The Prayer of Nabonidus

The Genesis Apocryphon, as we have just seen, represents a reworking of material in Genesis and forms one of a number of writings from Qumran of various kinds in which biblical material has been reworked. By contrast the Prayer of Nabonidus (4QPrNab) represents an older form of a tradition preserved in the Bible, namely the story of Nebuchadnezzar's madness (Dan. 4). The Prayer therefore is not strictly speaking 'exegetical', but it is included here because of its close relationship to Dan. 4.

The story of Nebuchadnezzar's madness forms part of the cycle of traditions associated with the figure of Daniel. This cycle includes not only the biblical book that bears his name, but also the stories in the Apocrypha of Daniel and Susanna, and Daniel, Bel, and the Snake. To this cycle have now to be added the fragments of three different writings in Aramaic that were found in Qumran Cave 4: (1) an apocalyptic work in which Daniel speaks before the king and his courtiers and gives an account of the history of the world from the flood onwards (4QPsDan ar^{a-c}); (2) a second apocalyptic work which is unclear in many respects, but is of interest because of its use of the terms 'Son of God' and 'Son of the Most High' (4QPsDan A^a (= 4Q243)); (3) the Prayer of Nabonidus. The Jewish hero of the Prayer is not in fact named in the fragments of this work that have survived, and it is by no means certain that he was named; but there is no question that this writing is related to the narrative of Dan. 4. The Prayer of Nabonidus and the other Danielic writings from Qumran are important, apart from anything else, because they enlarge our knowledge of the traditions associated with Daniel and enable us to see the Old Testament book of Daniel in a wider perspective.

Four fragments only of the Prayer of Nabonidus have survived, of which three belong to the first column of the work, and the fourth probably to another column; only the former are given here (4QPrNab 1–3 1). The fragments from column 1 provide the title (lines 1–2a), an introduction (lines 2b–5a), and the beginning of the narrative (lines 5b–8). According to this text Nabunai (Nabonidus, the last Babylonian king) was, by God's decision, afflicted with a disease while at Teiman, but after seven years was healed by a Jewish exorcist who told him to recount the story in order to glorify God (cp. Dan. 4:1–3). There is no evidence that these events ever occurred, and the narrative as a whole is fictitious; but the story has some basis in reality inasmuch as we know from Babylonian sources that Nabonidus spent a long period during his reign at a place called Teima, an oasis in the Arabian desert.

There are some obvious similarities between the Prayer of Nabonidus and the narrative of Dan. 4, but there are also some differences. Amongst the latter it may be observed that the Prayer concerns Nabonidus, not Nebuchadnezzar, that it is set in Teiman, not Babylon, and that the illness is physical, not mental – at least as far as the material that has survived is concerned. The manuscript of the Prayer dates from approximately the second quarter of the first century BC, but this does not mean that the composition itself is at late as this, and in fact, as already indicated, the Prayer appears to represent an older form of the narrative of Dan. 4. What is said about Nebuchadnezzar in Dan. 4 could more appropriately be referred to Nabonidus; the fact that we now have a writing similar to Dan. 4 in which Nabonidus is the central figure makes it plausible to think that in Dan. 4 a story which originally concerned Nabonidus has been altered so that it now refers to Nebuchadnezzar because the latter was a much better known figure.

As in the case of the Genesis Apocryphon, there is nothing sectarian about the contents of the Prayer of Nabonidus. It would appear to be a writing that was taken over by the Essene movement.

Bibliography

J. T. Milik, '"Prière de Nabonide", et autres écrits d'un cycle de Daniel, fragments araméens de Qumrân 4', *Revue Biblique* 63 (1956), 407–15.

B. Jongeling, C. J. Labuschagne and A. S. van der Woude (eds.), *Aramaic Texts from Qumran with Translations and Annotations* (Semitic Study Series, New Series, 4), Leiden, 1976, 121–31.

F. M. Cross, 'Fragments of the Prayer of Nabonidus', *Israel Exploration Journal* 34 (1984), 260–4.

THE PRAYER SPOKEN BY NABUNAI

1.1 The words of the prayer spoken by Nabunai, king of [Ba]bylon, [the great] king, [when he was afflicted] 2 with a malignant boil by the decision of G[o]d at Teiman. [I Nabunai] was afflicted [with a malignant boil] 3 for seven years, and from [that] (time) I became like [a beast; but I prayed to the Most High], ⁴ and my sin he forgave. An exorcist, a Jew fr[om the exiles, came to me and said], ⁵ 'Publish (this) in writing in order to render honour and great[ness] to the name of G[od Most High.' And I wrote as follows: I] ⁶ was afflicted with a ma[lignant] boil at Teiman [by the decision of God Most High. And I] ⁷ prayed for seven years [to] the gods of silver and gold, [of bronze, iron], ⁸ wood, stone, (and) clay, because [I though]t that t[hey] were gods [...

1.1–2a. The title. *the prayer*: the narrative no doubt served as the framework for a prayer of confession (cp. Dan. 4:34–5), but this has not survived. *Nabunai*: an abbreviated form of the name Nabu-naid (Nabonidus), the last king of Babylon, who reigned from 556 to 539 BC. Nabonidus was a religious reformer who fostered the cult of the moongod, Sin, and thereby incurred the hostility of the priests of Marduk in Babylon. After Cyrus had conquered the Babylonian empire in 539 BC, the Babylonian priests wrote a hostile account of the reign of Nabonidus which is known as the Verse Account of Nabonidus; the attitude of the priests towards Nabonidus is possibly reflected in Dan. 4 (see below). *a malignant boil*: the Hebrew equivalent of the Aramaic expression occurs in Deut. 28:35, 'May the LORD strike you...with malignant boils', and Job 2:7, 'and he smote Job with running sores'. By contrast, in Dan. 4 Nebuchadnezzar was afflicted with a form of madness (cp. verses 23–5, 32–3); this version of the tradition may ultimately reflect the hostile attitude of the Babylonian priests who, in the Verse Account of Nabonidus, state that the king is mad. *by the decision of G[o]d*: cp. Dan. 4:24, 'it is a decree of the Most High which touches my lord the king'. See also verse 17. *Teiman*: a variant form of Teima (or Tema, as it is called in the Old Testament; cp. e.g. Job 6:19; Isa. 21:14), the name of an oasis in northern Arabia. Nabonidus spent some seven or eight years at Teima (approximately from 552 to 545 BC) either because of the hostility of the Babylonians to his religious innovations, or in an attempt to build up trade in the western part of his empire. While he was in Teima, Nabonidus left his son Belshazzar in charge of affairs in Babylon; it is this Belshazzar who is falsely presented in Dan. 5 as the son of Nebuchadnezzar and the last king of Babylon.

2b–5a. A short introduction to the narrative.

2b–4a. [*I Nabunai*]: possible restoration. *for seven years*: this detail may be based on the historical fact that Nabonidus spent about this length of time (approximately 552–545 BC) at Teima; cp. the 'seven times' of Dan. 4:16, 23, 25, 32. *and from [that] (time) I became like [a beast*: the restoration is not certain, but cp. Dan. 5:21, 'his mind became like that of a beast'. *but I prayed to the Most High]*: possible restoration; some reference to God seems very likely because God must be the subject of 'forgave' in line 4. For the title 'the Most High' cp. 1QapGen 11.4; Dan. 4:17, 24, etc. *and my sin he forgave*: in Jewish thought sin and suffering were intimately linked (cp. e.g. Job 4:7; John 9:1–2), and so here Nabonidus's disease is implicitly presented as the result of his sin; it is the forgiveness of his sin which brings about the healing of his disease. A similar link between the forgiveness of sin and the healing of disease occurs in the story of the paralysed man (Mark 2:1–12 and parallels).

4b–5a. An exorcist: this is the probable meaning in the context of the Aramaic word *gāzēr*; the same word also occurs in Dan. 2:27; 4:7; 5:7, 11, where it is translated by the NEB as 'diviner'. *a Jew fr[om the exiles*: cp. Dan. 2:25; 5:13; 6:13. *Publish (this) in writing in order to render honour…to the name of G[od Most High*: in a somewhat similar way Nebuchadnezzar's account of his illness in Dan. 4 is presented as if it were a letter sent by the king to all his subjects and intended to glorify God; see Dan. 4:1–3. *G[od Most High*: for the title cp. Dan. 3:26; 4:2; 5:18, 21.

5b–8. The beginning of the narrative in which Nabonidus described what happened to him. *by the decision of God Most High*: for the restoration cp. line 2. *the gods of silver and gold, [of bronze, iron], wood, stone, (and) clay*: cp. the similar lists in Dan. 5:4, 23; for the inclusion of clay in the list cp. Dan. 2:35, 45.

We do not know how the narrative continued beyond this point. Column I effectively breaks off at line 8, and it is difficult to make very much of fragment 4, the only other part of the Prayer to have survived, although, in view of the parallels with Dan. 4, it is of interest that the fragment apparently refers to Nabonidus having a dream. However, it seems likely that the climax of the story consisted in a prayer of confession by Nabonidus addressed to the Most High as the only true god (cp. Dan. 4:34–5). There will then have followed his forgiveness and healing (cp. line 4; Dan. 4:36–7).

The Commentaries

The largest group of exegetical writings discovered at Qumran consists of the biblical commentaries. These writings are linked together by a common literary form: a biblical book (most often a prophetic book) is quoted section by section, and each portion of text is followed by an interpretation. The pieces of interpretation are introduced by a number of stereotyped formulas in which the word *pēšer* ('interpretation') is used, and from this usage the commentaries are often referred to by the Hebrew word *pᵉšārîm*, the plural form of the word *pēšer*. The pieces of interpretation were intended to make the biblical text refer to the history and circumstances of the Qumran community, within which the commentaries were composed. This was done on the basis that the prophetic books were understood to contain only a partial revelation. In an important passage in the Commentary on Habakkuk (1QpHab VII.1–5a) the words of the prophets are described as 'mysteries' (Hebrew *rāzîm*), whose full meaning was only disclosed to the teacher of righteousness.

Fragments of fifteen writings that can clearly be regarded as belonging to this literary genre are in existence. Twelve of these are commentaries on prophetic books (five on Isaiah, two each on Hosea and Zephaniah, one each on Micah, Nahum, and Habakkuk), while the remaining three are commentaries on the book of Psalms. Three of the most important of these commentaries – on Nahum, on Habakkuk, and the Commentary on Psalms known as 4QpPsᵃ – are given here.

The commentaries may be approached from two points of view. On the one hand comparisons may be drawn with the book of Daniel. The word *pišrā'*, the Aramaic equivalent of the Hebrew *pēšer*, is frequently used in Dan. 2 and 4 with reference to the interpretation of Nebuchadnezzar's dreams (cp. also 7:16), and in Dan. 5 with reference to the interpretation of the writing on the wall. There is a certain similarity between the view that the words of the prophets were 'mysteries' (Hebrew *rāzîm*), whose true meaning was only made known through the divine revelation given to the teacher of righteousness (see the comment on 1QpHab VII.1–5a), and the view that

Nebuchadnezzar's dream was a 'mystery' (Aramaic *rāzā*'; NEB 'secret'), whose true meaning was revealed to Daniel by God (Dan. 2:18–19, 27–30). Further, the kind of word-play that forms the basis of the interpretation of the writing on the wall (Dan. 5:25–8) is frequently used as a method of interpretation in the Qumran commentaries. It is, however, perhaps more important to observe that the exegetical techniques employed in the Qumran commentaries (e.g. word-play or the use of variant readings) were also employed in the later rabbinic commentaries, the midrashim (for these see above, pp. 184–5); and that the exegesis is often traditional in character and can be paralleled in other ancient Jewish sources such as the Septuagint, the targums, and the rabbinic writings. The Qumran biblical commentaries may be compared with the later rabbinic midrashim, but their form is not the same as that of the midrashim.

The teacher of righteousness is twice said in the Habakkuk Commentary to be the one through whom God had made known the hidden meaning of prophecy (1QpHab II.7–10a; VII.1–5a). This does not necessarily mean that the teacher was the author of the Qumran commentaries, but rather that the interpretative tradition reflected in them stems from him.

Attempts have often been made to exploit the commentaries in order to reconstruct the history of the Qumran community. This is, however, more difficult to do than is often assumed because the pieces of interpretation frequently follow traditional lines of interpretation and their language is opaque.

The biblical text given in the commentaries frequently differs, to a greater or lesser extent, from the Massoretic text, and it is for this reason that the translation of the biblical text in the following pages often differs considerably from such translations as the Revised Standard Version or the New English Bible. Important examples of such differences from the Massoretic text have been noted below, but many cases have had to be passed over without comment. It should also be noted here that in some cases the commentaries appear to show knowledge of a biblical text different from the one actually quoted.

The Commentary on Nahum

The five fragments of the Commentary on Nahum (4QpNah) contain the remains of seven columns of text, but little or nothing has survived of two of the columns, and a third is seriously damaged. Here only the four columns contained in fragment 3 (a small piece) and fragment 4 (a quite substantial piece) are presented (4QpNah 3–4 I–IV). These two fragments cover Nahum 2:11–3:12, which forms part of a loosely structured poem on the theme of the destruction of Nineveh (Nahum 2:1, 3–13; 3:1–19). No formal divisions are made in the Commentary, but the content of fragments 3 and 4 may be seen to follow the strophic structure of the biblical material and to divide fairly naturally into three sections: I.1–II.1a, covering Nahum 2:11–13; II.1b–III.8a, covering 3:1–7; III.8b–IV.8a, covering 3:8–11 (lines 8b–9a begin Nahum 3:12, but the text breaks off at this point).

The Commentary on Nahum is important for its covert references in I.1–II.1a to events in the first half of the first century BC, particularly during the reign of Alexander Jannaeus (103–76 BC), and also for its equally covert references to two contemporary religious groups, the Pharisees and the Sadducees. The former, referred to here as 'the seekers after smooth things' and as 'Ephraim', are mentioned throughout the text, but are the particular subject of the commentary in II.1b–III.8a; the latter, referred to here as 'Manasseh', are dealt with in III.8b–IV.8a. From another point of view it may be observed that whereas I.1–II.1a for the most part looks back on past events and is retrospective in character, II.1b–IV.8a has an eschatological perspective.

The manuscript dates from the latter part of the first century BC, and this was probably also the time when the work was composed, because I.3 apparently refers to Pompey's capture of Jerusalem in 63 BC.

Bibliography

J. M. Allegro, *Qumrân Cave 4, I (4Q158–4Q186)* (Discoveries in the Judaean Desert of Jordan, 5), Oxford, 1968, 37–42 and plates XII–XIV (see on this J. Strugnell, 'Notes en marge du volume V des "Discoveries in the Judaean Desert of Jordan"', *Revue de Qumrân* 7 (1969/71), 204–10).

M. P. Horgan, *Pesharim: Qumran Interpretations of Biblical Books* (The Catholic Biblical Quarterly Monograph Series, 8), Washington, DC, 1979, 158–91.

J. M. Baumgarten, 'Does *TLH* in the Temple Scroll Refer to Crucifixion?', *Journal of Biblical Literature* 91 (1972), 472–81.

J. A. Fitzmyer, 'Crucifixion in Ancient Palestine, Qumran Literature, and the New Testament', *Catholic Biblical Quarterly* 40 (1978), 493–513.

Y. Yadin, 'Pesher Nahum (4QpNahum) Reconsidered', *Israel Exploration Journal* 21 (1971), 1–12.

THE FURIOUS YOUNG LION

I.1 [...] a dwelling for the wicked of the nations.

Where the lion went to enter, the lion's cub, ² [and no one to disturb.

Its interpretation concerns Deme]trius king of Greece who sought to enter Jerusalem on the advice of the seekers after smooth things, ³ [but God did not give Jerusalem] into the hand of the kings of Greece, from Antiochus until the appearance of the rulers of the Kittim. But afterwards it will be trampled ⁴ [...]

The lion tears enough for its cubs and strangles prey for its lionesses.

⁵ [Its interpretation concerns...] against the furious young lion who attacks with his great men and with the men of his council ⁶ [...

And it fills] its cave [with prey] and its den with torn flesh.

Its interpretation concerns the furious young lion ⁷ [...]...on the seekers after smooth things, who hangs men alive ⁸ [...] in Israel in former times. For in the case of a man hanged alive upon a tree [it re]ads: Behold, I am against yo[u], ⁹ says[s the LORD of hosts. I will burn you]r [multitude in smoke], and the sword will devour your young lions; [I] will cut off its [p]rey [from the earth], ¹⁰ and [the voice of your messengers] will no [more be heard].

Its [interpret]ation: 'Your multitude' are the troops of his army t[hat are in Jerusale]m; and 'his young lions' are ¹¹ his great men [...]; and 'his prey' is the wealth which [the prie]sts of Jerusalem have ama[ssed], which ¹² they [will] give .[...E]phraim, Israel will be given[...];
II.1 and 'his messengers' are his envoys, whose voice will no more be heard among the nations.

The commentary material on Nahum 2:11–13 includes the mention of two named individuals, Demetrius and Antiochus. The identification of the former as the Seleucid ruler Demetrius III Eucaerus (95–88 BC) makes it possible to make reasonable sense of all the historical allusions in column 1, and there is general agreement amongst scholars that this passage refers to events of the reign of Alexander Jannaeus (103–76 BC), in particular the civil war against Alexander in which Demetrius became involved; see the notes below for further details. Alexander Jannaeus is 'the furious young lion' of the commentary. This passage is important because it indicates that 'the seekers after smooth things' are the Pharisees.

1.1*a*. The end of the interpretation of Nahum 2:11*a*, 'Where is the lions' den, the cave of the young lions?' (RSV, following a common emendation of the Hebrew text). In Nahum the lions represent the Assyrians, and the den or cave is Nineveh; in the Commentary on Nahum the lion-symbolism has been applied to Alexander Jannaeus and his supporters, and the den or cave is now Jerusalem. *a dwelling*: presumably Jerusalem is meant. *for the wicked of the nations*: perhaps a reference to the mercenaries used by Alexander Jannaeus.

1*b*–4*a*. Nahum 2:11*b* and interpretation. The form of the biblical text agrees with the Septuagint ('went to enter') rather than the Massoretic text, and the interpretation makes use of this variant. *Deme]trius king of Greece...Antiochus*: this is one of only two cases in the scrolls in which individuals are mentioned by their actual names, the two here being by general agreement identified as the Seleucid rulers Demetrius III Eucaerus and Antiochus IV Epiphanes. In about 88 BC, after six years of civil war, Jews who were in open revolt against Alexander Jannaeus enlisted the aid of Demetrius III. Alexander was defeated in battle by the combined forces of Demetrius and the rebel Jews, but the defeat had the effect of rallying national support for Alexander. Demetrius withdrew and Alexander was then able to put down the revolt. (The events are described in Josephus, *Ant.* XIII.13.5–14.2 (372–83); *War* 1.4.4–6 (90–8).) The opposition to Alexander was led by the Pharisees, and it is they who are *the seekers after smooth things*. According to the present passage Demetrius attempted to capture Jerusalem on the advice of the Pharisees, but was unsuccessful. *who sought to enter Jerusalem*: it is interesting that whereas the lion-symbolism of the biblical text is primarily applied to Alexander Jannaeus, 'Where the lion went to enter' of the biblical text is referred not to Alexander, but to Demetrius. [*but God did not give Jerusalem*] *into the hand of*: the restoration gives the sense demanded by the passage; the interpretation at this point is based on 'and no one to disturb' in the biblical text. *the kings of Greece*: the Ptolemies and the Seleucids, but here particularly the latter. *from Antiochus*: almost certainly Antiochus IV Epiphanes. *until the appearance of the rulers of the Kittim*: the Kittim, originally the inhabitants of Cition in Cyprus, were the people of Cyprus (cp. Isa. 23:1, 12). But the word came to be used in a wider sense to refer to the Mediterranean peoples in general, firstly the Greeks (cp. I Macc. 1:1; 8:5), then the Romans (cp. Dan. 11:30), and in the scrolls the Kittim are always the Romans. The present passage apparently refers to the events of 63 BC, when, at the end of the civil war between Hyrcanus II and Aristobulus II, Pompey intervened directly in Jewish affairs, captured Jerusalem, and imposed a political settlement on the Jews. *But afterwards it will be trampled* [...]: apparently the beginning of a description of the future destruction of Jerusalem, perhaps as part of the events of the end time.

4*b*–6*a*. Nahum 2:12*a* and interpretation. [*Its interpretation concerns*...] *against the furious young lion*: it is tempting to restore the text '[Its interpretation] concerns the furious young lion' (cp. line 6*b*), but it is difficult to explain the blank space that has then to be assumed at the beginning of line 5. There is general agreement that 'the furious young lion' is Alexander Jannaeus. *with his great men*: Alexander's supporters, perhaps specifically the Sadducees; cp. lines 10*b*–11*a*, 'and "his young lions" are his great men', and III.9.

6*b*–8*a*. Nahum 2:12*b* and interpretation. There is general agreement about the events referred to in the interpretation, but considerable uncertainty about how the events were regarded by the author. When Alexander Jannaeus put down the revolt that is described above, he took terrible revenge on those who had opposed him. Josephus reports: 'He had eight hundred of his captives crucified in the midst of the city [i.e. Jerusalem], and their wives and children butchered before their eyes, while he looked on, drinking, with his concubines reclining beside him' (*War* 1.4.6 (97); cp. *Ant.* XIII.14.2 (380)). It is commonly agreed that in the Commentary on Nahum *the furious young lion* is Alexander Jannaeus, *the seekers after smooth things* are the Pharisees, who were the leading opponents of Alexander, and that *who hangs men alive* refers to Alexander's crucifixion of his opponents. But there is considerable disagreement about how the gaps at the beginning of lines 7 and 8 should be restored, and hence disagreement as to whether Alexander's action was regarded by the author as a shocking and novel form of punishment, or as a penalty prescribed by the law. In the light of the Temple Scroll (11QTemple LXIV.6*b*–13*a*) it does seem that the community would have regarded execution by means of crucifixion or hanging – the Temple Scroll could mean either – as the proper punishment for crimes against the state, but the extensive gaps in lines 7 and 8 make it impossible to say whether Alexander's action in this particular case was or was not condemned. *For in the case of a man hanged alive upon a tree [it re]ads*: there is disagreement as to how the Hebrew should be translated. The present translation assumes that the interpretation of Nahum 2:12b ran straight on into the quotation of the next piece of text, Nahum 2:13; this is unusual, but not totally without parallel. There is an allusion to Deut. 21:22–3, although Deuteronomy is concerned with hanging a man on a tree after death, not before.

   I.8b–II.1a. Nahum 2:13 and interpretation. *Behold, I am against yo[u], say[s the* LORD *of hosts*: this part of the text goes with what precedes and refers to the 'man hanged alive upon a tree'; it is not commented on in the following interpretation. The remainder of the passage is interpreted with reference to 'the furious young lion', i.e. Alexander Jannaeus, and with reference to the Hasmonaean high priests generally. *you]r [multitude*: for this restoration, which corresponds to the text of the Septuagint, see line 10; the Massoretic text differs. In the Massoretic text the occurrences of the possessive 'your' are all feminine and refer to Nineveh; in the Commentary on Nahum the 'your' in 'your multitude' and 'your young lions' is masculine, probably because the verse is interpreted to refer to Alexander Jannaeus, 'the furious young lion'. *its [p]rey*: possibly a mistake for 'your [p]rey'. *and 'his young lions' are his great men*: see the comment on I.4b–6a. *and 'his prey' is the wealth which [the prie]sts of Jerusalem have ama[ssed]*: '[the prie]sts of Jerusalem' are the Hasmonaean high priests, of whose dynasty Alexander was a member; for the wealth acquired by the Hasmonaeans as a result of their wars of conquest see also 1QpHab IX.4–7. *E]phraim*: here a symbolic name for the Pharisees, as is clear from II.2. *and 'his messengers' are his envoys, whose voice will no more be heard among the nations*: the wording of the interpretation is obviously strongly influenced by the biblical text; the 'his' probably still refers to Alexander Jannaeus. The whole context in I.11b–II.1a appears to allude to events that were expected to happen at the eschatological judgement, but much is unclear because of the loss of the greater part of I.12.

JUDGEMENT ON THE SEEKERS AFTER SMOOTH THINGS

II.1 Woe to the city of blood, all of it full of [deceit and pilla]ge!

2 Its interpretation: This is the city of Ephraim, the seekers after smooth things at the end of days, who walk in deceit and falseho[od].

3 No end to the prey! The crack of the whip and the rattle of wheels! Horses dashing, chariots bounding, horsemen charging! The flash 4 and glitter of spears! A multitude of slain and a mass of corpses! There is no end to the dead bodies, and they stumble over their bodies!

Its interpretation concerns the rule of the seekers after smooth things, 5 from the midst of whose congregation the sword of the nations will not depart. Captivity, plundering, and burning will be among them, and exile from fear of the enemy. A multitude 6 of guilty corpses will fall in their days, and there will be no end to the sum of their slain. Indeed, they will stumble over their dead flesh because of their guilty counsel.

7 Because of the countless harlotries of the graceful harlot, the mistress of sorceries, who betrays nations through her harlotry and families through her sorceries.

8 [Its] interpretation [con]cerns those who lead Ephraim astray, who through their false teaching, their lying tongue and deceitful lips lead many astray 9 – th[eir] kings, princes, priests, and people, together with the alien who joins (them). Cities and families will perish through their counsel; ho[nou]red men and ru[lers] 10 will fall [because of the inso]lence of their tongue.

Behold, I am against you, says the LORD of h[ost]s, and you will lift up 11 [your] skirts over your face, and you will show nations [your] nakedness and kingdoms your shame.

Its interpretation [...] 12 [...] cities of the east, for 'the skirts' [...] III.1 the nations because of their impurity [and because of] their abominable [fi]lth.

I will cast filth over you, [and] I [will] treat you with contempt. I will make you 2 repulsive, and all who see you will flee from you.

3 Its interpretation concerns the seekers after smooth things whose evil deeds will be revealed to all Israel at the end of time. 4 Many will understand their iniquity, and will hate them and consider them

repulsive because of their guilty insolence. When the glory of Judah is [re]vealed, ⁵ the simple of Ephraim will flee from the midst of their assembly, and will forsake those who lead them astray, and will join [I]srael.

And they will say: ⁶ 'Nineveh is laid waste; who will grieve over her?' Whence shall I seek comforters for you?

Its interpretation [concerns] the seekers after ⁷ smooth things, whose counsel will perish, and whose congregation will be dispersed. They will never again lead [the] assembly astray, and the sim[ple] ⁸ will support their counsel no more.

The commentary material on Nahum 3:1–7 is primarily concerned with the Pharisees. Judgement on Nineveh, 'the city of blood' (Nahum 3:1–3), the prostitute and sorceress (3:4–7), has become judgement on Jerusalem understood as the city of Ephraim, the seekers after smooth things who lead men astray by their false teaching.

II.1*b*–2. Nahum 3:1*a* and interpretation. *This is the city of Ephraim, the seekers after smooth things*: 'Ephraim' and 'the seekers after smooth things' are here identified, and thus it is clear that 'Ephraim' is a symbolic name for the Pharisees. It follows from this that 'Manasseh' (III.9, etc.) is a symbolic name for the Sadducees. 'The city of Ephraim' means Jerusalem, so described because it was a place where Pharisees exercised considerable influence from the time of Alexandra (76–67 BC) onwards. It was the equation of Nineveh with Jerusalem understood as the city of the Pharisees that enabled the author to interpret Nahum 3:1–7 in terms of judgement on the Pharisees. *at the end of days*: a clear indication that the commentary material which follows refers to the last time. Much of the material is intended as a description of the fate of the Pharisees (and of others) at the eschatological judgement.

3–6. Nahum 3:1*b*–3 and interpretation. *No end to the prey!*: in the Massoretic text part of the description of 'the city of blood' (verse 1), but here linked with the description of the defeat of Nineveh in battle (verses 2–3). *The flash and glitter of spears!*: the 'sword' of the Massoretic text was omitted by mistake (cp. line 5). *Its interpretation concerns the rule of the seekers after smooth things from the midst of whose congregation the sword of the nations will not depart*: the account of the battle is taken to refer to the judgement of the Pharisees as part of the events of the last days; see the comparable statement about the Sadducees in IV.3. *the sword...will not depart*: an interpretation of 'No end to the prey!'. In the Hebrew 'No end to' and 'will not depart' are the same. The 'sword' comes from verse 3 of the biblical text. *Captivity, plundering ...from fear of the enemy*: the thought of judgement is inspired by verses 2, 3a of the biblical text, although the exact basis of the interpretation is unclear. *their dead flesh*: literally 'the corpses of their flesh', cp. 1QpHab IX.2a. *because of their guilty counsel*: a recurrent theme in the accusations made against the seekers after smooth things concerns their false teaching by which they lead men astray: cp. e.g. lines 8–9.

7–10a. Nahum 3:4 and interpretation. *betrays*: there are uncertainties about the translation, but 'betrays' makes good sense in the context: cp. in the interpretation 'lead astray', 'will perish', 'will fall'. *[Its] interpretation [con]cerns those who lead Ephraim astray*: i.e. the leaders of the Pharisees ('Ephraim'). The 'harlotries' and 'sorceries' of the biblical text are taken in the interpretation to signify Pharisaic 'false teaching' and evil 'counsel', and the latter in turn are said to mislead and harm the nation. *will perish...will fall*: in the events of the eschatological judgement. *will fall [because of the inso]lence of their tongue*: cp. Hos. 7:16 (see the RSV; NEB understands the passage differently).

II.10b–III.1a. Nahum 3:5 and interpretation. The bottom of column II has suffered serious damage, but it is likely that the interpretation referred to the future disgrace and punishment of the Pharisees.

III.1b–5a. Nahum 3:6–7a and interpretation. *repulsive*: the Massoretic text has 'I will make you a spectacle' or, differently understood, 'I will treat you like excrement' (so NEB). The word used in the scroll is similar to the one in the Massoretic text, but is spelt differently. Since the same word is also used in line 4, the choice of the word in the quotation of the biblical text was probably deliberate. *will be revealed*: the choice of word was perhaps suggested by the use of the same Hebrew word in Nahum 3:5, translated (in II.10) as 'lift up'. *at the end of time*: a further reminder of the eschatological perspective of the interpretation. *Many will understand...their guilty insolence*: based on 'I will make you repulsive.' *When the glory...will join [I]srael*: based on 'and all who see you will flee from you'. *When the glory of Judah is [re]vealed*: 'Judah' is here a symbolic name for the community (cp. CD IV.11; 1QpHab VIII.1), and the thought is of the vindication and triumph of the community in the events of the end. *the simple of Ephraim*: the followers of the Pharisees. *[I]srael*: the true Israel constituted by the community.

5b–8a. Nahum 3:7b and interpretation. The 'laying waste' of Nineveh of the biblical text is taken to refer to the demise of the Pharisees at the time of judgement.

JUDGEMENT ON 'MANASSEH'

III.8 Will you do better than Am[on which lay by the] rivers?

⁹ Its interpretation: 'Amon' is Manasseh, and 'the rivers' are the great men of Manasseh, the honoured men of the […]…[…]

¹⁰ Waters surrounded her, whose rampart was the sea, whose walls were waters.

¹¹ Its interpretation: They are the men of her [ar]my, her [w]arlike warrior[s].

Cush was her strength, [and Egypt too, without limit].

¹² [Its interpretation…

P]ut and the [Lybians were your help].

IV.1 Its interpretation: They are the wicked one[s of…]., the house of Peleg, who joined Manasseh.

Yet she too w[ent] into exile, [into captivity. Even] ² her infants were dashed to the ground at every street-corner. For her honoured men they cast lots, and all [her] g[rea]t [men were bound] ³ in fetters.

Its interpretation concerns Manasseh at the last time, whose rule over Is[rael] will be laid low […] ⁴ his wives, his infants, and his children will go into captivity. His warriors and his honoured men [will perish] by the sword.

[You too will be drunk], ⁵ and you will be in black despair.

Its interpretation concerns the wicked of E[phraim…] ⁶ whose cup will come after Manasseh […

You too will seek] ⁷ refuge in the city from the enemy.

[Its] inter[pretation con]cerns […] ⁸ their enemies in the city […

All your fortresses] ⁹ are (like) fig-trees with [first-ripe figs…

Nahum 3:8–11 is concerned to argue that Nineveh would be no more able to escape destruction than was the Egyptian city No-amon, i.e. Thebes. In the commentary material 'No-amon', or rather 'Amon', is identified by means of word-play as 'Manasseh', which is itself a covert name for the Sadducees. The destruction of Amon thus becomes judgement on the Sadducees.

III.8b–9. Nahum 3:8a and interpretation. *Will you do better than Am[on?]*: the Massoretic text has 'Will you fare better than No-amon?' and makes a comparison between the impending fate of Nineveh and that of No-amon, i.e. Thebes. The text of the scroll differs slightly and apparently refers to 'Amon' (cp. line 9) instead of 'No-amon', no doubt in order to facilitate the word-play with Manasseh. The Septuagint, although it differs considerably, also gives the name as 'Amon'. *'Amon' is Manasseh*: from the fact that 'Ephraim' is a symbolic name for the Pharisees it appears that 'Manasseh' is a symbolic name for the Sadducees. *the great men of Manasseh*: see the comment on 1.4*b*–6*a*.

10–11*a*. Nahum 3:8*b* and interpretation. *whose rampart*: the Hebrew word, understood differently, could also be translated as 'whose army'. The interpretation makes use of this play on meanings in that the Hebrew word is used with the meaning 'her army' in line 11*a*.

11*b*–12*a*. Nahum 3:9*a* and interpretation – but little has survived.

III.12*b*–IV.1*a*. Nahum 3:9*b* and interpretation. *the wicked one[s of…].*, *the house of Peleg*: the identity of 'the house of Peleg', also mentioned in CD xx.22*b*, is unknown; see the comment on CD xx.22*b*–25*a*.

IV.1*b*–4*a*. Nahum 3:10 and interpretation. *Its interpretation concerns Manasseh at the last time, whose rule over Is[rael] will be laid low*: the commentary material on Nahum 3:8–9 consists of a series of straight-forward identifications (cp. III.9, 11; IV.1; probably also III.12), no doubt because the biblical text itself consists largely of a description of No-amon. In contrast the reference to the fall of No-amon in Nahum 3:10 provided the opportunity for the announcement of judgement on 'Manasseh', i.e. the Sadducees, 'at the last time'; a comparable statement about the Pharisees is made in II.4*b*–5*a*.

4*b*–6*a*. Nahum 3:11*a* and interpretation. [*You too will be drunk*]: the restoration and translation are based on the Massoretic text as traditionally understood and are made probable for the Commentary on Nahum by the reference to the 'cup' in line 6; for the thought cp. Isa. 51:21–2; Jer. 25:27. NEB 'You too shall hire yourself out' reflects a different understanding of the consonants of the Hebrew. *and you will be in black despair*: the translation is uncertain; another possibility is 'you will be dazed' (RSV). For the NEB see the Cambridge Bible Commentary on Nahum, p. 119. *Its interpretation concerns the wicked of E[phraim…] whose cup will come after Manasseh*: the 'cup' is a symbol of judgement, cp. e.g. Isa. 51:17, 22; Jer. 25:15–17. Just as the biblical text compares the impending fate of Nineveh with that of No-amon, so the interpretation links the theme of judgement on the Pharisees ('Ephraim') with that of judgement on the Sadducees ('Manasseh').

6b–8a. Nahum 3:11*b* and interpretation. *refuge in the city from the enemy*: 'in the city' is not in the Massoretic text; it was probably included with the interpretation (line 8) in mind; cp. 'repulsive' in III.2, 4.

8b–9a. Nahum 3:12*a*. Fragment 4 breaks off here.

The Commentary on Habakkuk

The Commentary on Habakkuk (1QpHab) is the best preserved and in many ways the most important of the Qumran biblical commentaries. It consists of twelve and a half columns of text, each column apparently seventeen lines in length; but the right-hand side of column I and the bottom of the entire manuscript have been lost. As in the Commentary on Nahum no divisions are marked in the text, but the Commentary can be seen to follow the structure of the book of Habakkuk itself. Thus the material presented here can be divided into the following sections: I.(16)–II.10a, covering Hab. 1:5; II.10b–IV.(16a), covering Hab. 1:6–11; IV.(16b)–VI.12a, covering Hab. 1:12–17; VI.12b–VIII.3a, covering Hab. 2:1–4; VIII.3b–XIII.4, covering Hab. 2:5–20. The Commentary does not cover Hab. 3, perhaps because this chapter was not appropriate for the author's immediate purposes.

The Commentary is primarily important for the very full illustration it provides of methods of biblical exegesis employed by the Qumran community. These are discussed in the appropriate places below, but here it should be noted that links may often be observed with traditional Jewish exegesis of Habakkuk as represented, for example, by the Septuagint or the Targum of Jonathan on the Prophets (for the targums see above, p. 184). The Commentary is also important for the historical allusions it contains, particularly in VIII.3b–XII.10a, but the information given is more opaque than is often assumed (see below, pp. 235–6).

The manuscript dates from the second half of the first century BC, but the work was probably composed before this. There are indications in the Commentary that it was composed in the last decades before the time of Hyrcanus II and Aristobulus II (see p. 240), possibly in the last years of the reign of Alexander Jannaeus (see pp. 236, 245).

Bibliography

M. Burrows, with the assistance of J. C. Trever and W. H. Brownlee, *The Dead Sea Scrolls of St Mark's Monastery*. Volume I: *The Isaiah Manuscript and the Habakkuk Commentary*, New Haven, 1950.

W. H. Brownlee, *The Midrash Pesher of Habakkuk* (Society of Biblical Literature Monograph Series, 24), Missoula, Montana, 1979.

M. P. Horgan, *Pesharim: Qumran Interpretations of Biblical Books* (The Catholic
    Biblical Quarterly Monograph Series, 8), Washington, DC, 1979, 10–55.
F. F. Bruce, *Biblical Exegesis in the Qumran Texts*, London, 1960.
A. Finkel, 'The Pesher of Dreams and Scriptures', *Revue de Qumrân* 4
    (1963/64), 357–70.
L. H. Silberman, 'Unriddling the Riddle: A Study in the Structure and
    Language of the Habakkuk Pesher (1QpHab.)', *Revue de Qumrân* 3
    (1961/62), 323–64.
A. S. van der Woude, 'Wicked Priest or Wicked Priests? Reflections on the
    Identification of the Wicked Priest in the Habakkuk Commentary',
    Journal of Jewish Studies 33 (1982), 349–59.

THE TRAITORS

1.(16) [...Look, you traitors, and see, (17) astonish yourselves and be
astounded; for I am doing a deed in your days that you will not believe
when] 11.1 it is told.

[The interpretation of the passage concerns] the traitors with 2 the
liar, for [they did] not [believe the words] of the teacher of righteousness
(which he received) from the mouth 3 of God. And it concerns those
who betr[ayed] the new [covenant], for they have not 4 believed in
the covenant of God [and have profaned] his holy name. 5 And likewise,
the interpretation of the passage [concerns the trai]tors at the end 6 of
days. They are those who act ruth[lessly against the covena]nt, who
do not believe 7 when they hear all the things that [are to come upon]
the last generation from the mouth 8 of the priest in whose [heart] God
put [understand]ing that he might interpret all 9 the words of his
servants the prophets, through [whom] God foretold 10 all the things
that are to come upon his people and [his congregation].

Column 1 of the Commentary dealt almost entirely with Hab. 1:1–4,
the lament of the prophet about the lack of justice in society; but
because only the left-hand side of the column has survived, this material
is not presented here. Hab. 1:5 introduces God's reply to the prophet
(1:5–11), and the wording of this verse provided the opportunity for
the commentator to refer to those who had betrayed the community.

1.(16)–11.10a. Hab. 1:5 and interpretation. [*Look, you traitors*: the
Massoretic text has 'Look among the nations', but the Septuagint (cp.
Acts 13:41) presupposes 'Look, you traitors', and this has been restored
here because the interpretation is entirely concerned with traitors (see

II.1, 3, 5). It is, however, conceivable that the commentator had 'among the nations' in his text, but made use of a variant known to him ('you traitors') in his interpretation *you will not believe*]: a key phrase which was used in the interpretation in II.4, 6 and perhaps also in line 2. [*The interpretation of the passage concerns*] the traitors with the liar: the interpretation appears to refer to three different groups of apostates. The first of these is a group that broke away at a very early stage in the community's history under the leadership of 'the liar' (cp. v.8*b*–12*a*). This individual, also called 'the preacher of lies' and 'the scoffer', is referred to several times in the commentaries and in the Damascus Document; see the passages listed above, p. 23. The act of treachery is probably the same as that mentioned in CD I.13–18*a*; XIX.33*b*–XX.1*a*; XX.10*b*–11*a*, 14*b*–15*a*. *And it concerns those who* betr[ayed] the new [covenant]: the second group are apparently those who apostatised during the course of the community's history. For 'the new covenant' cp. CD VI.19; VIII.21*b* = XIX.33*b*–34*a*; XX.12. *And likewise, the interpretation of the passage* [*concerns the trai*]*tors at the end of days*: the third group consists of the apostates of the last days before the final judgement. If it is right to think that the author believed himself to be living in the last days, then they are the apostates of the author's own day. *those who act ruth*[*lessly against the covena*]*nt*: see the comment on 1QH II.10*b*–11*a*. *who do not believe*: or 'who will not believe'. *the priest*: almost certainly the reference is to the teacher of righteousness; cp. 4QpPs[a] 1–10 III.15, 'the priest, the teacher of [righteousness'. In post-exilic literature 'the priest', used as a title, means 'the high priest'; this raises the possibility that at one stage the teacher of righteousness functioned as high priest in Jerusalem; see further, p. 10. *that he might interpret all the words of his servants the prophets*: for the role of the teacher of righteousness as interpreter of the hidden meaning of prophecy see VII.1–5*a*; cp. CD VI.7*b*–8*a*. For the Old Testament cliché 'his servants the prophets' cp. for instance 2 Kings 17:23; 21:10.

THE KITTIM

II.10 For behold, I am raising up 11 the Chaldeans, that cru[el and impetu]ous nation.

12 Its interpretation concerns the Kittim [who are] quick and valiant 13 in war, causing many to perish [...] under the dominion 14 of the Kittim, and [...], and they will not believe 15 in the statutes [of God... (16–17) ...

They march through the wide tracts of the earth to take possession of dwellings which are not their own.

Its interpretation concerns the Kittim who...] III.1 and through the plain they march to attack and plunder the cities of the earth, 2 for this is what it says: 'to take possession of dwellings which are not their own'.

Dread 3 and fearsome are they; their justice and their guile proceed from themselves.

4 Its interpretation concerns the Kittim, fear and dread of whom are upon all 5 the nations. By intention all their plans are to do evil, and with cunning and deceit 6 they deal with all the peoples.

Their horses are swifter than leopards and fiercer 7 than wolves of the plain; they prance about, and their horsemen spring forward. From afar 8 they fly like an eagle hastening to devour all. They come intending violence; their massed faces 9 are (like) the east wind.

Its in[terpretation] concerns the Kittim who 10 trample the earth with [their] horses and with their cattle. They come 'from afar', 11 from the coasts of the sea, to devou[r a]ll the peoples 'like an eagle', 12 but they are not satisfied. And with fury [... and with bur]ning anger and fierce 13 rage they speak with [all the peoples, fo]r this is what 14 it says: '[their] m[assed faces are (like) the east wind'.

They gather] captives [like san]d.

15 Its [interpret]ation [...(16–17)...

Kings] IV.1 they deride, and rulers are a laughing-stock to them.

Its interpretation is that 2 they mock the great and despise those who are honoured; at kings 3 and princes they scoff, and they deride great armies.

They 4 laugh at every fortress; they heap up earthworks and take it.

5 Its interpretation concerns the rulers of the Kittim who despise 6 the fortresses of the peoples and in mockery laugh at them. 7 They encircle them with a great army to capture them, and in fear and dread 8 they are given into their hand. And they raze them to the ground because of the iniquity of those who dwell 9 in them.

Then the wind sweeps on and passes; and they make their strength [10] their god.

Its interpretation concerns the rulers of the Kittim [11] who by the decision of [their] house of guilt pass one [12] before another; [o]ne after another [their] rulers come [13] to destroy the e[arth.

And they make] their strength their god.

[14] Its interpretation [...al]l the peoples [(15–16)] [...]

The main part of God's reply to the prophet's lament consists of an announcement that he was raising up the Chaldeans to carry out his purposes (Hab. 1:6–11). The commentator applies the description of the Chaldeans to the Kittim, i.e. the Romans.

II.10*b*–(16*a*). Hab. 1:6*a* and interpretation. *the Kittim*: for the meaning of this term in the Old Testament and its use in the scrolls as a covert name for the Romans (cp. Num. 24:24; Dan. 11:30) see the comment on 4QpNah 3–4 1.3. The identification of the Chaldeans as the Kittim was perhaps based on the equation of 'Kittim' in Isa. 23:12 with 'the land of the Chaldeans' in Isa. 23:13 (see the RSV, where 'Kittim' is translated as 'Cyprus'). *quick and valiant in war*: the description of the Kittim as 'quick' reflects the 'impetuous' of the biblical text, while the description of them as 'valiant' apparently reflects knowledge of an addition to the text presupposed by some manuscripts of the Septuagint according to which the Chaldeans were 'warriors'. *and they will not believe*: the subject of this verb was probably not the Kittim, but wicked Jews or apostates (as in lines 1–10*a*). But the details are unclear because it is impossible to restore lines 13–14 with any degree of certainty.

II.(16*b*)–III.2*a*. Hab. 1:6*b* and interpretation. The interpretation follows the thought of the biblical text. *and through the plain they march*: based on 'They march through the wide tracts of the earth.'

III.2*b*–6*a*. Hab. 1:7 and interpretation. *their guile*: the meaning of the Hebrew word is uncertain. The NEB takes it as 'judgement', the RSV as 'dignity'. But it appears that the commentator understood the word quite differently and connected it with the verb 'to beguile, deceive'. The two parts of the interpretation reflect the thought of the two halves of the verse. *By intention*: or 'In counsel'.

6*b*–14*a*. Hab. 1:8, 9*a* and interpretation. The biblical text as given here differs in a number of significant respects from the Massoretic text. *than wolves of the plain*: or 'of the evening'. *From afar they fly*: the

Massoretic text has 'from afar they come flying'. The Commentary omits 'they come' in its quotation of the biblical text (cp. the Septuagint), but presupposes it in the interpretation (see lines 10b–11a). *hastening to devour all. They come intending violence*: this translation seems to be indicated by the interpretation (line 11), but the Hebrew could also be translated 'hastening to devour. They all come intending violence.' *their massed faces are (like) the east wind*: the translation is uncertain; 'the mutterings of their face are the east wind' is one of a number of other suggestions. The hot 'east wind' is mentioned because of its devastating power; cp. Ezek. 19:12; Hos. 13:15. *who trample…their cattle*: based on what is said in Hab. 1:8a about the horses and their prancing. *They come…not satisfied*: based on the thought and language of Hab. 1:8b. *from the coasts of the sea*: the coasts of Italy are probably meant. *And with fury…[the east wind*: derived from Hab. 1:9a. The sentence refers to the despotic treatment by the Romans of other nations.

14b–(17a). Hab. 1:9b and interpretation.

III.(17b)–IV.3a. Hab. 1:10a and interpretation. The interpretation refers to Roman contempt for their enemies and follows the thought and language of the biblical text.

IV.3b–9a. Hab. 1:10b and interpretation. *they are given*: the subject is 'the fortresses'. *because of the iniquity of those who dwell in them*: these words appear to offer a justification for Roman treatment of other nations, which is surprising in view of the generally unsympathetic picture given of them in this document. But perhaps the author was influenced here by the typical Old Testament view that defeat was the inevitable consequence of sin.

9b–13a. Hab. 1:11 and interpretation; Hab. 1:11b is repeated and given a separate interpretation (lines 13b–(16a)). The translation and explanation of Hab. 1:11 pose considerable problems. It should be noted that the text of this verse as given in the Commentary on Habakkuk differs in a significant respect from the Massoretic text. *Then the wind sweeps on and passes*: probable translation in the light of the interpretation. This apparently refers to the regular succession of the Roman governors, who were appointed by the Senate and sent out to the provinces in command of the armies. The verb 'to pass' is used in both text and interpretation. *and they make their strength their god*: the Massoretic text has 'guilty men, whose strength is their god' (cp. RSV; NEB understands the text differently), but this has sometimes been emended so that it corresponds more or less to the wording of the Commentary on Habakkuk. *[their] house of guilt*: probably the

Roman Senate. The occurrence of the word for 'guilt' is important because it shows that the commentator was familiar with the textual tradition preserved in the Massoretic text, even though he quotes the verse in a different form. *to destroy the e[arth*: perhaps inspired by an alternative understanding of 'and they make' of the biblical text, namely as if it were from the verb 'to ravage'.

13*b*–(16*a*). Hab. 1:11*b* and interpretation. Elsewhere in the Commentary (e.g. VI.2) the repetition of a piece of text with a view to a further piece of interpretation is introduced by the formula 'And when it says'.

THE JUDGEMENT OF ALL THE NATIONS AND MORE ABOUT THE KITTIM

IV.(16) [Are you not from of old, (17) O LORD, my God, my holy one? We shall not die. O LORD,] V.1 you appointed them to execute judgement; O rock, you established them as their reprover. Their eyes are too pure 2 to look upon evil; and you cannot countenance wrongdoing.

3 The interpretation of the passage is that God will not destroy his people by the hand of the nations, 4 but in the hand of his chosen ones God will place the judgement of all the nations. Through their reproof 5 all the wicked of his people will be found guilty – (the reproof of those) who have kept his commandments 6 in their distress, for this is what it says: Their eyes are too pure to look 7 upon evil.

Its interpretation is that they have not lusted after their eyes during the time 8 of wickedness.

Why do you look on, O traitors, and are silent when the wicked swallows up 9 one more righteous than he?

Its interpretation concerns the house of Absalom 10 and the men of their council who were silent at the reproof of the teacher of righteousness 11 and did not help him against the liar who rejected 12 the law in the midst of their whole con[gregation].

You make men like the fish of the sea, 13 like gliding creatures, to rule over them. They draw al[l of them] up [with hoo]ks, they drag them out with their nets, 14 they gather them in [their] tr[awl-nets. Therefore they sacrif]ice to their nets. Therefore they make merry [15] [and rejoice and burn incense to their trawl-nets; for by them] their portion is fat, [16] [and their food is rich.

Its interpretation... [(17)] ...] [VI.1] the Kittim, and they gather in their wealth together with all their spoil [2] 'like the fish of the sea'.

And when it says: Therefore they sacrifice to their nets [3] and burn incense to their trawl-nets.

Its interpretation is that they [4] sacrifice to their standards, and their weapons of war are [5] the objects of their reverence.

For by them their portion is fat, and their food is rich.

[6] Its interpretation is that they apportion their yoke and [7] their tribute – their food – on all the peoples year by year, [8] laying waste many lands.

Therefore they unsheathe the sword continually [9] to slaughter the nations, and they have no pity.

[10] Its interpretation concerns the Kittim who cause many to perish by the sword [11] – youths, grown men, the aged, women and children – and even for the fruit [12] of the womb they show no compassion.

Habakkuk is not satisfied by God's reply and renews his complaint (Hab. 1:12–17). Can the just God really have appointed the Chaldeans to maintain justice (verses 12–13)? Habakkuk accuses God of treating men as no better than fish (verse 14) and depicts the Chaldeans as dealing with other nations in the way that fishermen deal with fish (verses 15–17). The commentator interprets all of verses 14–17 with reference to the Kittim, but he takes verses 12–13 in a way quite different from their original meaning and interprets them to refer to the judgement exercised by the members of the community, and to the house of Absalom.

IV.(16b)–V.8a. Hab. 1:12–13a and interpretation. The translation of the biblical text reflects the understanding of the text presented in the interpretation, although the actual wording of the Commentary on Habakkuk differs in only minor respects from that of the Massoretic text. In the Massoretic text the complaint is made that God has appointed the Chaldeans – although not named, in the context it must be they who are meant – to maintain justice. Further, it is God whose 'eyes are too pure to look upon evil', who 'cannot countenance wrongdoing'. In the Commentary on Habakkuk, by contrast, the element of complaint is lacking (at least for verses 12–13a), and the

passage was understood to mean that God had appointed faithful
members of the community to maintain justice, specifically to execute
judgement on the nations (line 4*a*) and on the wicked in Israel (lines
4*b*–5*a*). Further, it is the faithful members of the community whose
'eyes are too pure to look upon evil' (lines 5*b*–8*a*). Only the clause
'and you cannot countenance wrongdoing', which is not interpreted,
is left referring to God. This section, like the following one (lines
8*b*–12*a*), is important for the principle of atomisation, that is the
principle by which in the biblical commentaries verses or parts of verses
can be interpreted in isolation rather than in relation to their biblical
context. *We shall not die*]: the original reading in the book of
Habakkuk was probably 'You shall not die'; see the footnote in the
NEB. But it is plausible to think that the Commentary on Habakkuk
read 'We shall not die' because the sentence 'God will not destroy his
people by the hand of the nations' (line 3) looks like an interpretation
of this reading. *but in the hand of his chosen ones...all the nations*: an
interpretation of 'O LORD, you appointed them to execute judgement.'
'His chosen ones' are the members of the community; see the comment
on 1QH II.13*b*–14*a*. The role of the community in the judgement of
the nations is described in the War Scroll. *Through their reproof...be
found guilty*: an interpretation of 'O rock, you established them as their
reprover.' *they have not lusted after their eyes*: cp. CD II.16; 1QS 1.6.
during the time of wickedness: see the comment on CD VI.10. Here 'the
time of wickedness' is the same as the time of 'distress' (line 6).

v.8*b*–12*a*. Hab. 1:13*b* and interpretation. *Why do you look on, O
traitors, and are silent*: in the Massoretic text both verbs are singular,
and it is God who looks silently on at the activities of the traitors. In
the Commentary on Habakkuk the first verb is plural, and the second
interpreted as such, and it is the traitors who look silently on. This
change in meaning reflects the understanding given to the passage in
the interpretation; for the principles involved see also the comment on
the preceding section. In the interpretation the 'traitors' are identified
as 'the house of Absalom', 'the wicked' as 'the liar', and the 'one more
righteous than he' as 'the teacher of righteousness'. *the house of Absalom
and the men of their council*: this could be a cryptic name for a
contemporary religious group, the name being suggested by the
treachery of Absalom; but if so, the real identity of this group is
unknown. Alternatively, Absalom could be the name of an actual
person, and the reference would then be to the family and supporters
of this man; in this case it is often assumed that Absalom is the person
mentioned in 1 Macc. 11:70; 13:11; 2 Macc. 11:17 as an important

figure in the early Hasmonean period. *who were silent at the reproof of the teacher of righteousness*: it is not clear whether the reproof was received or uttered by the teacher of righteousness. The former view is suggested by the wording of the biblical text ('when the wicked swallows up one more righteous than he'), and on this view we are to imagine that the teacher of righteousness was reproved by 'the liar'. The latter view would be the more natural one, if it were not for the context provided by the biblical text. On this view the passage refers to the silence of the house of Absalom on an occasion when the teacher of righteousness reproved either them or 'the liar', but it does not really offer an interpretation of 'when the wicked swallows up one more righteous than he'. *the liar*: see the comment on II.2.

v.12*b*–VI.2*a*. Hab. 1:14–16 and interpretation. Hab. 1:16*a* and 16*b* are repeated and given separate interpretations (VI.2*b*–5*a*, 5*b*–8*a*), and the material in v.16*b*–VI.2*a* will have formed an interpretation of verses 14–15 only. *to rule over them*: the Massoretic text has 'which have no ruler'. In the Massoretic text Hab. 1:14 continues the complaint addressed to God in verses 12–13: you, God, treat men as no better than fish which have no ruler to protect them. In the Commentary on Habakkuk the fact that the interpretation of Hab. 1:14 has been all but completely lost makes it difficult to know how 'to rule over them' was understood. If Hab. 1:14 was still understood as being addressed to God, then 'to rule over them' could refer to God's ruling over men. But it seems more natural to take the words as referring to the rule of the Chaldeans (i.e. the Kittim) over men. The thought would then be: you, God, treat men like fish in allowing the Chaldeans to rule men. It is also possible that Hab. 1:14 as a whole was understood as being addressed to the Chaldeans. Either explanation would provide a natural transition to verses 15–16, in which the Chaldeans are depicted as treating other nations in the way that fishermen deal with fish. In the interpretation the fishermen-imagery is applied to 'the Kittim', that is to the Romans. *Therefore they sacrif]ice to their nets. Therefore they make merry [and rejoice*: the end of verse 15 and the beginning of verse 16 were copied in the wrong order by mistake. The text of verse 16*a* is given correctly in VI.2*b*–3*a*. *and they gather in ...'like the fish of the sea'*: primarily an interpretation of Hab. 1:15*a*, although the final words come from verse 14. The reference is to the spoil accumulated by the Romans as a result of their wars.

VI.2*b*–5*a*. Hab. 1:16*a* and interpretation. The interpretation is commonly taken to refer to Roman worship of their military standards (*signa*). (Josephus (*War* VI.6.1(316)) records that when the Romans had captured the temple in AD 70, they 'carried their standards into the temple court and, setting them up opposite the eastern gate, there sacrificed to them'.)

5b–8a. Hab. 1:16b and interpretation. *their tribute*: or 'their forced labour'. But the interpretation is more naturally taken as referring to the oppressive annual imposition of tribute by the Romans on their subject peoples.

8b–12a. Hab. 1:17 and interpretation. *Therefore they unsheathe the sword*: the Massoretic text continues the imagery of verses 15–16 and has 'Are they then to empty the net?' ('Unsheathe' and 'empty' are the same word in Hebrew.) The reading 'sword' instead of 'net' (a difference of one letter in Hebrew) was probably the original reading in the book of Habakkuk and has been adopted by the NEB; it is also found in one manuscript of the Septuagint and in the Bohairic version (one of the Coptic versions of the Bible). The Massoretic text is in the form of a question, the climax of the complaint of Hab. 1:12–17, but the Commentary on Habakkuk, like the Septuagint, has a statement. The interpretation reflects the thought of the biblical text as it is given in the Commentary on Habakkuk and refers to the cruelty of the Romans. *and even for the fruit of the womb they show no compassion*: probably quoted from Isa. 13:18.

THE TRUE MEANING OF PROPHECY

VI.12 I will stand at my post 13 and will take my place on my watch-tower; I will watch to see what he will say 14 to me, and wh[at (answer) I will receive con]cerning my complaint. And the LORD answered me 15 [and said, Write down the vision, make it plai]n on tablets, that [the one who reads it] may run (with it).

16 [Its interpretation... (17) ...] VII.1 and God told Habakkuk to write down all the things that are to come on 2 the last generation, but the end of the time he did not make known to him.

3 And when it says: That the one who reads it may run (with it).

4 Its interpretation concerns the teacher of righteousness to whom God made known 5 all the mysteries of the words of his servants the prophets.

For the vision still (waits) 6 for the appointed time; it will testify of the end and will not fail.

7 Its interpretation is that the last time will be prolonged and will

go beyond all [8] that the prophets said; for the mysteries of God are a source of wonder.

[9] If it delays, wait for it; for it will surely come and will not [10] be late.

Its interpretation concerns the men of truth, [11] those who observe the law, whose hands do not slacken in the service [12] of truth when the last time is drawn out for them; for [13] all the times of God come according to their fixed rule, as he has decreed [14] for them in the mysteries of his discernment.

Behold, [his soul] is heedless, it is not upright [15] [within him].

Its interpretation is that they will double upon themselves [16] [...and] they will n[ot] be accepted when they are judged. [... (17) ...

But the righteous man will live by his faithfulness].

VIII.[1]Its interpretation concerns all those who observe the law in the house of Judah, whom [2] God will save from the house of judgement because of their suffering and their faithfulness [3] to the teacher of righteousness.

In the fourth section of Habakkuk (Hab. 2:1–4) the prophet goes to the watch-tower to await a reply from God (verse 1). The reply is given in verses 2–4, but verses 2–3 are instructions to Habakkuk, and the actual reply to his complaint only comes in verse 4. The commentator took the opportunity provided by Hab. 2:1–3 to discuss the true meaning of prophecy, and thus the character of his own work, and also to discuss the fulfilment of prophecy as it related to 'the last time'. The divine reply of Hab. 2:4 was interpreted to refer to the fates of the wicked and the righteous at the judgement.

VI.12b–VII.2. Hab. 2:1–2 and interpretation; Hab. 2:2b is repeated and given a separate interpretation (VII.3–5a). *and wh[at (answer) I will receive con]cerning my complaint*: the restoration follows the Massoretic text, and the translation (literally 'and what I will bring back concerning my complaint') gives the sense required by the context; but the Massoretic text has often been emended to 'and what he (i.e. God) will answer concerning my complaint'. The Massoretic text could be translated 'and what I will reply concerning the complaint made against me' (cp. RSV, NEB), but this does not fit the context. *the LORD*: here, as in some other places in the commentaries (e.g. 4QpPs[a] 1–10 II.4), the name 'Yahweh' (rendered in the RSV and NEB as 'the LORD') was, out of reverence, written in the Old Hebrew script instead of the familiar square characters that are used for most of the scrolls; see the comment on 1QS VIII.12b–14. *make it plai]n on tablets*: the restoration follows the Massoretic text, but the interpretation (VII.2) indicates that the vision was not 'made plain'. Perhaps there was a play on words between Hebrew *bāʾēr* ('make plain') and *bāʿēr*; the latter could mean 'make empty' or, understood differently, be linked with the verb 'to be stupid'. *that [the one who reads it] may run (with it)*: for the restoration of the text see VII.3. The Hebrew verb *qārāʾ* can mean both 'to call' and 'to read', and in the book of Habakkuk the clause is better translated 'that the one who calls it out (i.e. the herald) may run (with it)'; the thought is apparently of a herald carrying the divine reply received by Habakkuk. The interpretation of the clause in the Commentary on Habakkuk is concerned with the meaning of prophecy (VII.4–5a), and this suggests that 'the one who reads it' is more appropriate here. [*Its interpretation*...]: the bottom of column VI will have contained whatever interpretation there was of Hab. 2:1. The first two lines of column VII are an interpretation of 'Write down the vision, make it plain on tablets' (Hab. 2:2a). *and God told Habakkuk...did not make known to him*: this passage casts an important light on the author's views about the nature of prophetic inspiration and the character of his own work; no doubt what is said here also applies to the other Qumran commentaries (for those on the prophets cp. lines 4–5a). According to this passage Habakkuk wrote under divine inspiration, and his words referred to 'the last generation', but the revelation to Habakkuk was only partial. In lines 4–5a we are further told that the words of the prophets were 'mysteries' (Hebrew *rāzîm*), and that their true meaning was only made known through the divine revelation given to the teacher of righteousness. In a somewhat similar way Nebuchadnezzar's dream was a 'mystery' (NEB, 'secret'), whose meaning was revealed to Daniel by God (Dan. 2:18–19), 'the revealer of mysteries' (Dan. 2:28–9, 47). *the end of the time*: by 'the time' is meant 'the last time', the same as 'the last generation'.

VII.3–5a. Hab. 2:2b and interpretation. *That the one who reads it may run (with it)*: from the interpretation it appears that the verb 'to run' was taken as 'to explain, interpret', but it is not quite clear how this was done. One suggestion is that the verb 'to run' (*rûṣ*) was linked to the verb 'to crash, shatter' (*rāṣaṣ*), and that this latter verb was understood in a transferred sense as 'to interpret'. Support for this explanation is provided, at least by analogy, by a rabbinic tradition. Another possibility is that there was a play on words with the Aramaic verb *t^eraṣ*, which can mean 'to explain'. It is perhaps significant that the word for 'may run' was omitted by the original copyist and only later added by a different person; without the verb the translation is 'for the sake of the one who reads it', that is for the sake of the teacher of righteousness. *the teacher of righteousness to whom God made known all the mysteries*: this does not necessarily mean that the teacher was the author of the commentaries, but rather that the interpretative tradition reflected in them stems from the teacher. For the role of the teacher as the interpreter of prophecy see also II.7–10a.

5b–8. Hab. 2:3a and interpretation. *For the vision still (waits) for the appointed time*: in the book of Habakkuk the concern is apparently about the delay in the reception of the prophetic vision, and the words are an assurance that an answer will eventually be given. In the Commentary on Habakkuk the concern is rather about the delay in the fulfilment of the prophetic vision, i.e., as it becomes in the interpretation, about the prolongation of 'the last time'. *it will testify of*: or 'it will hasten to'. *the last time*: probably the age in which the author and his contemporaries were living, the same as 'the time of wickedness' (v.7b–8a) and 'the last generation' (VII.2). Both this and the following section (lines 9–14a) are apparently concerned with the problem that the new age had not dawned, and 'the last time' seemed to be prolonged indefinitely. However, some scholars think that 'the last time' is a term for the new age itself.

9–14a. Hab. 2:3b and interpretation. The two parts of the interpretation correspond, and are related in thought, to the two parts of the biblical text. The interpretation continues the theme of lines 5b–8 and offers encouragement and assurance to those who might be discouraged by the prolongation of 'the last time' and the delay in the dawning of the new age. *the men of truth, those who observe the law*: the members of the community; for 'those who observe the law' cp. VIII.1; XII.4b–5a; 4QpPs^a 1–10 II.15, 23.

14b–(17a). Hab. 2:4a and interpretation. The two parts of God's reply to Habakkuk's complaint (Hab. 2:4a and 4b) are made the basis of contrasting statements about the fate of the wicked and of the righteous at the judgement. These statements follow naturally on the preceding pieces of the interpretation, which have been concerned with 'the last time'. *Behold, [his soul]...[within him]*: the scroll apparently followed the Massoretic text, but the translation and meaning are obscure. *Its interpretation is that they will double upon themselves*: the subject, whether it was expressed or implied, was 'the wicked', and the object something like 'their guilt'. The idea of 'doubling' was

perhaps derived from the biblical text on the basis of a pun. *and] they
will n[ot] be accepted when they are judged*: there is a link with the reading
of the Septuagint, which differs considerably from the Massoretic text.
The Septuagint speaks of God not being 'pleased with' the man who
shrinks back (cp. Heb. 10:38), and may even presuppose the Hebrew
verb here translated 'accept' (*rāṣāh*).

VII.(17*b*)–VIII.3*a*. Hab. 2:4*b* and interpretation. *all those who observe
the law in the house of Judah*: i.e. the members of the community; for
'the house of Judah' cp. CD IV.11. *the house of judgement*: the place
where the final judgement will take place, but here almost meaning
the judgement itself. The thought of the interpretation derives from
that of the biblical text, and 'faithfulness' is common to both; cp. the
use of Hab. 2:4*b* in Rom. 1:17; Gal. 3:11; Heb. 10:37–8.

THE FIVE WOES

The last section of Habakkuk dealt with in the Commentary (2:5–20)
consists of a series of five woes. (There is some dispute as to whether
Hab. 2:5 forms the end of the previous section or the start of the present
section, but in the Commentary it is clearly taken with the series of
woes.) In the context of the book of Habakkuk the woes were no doubt
meant to refer to the Chaldeans, perhaps specifically as represented by
their king, but in the Commentary they are for the most part referred
to 'the wicked priest'. This individual, who from what is said about
him was fairly obviously the high priest, is mentioned in other
commentaries (4QpPs[a] 1–10 IV.8; 4QpIsa[c] 30 3), but not in other
Qumran writings. Reference is also made in the Commentary to 'the
priest' (VIII.16; IX.16; XI.12), to 'the last priests of Jerusalem' (IX.4),
and to 'the preacher of lies' (X.9). It is often assumed that 'the priest'
is the same person as 'the wicked priest', but it is not certain that this
is so. It seems virtually certain that 'the preacher of lies' (who is
mentioned in other Qumran writings; see above, pp. 23–4) is a quite
different person from 'the wicked priest' and 'the priest', because quite
different things are said about him than are said about the other two.
Apart from the references to these individuals, the Commentary
interprets Hab. 2:18–20 with reference to the idolatry of the nations,
no doubt thinking particularly of the Kittim.

Scholars have employed much ingenuity in trying to identify 'the
wicked priest' from the references to him in the Habakkuk
Commentary in the hope thereby of casting light on the early history
of the Qumran community. One dominant view that has emerged is

that 'the wicked priest' was either Jonathan (high priest from 152 to 143) or Simon (high priest from 143 to 134), and the view followed in this work is that 'the wicked priest' was Jonathan (see above, pp. 6–10). But it has to be recognised that the Habakkuk Commentary itself provides only limited support for this view, which depends on a number of different considerations. The content of the pieces of interpretation was strongly influenced by the underlying biblical text, not by the real nature of the characters and events to which reference is made. Further, the language used in the pieces of interpretation is frequently opaque (rather like Dan. 11), and the things that are said could have been applied to almost any one of the Hasmonaean high priests.

It has recently been suggested that this section of the Habakkuk Commentary is concerned not just with one wicked priest, but with a succession of wicked high priests, who are described in chronological order: Judas (VIII.3*b*–13*a*; according to one tradition in Josephus (*Ant.* XII.10.6(414)) the people gave the high priesthood to Judas, but see above, p. 10); Alcimus (VIII.13*b*–IX.2*a*); the last priests of Jerusalem, understood as the Hasmonaeans (IX.2*b*–7); Jonathan (IX.8–12*a*); Simon (IX.12*b*–X.5*a*); (the preacher of lies, not part of the series of wicked priests, X.5*b*–XI.2*a*); John Hyrcanus (XI.2*b*–8*a*); Alexander Jannaeus, in the last years of whose reign (103–76 BC) the Commentary is held to have been written (XI.8*b*–XII.10*a*). This is an attractive view, and it deserves serious consideration. Apart from anything else it serves to emphasise that it is by no means clear that this section of the Habakkuk Commentary is concerned with just one individual. As an alternative view it may be suggested that the things said about 'the wicked priest' do all refer to the same high priest, namely Jonathan, but that the sections dealing with 'the priest' (VIII.13*b*–IX.2*a*; IX.12*b*–X.5*a*; XI.8*b*–(17*a*)) are concerned with another person, a contemporary of the author, who is to be identified with Alexander Jannaeus. A date for the composition of the Habakkuk Commentary in the last years of the reign of Alexander Jannaeus would make good sense of the material.

For convenience the material is treated in two sections here: VIII.3*b*–X.5*a*; X.5*b*–XIII.4.

THE WICKED PRIEST

VIII.3 Moreover, wealth causes the arrogant man to be a traitor, and he will not 4 remain; he opens his throat wide like Sheol, and like death he is never satisfied. 5 All the nations are gathered to him, and all the peoples are assembled to him. ⁶ Will not all of them take up a taunt against him and interpreters of riddles (utter riddles) about him, ⁷ and say: 'Woe to the one who heaps up what is not his own! How long will he load himself up ⁸ with goods taken in pledge?'

Its interpretation concerns the wicked priest who ⁹ was called by the name of truth when he first appeared. But when he ruled ¹⁰ over Israel, his heart became presumptuous, and he forsook God and betrayed the statutes for the sake of ¹¹ wealth. He stole and amassed the wealth of the men of violence who rebelled against God, ¹² and he took the wealth of the peoples, heaping on himself guilty iniquity. And he followed abominable ways ¹³ amid every kind of unclean impurity.

Will not your cre[dit]ors suddenly arise, ¹⁴ and will not those who make you tremble awake, and will you not become their prey? ¹⁵ For you have plundered many nations, but all the rest of the peoples will plunder you.

¹⁶ The in[terpretation of the passage con]cerns the priest who rebelled ¹⁷ [and transgr]essed the statutes [of God...in order to] ᴵˣ·¹ chastise him by means of the judgements of wickedness. And they inflicted horrors of evil diseases ² upon him and acts of vengeance upon his body of flesh.

And when ³ it says: For you have plundered many nations, but all the rest of the peoples will plunder you.

⁴ Its interpretation concerns the last priests of Jerusalem ⁵ who amass wealth and ill-gotten gain by plundering the peoples. ⁶ But at the end of days their wealth and their plunder will be given into the hand ⁷ of the army of the Kittim, for they are 'the rest of the peoples'.

⁸ Because of human bloodshed and violence done to the land, to the city, and to all who dwell in it.

⁹ Its interpretation concerns the wicked priest whom, because of the iniquity committed against the teacher ¹⁰ of righteousness and the men of his council, God gave into the hand of his enemies that they might humble him ¹¹ with a destroying blow, in bitterness of soul, because he had acted wickedly ¹² against his chosen ones.

Woe to the one who gets evil gain for his house, to set ¹³ his nest on high, to be safe from the reach of evil! You have planned shame [14] for your house, the borders of many peoples, and you forf[eit] your [lif]e. For [15] the st[one] will cry out [from] the wall, [and] the beam from the woodwork will an[swer].

[16] [The interpretation of the passa]ge concerns the p[riest] who [...[(17)]...] [X.1] so that its stones lay amidst extortion and the beam of its woodwork amidst robbery.

And when [2] it says: The borders of many peoples, and you forfeit your life.

[3] Its interpretation: This is the house of judgement. God will give [4] his judgement in the midst of many peoples, and from there he will bring him up for judgement; [5] he will declare him guilty in their midst and will punish him with fire of brimstone.

VIII.3*b*–13*a*. Hab. 2:5–6 and interpretation. *Moreover, wealth causes the arrogant man to be a traitor, and he will not remain*: the text of Hab. 2:5–6 in the Commentary on Habakkuk differs in several respects from the Massoretic text, perhaps most significantly in the reading 'wealth' (*hôn*) instead of 'wine' (*hayyayin*); cp. RSV, 'Moreover, wine is treacherous; the arrogant man shall not abide.' But the meaning of Hab. 2:5*a* is obscure, and the text has often been emended, as for instance in the NEB. 'Wealth' is a key-word in the interpretation. *and he will not remain*: the translation is uncertain, but appears to be supported by 'forsook' (line 10) in the interpretation. Another possibility is 'and he will not succeed'. *the wicked priest...for the sake of wealth*: an interpretation of 'Moreover, wealth...is never satisfied', based on the identification of 'the arrogant man' as 'the wicked priest'. 'Wealth' and the theme of betrayal are common to text and interpretation, 'his heart became presumptuous' is perhaps based on 'arrogant', and 'he forsook God' perhaps goes back to 'he will not remain'. It is assumed here that 'the wicked priest' was Jonathan, and that the two stages in his career, the former approved, the latter not, are the period from approximately 166 down to 152 BC, when Jonathan began by playing a leading part in the Maccabean revolt and then in 160 became the leader of the nationalist forces opposed to the Hellenisers and the Seleucids (cp. 1 Macc. 9:28–31), and the period from 152 BC, when Jonathan assumed the office of high priest (cp. 1 Macc. 10:18–21), although he did not belong to the legitimate high-priestly family. *called by the name of truth when he first appeared*: 'to be called by the name of' means 'to be reckoned to' (Gen. 48:6).

Initially the community felt able to regard the wicked priest as an adherent of the truth, i.e. as being in some way associated with its aims (cp. VII.10*b*–12*a*). This could have been said of Jonathan during the Maccabean revolt, but less and less so after 160 when, as leader, he assumed increasing power and pursued a policy of political independence for the Jews. The assumption by him of the office of high priest in 152 would have been anathema to the members of the community; it marked the final break between the community and the wicked priest. *He stole . . . the wealth of the men of violence who rebelled against God*: an interpretation of 'All the nations are gathered to him', in which 'the nations' (*gôyîm*) are identified as apostate Jews, i.e. Hellenisers. For Jonathan's treatment of the Hellenisers see 1 Macc. 9:73 (here called 'the godless'), and for the theft of their property see 1 Macc. 6:24 (although this relates to Judas). *and he took the wealth of the peoples*: an interpretation of 'and all the peoples are assembled to him'. For the spoil obtained by Jonathan in the course of his wars see 1 Macc. 10:87; 11:51; 12:31. *heaping on himself guilty iniquity*: based on 'Woe to the one who heaps up what is not his own!', but 'heaping' and 'heaps up' are from two different verbs in the Hebrew. *And he followed . . . unclean impurity*: based on 'How long . . . goods taken in pledge?'. The word for 'goods taken in pledge' (*'abṭîṭ*) was apparently understood as 'cloud of mud' (*'āb ṭîṭ*), as in some Hebrew manuscripts of the Old Testament and as it was translated in the Syriac version.

VIII.13*b*–IX.2*a*. Hab. 2:7–8*a* and interpretation; Hab. 2:8*a* is repeated and given a separate interpretation (IX.2*b*–7), and the material in this section is only an interpretation of Hab. 2:7. *your cre[dit]ors*: or 'your de[bt]ors', but the interpretation presupposes the idea of 'those who exact payment from you'. *The in[terpretation of the passage con]cerns the priest who rebelled*: it is not certain that 'the priest who rebelled' is the same as 'the wicked priest', although it is often assumed that this is so. What is said about the illness of this priest (IX.1–2*a*) does not fit what is known of Jonathan, but would fit Alcimus (see 1 Macc. 9:54–6) or Alexander Jannaeus (see Josephus, *Ant.* XIII.15.5(398)). *. . . in order to] chastise him by means of the judgements of wickedness. And they inflicted horrors of evil diseases upon him*: the translation is uncertain because of the loss of the foot of column VIII, but the 'they' are probably 'destroying angels', who in CD II.6 and 1QS IV.12 are responsible for the infliction of chastisements on the wicked. The idea of illness was perhaps derived from the text by taking the word for 'awake' to be from a different verb with the meaning 'make (you) feel sick'. *his* *body of flesh*: same expression in 4QpNah 3–4 II.6, there translated 'their dead flesh' ('the corpses of their flesh').

IX.2*b*–7. Hab. 2:8*a* and interpretation. *the last priests of Jerusalem*: the high priests contemporary with the author, probably the later members of the Hasmonaean dynasty. That at least Alexander Jannaeus was included under this designation is suggested by the fact that 4QpHos^b 2 2–3 apparently identifies 'the furious young lion' (i.e. Alexander Jannaeus; see above, p. 212) as 'the last priest'. For the wealth acquired by the Hasmonaeans see also 4QpNah 3–4 I.11. *at the end of days*: the fact that the confiscation of the wealth by the Kittim still lies in the future suggests that the Commentary was composed in the last decades before the direct intervention of the Romans in Jewish affairs in the time of Hyrcanus II and Aristobulus II.

8–12*a*. Hab. 2:8*b* and interpretation. *because of the iniquity committed against the teacher of righteousness and the men of his council*: for attacks on the teacher and the community by the wicked priest see also XI.4–8*a*; XII.2–6*a*, 7*b*–10*a*; and particularly 4QpPs^a IV.8–10*a*. *God gave...bitterness of soul*: the description fits the identification of the wicked priest as Jonathan, who was captured by Trypho through a trick and subsequently murdered (1 Macc. 12:39–48; 13:23). *his chosen ones*: see the comment on 1QH II.13*b*–14*a*.

IX.12*b*–X.1*a*. Hab. 2:9–11 and interpretation; Hab. 2:10*b* is repeated and given a separate interpretation (X.1*b*–5*a*). *the borders of many peoples*: this translation appears to be supported by the interpretation (X.4), the sense being 'within the borders of many peoples'. The text of the Habakkuk Commentary differs here (although not in X.2) from the consonantal form of the Massoretic text; the latter is obscure, but is often understood as 'by cutting off many peoples' (cp. RSV). *and you forf[eit] your [lif]e*: probable translation. The text in X.2 (less certainly here) differs in one respect from the Massoretic text and has sometimes been translated 'and the cords (or 'threads') of your life'; but it is not quite clear that such a translation can be related to the interpretation. *the p[riest] who*: it is again not clear whether this 'priest' is the same as 'the wicked priest'. *so that its stones lay amidst extortion and the beam of its woodwork amidst robbery*: 'lay amidst' is literally 'were in'. This piece of interpretation draws on elements in Hab. 2:9*a*, 11. The lost antecedent of 'its' was probably a word like 'city', of which the 'stones' and the 'beam' are poetic representations. It is often assumed that this passage refers to some form of building activity on the part of 'the priest', but it is not at all clear from what survives of the interpretation that this is so.

x.1*b*–5*a*. Hab. 2:10*b* and interpretation. *the house of judgement*: the scene of the final judgement (cp. VIII.2). The following passage appears to refer to judgement in two stages, judgement of 'the priest' at the end of his life, and the eschatological judgement. *God will give his judgement in the midst of many peoples*: the 'his' appears to refer back to 'the priest' (IX.16), while 'in the midst of many peoples' (an interpretation of 'the borders of many peoples') suggests that the priest met/was to meet his death outside the territory of Judah. It is not clear from the use of the imperfect tense whether the priest had, or had not, yet died. *and from there*: from judgement 'in the midst of many peoples'. *he will bring him up for judgement; he will declare him guilty in their midst*: the eschatological judgement; 'declare him guilty' is an interpretation of 'and you forfeit your life'. *and will punish him with fire of brimstone*: for burning as the form of punishment cp. Matt. 5:22; 18:9; 1 En. 10:6, 13; 90:26–7.

THE PREACHER OF LIES AND MORE ABOUT THE WICKED PRIEST

x.5 Woe to 6 the one who builds a city with bloodshed and founds a town on injustice! Are not 7 these things from the LORD of hosts? Peoples toil only for fire, 8 and nations weary themselves for nothing.

9 The interpretation of the passage concerns the preacher of lies who led astray many 10 that he might build a city of vanity with bloodshed and establish a congregation on falsehood. 11 For the sake of its glory he made many toil in the service of vanity and sated them 12 with w[or]ks of falsehood, so that their labour was for nothing, that they might come 13 to the judgements of fire because they reviled and taunted the chosen ones of God.

14 For the earth will be full with the knowledge of the glory of the LORD as the waters 15 cover the sea.

The interpretation of the passage [is that] 16 when they return [...(17)...the preacher] XI.1 of lies. And afterwards knowledge will be revealed to them in abundance, like the waters 2 of the sea.

Woe to the one who makes his companions drink the outpouring 3 of his fury, making (them) drunk, that he might gaze at their feasts!

4 Its interpretation concerns the wicked priest who 5 pursued the

teacher of righteousness to his place of exile that he might confuse him in his furious anger. 6 And at the time of the feast, the rest 7 of the day of atonement, he appeared to them to confuse them 8 and to make them stumble on the day of fasting, their sabbath of rest.

You have sated yourself 9 with dishonour rather than with glory. Drink then, and stagger! 10 The cup of the LORD's right hand will come round to you, and shame (will come) 11 upon your glory.

12 Its interpretation concerns the priest whose dishonour was greater than his glory, 13 for he did not circumcise the foreskin of his heart, but walked in the ways 14 of drunkenness that his thirst might be quenched. But the cup of the wrath 15 of [Go]d will confuse him, increasing [...] and the pain 16 [...(17)...

For the violence done to Lebanon will overwhelm you, and the havoc done to the beasts] xii.1 will terrify you, because of human bloodshed and violence done to the land, to the city, and to all who dwell in it.

2 The interpretation of the passage concerns the wicked priest – to pay him 3 the reward with which he rewarded the poor. For 'Lebanon' is 4 the council of the community, and 'the beasts' are the simple of Judah who observe 5 the law. God will condemn him to destruction 6 because he plotted to destroy the poor.

And when it says: Because of the blood 7 of the city and the violence done to the land.

Its interpretation: 'The city' is Jerusalem 8 where the wicked priest committed abominable deeds and made the sanctuary of God unclean. 9 'And the violence done to the land' means the cities of Judah, where 10 he stole the wealth of the poor.

What use is an idol when its maker has shaped it, 11 a molten image, a fatling of falsehood? For the maker puts his trust in the things he has made 12 when he makes dumb idols.

The interpretation of the passage concerns all 13 the idols of the nations which they make so that they may serve them and worship 14 them. But they will not save them on the day of judgement.

Woe, 15 w[oe to the one who says] to wood, 'Wake up', to dumb [sto]ne, 'B[estir yourself'!] 16 [Can such a thing teach? Behold, it is encased in gold and silver and has no (17) breath in it. But the LORD is in his holy temple;] xiii.1 let all the earth be silent before him.

Its interpretation concerns all the nations 2 who serve stone and wood. On the day 3 of judgement God will destroy all those who serve idols 4 and the wicked from the earth.

x.5*b*–13. Hab. 2:12–13 and interpretation. *Peoples toil only for fire*: or 'for a pittance' (so NEB), but the interpretation (line 13) indicates that the word was understood as 'fire'. *the preacher of lies*: for references to this individual – elsewhere called 'the liar' or 'the scoffer' – see above, pp. 23–4. He is not to be identified with 'the wicked priest', but – as stated in the comment on ii.1*b*–2*a* – was the leader of a group which broke away from the community at an early stage in its history. *that he might build a city of vanity with bloodshed and establish a congregation on falsehood*: these words refer to the setting-up of the break-away group under the leadership of 'the preacher of lies'. The expression 'build a city' has been taken from the biblical text, and it is unlikely that it is to be understood literally – as the parallel 'establish a congregation' indicates; cp. the use of 'build' in a metaphorical sense in 4QpPs^a 1–10 iii.16. For the congregation of 'the preacher of lies' cp. CD viii.13 = xix.25*b*–26*a*. *with bloodshed*: this expression is likewise taken from the biblical text, and it is not clear whether, or to what extent, it should be taken literally. *that they might come to the judgements of fire*: for punishment by burning following the eschatological judgements see the comment on line 5*a*. *the chosen ones of God*: see the comment on 1QH ii.13*b*–14*a*.

x.14–xi.2*a*. Hab. 2:14 and interpretation. *when they return*: or 'when they turn aside'. This section was apparently concerned with the same group as the previous one, but the loss of the bottom of the column makes it difficult to determine the thrust of the passage.

xi.2*b*–8*a*. Hab. 2:15 and interpretation. *their feasts*: the Massoretic text has 'their nakedness' (NEB, 'their naked orgies'), only a slight difference in the Hebrew. The reading of the Commentary on Habakkuk was chosen with the interpretation (see line 6) in mind. *his place of exile*: probably the settlement at Qumran. *confuse him in his furious anger*: based on 'makes his companions drink the outpouring of his fury, making (them) drunk'. The word for 'confuse', both here and in line 7, could also be translated 'swallow up', but the parallel in line 8 ('make stumble') makes this less likely. *And at the time of the feast, the rest of the day of atonement, he appeared to them to confuse them* *and to make them stumble*: the 'he' is the wicked priest and the 'them' the teacher of righteousness and his supporters. It is not clear what happened on the occasion of this clash between the wicked priest and the teacher of righteousness, but this passage is important because it provides further evidence that the community followed a calendar different from the one observed in Jerusalem. It is commonly assumed that the wicked priest was the high priest in office at the time, and as such he would have had to have officiated in the temple on the day of atonement (see Lev. 16). Only on the assumption that this passage refers to the day of atonement according to the calendar followed by the community is it possible to explain the absence of the wicked priest (the high priest) from Jerusalem. Perhaps the wicked priest was attempting to dissuade the teacher of righteousness and his followers from continuing to observe the law (of which the calendar forms an important part) according to their own particular interpretation. On the calendar see also above, p. 34. *and to make them stumble*: perhaps derived from the biblical text by taking the word for 'their feasts' in a secondary sense as if it were from the verb *mā'ad*, 'to slip, totter'. *on the day of fasting, their sabbath of rest*: for the description of the day of atonement as a 'sabbath of rest' cp. Lev. 23:32.

8*b*–(17*a*). Hab. 2:16 and interpretation. *and stagger*: the Massoretic text has 'and be uncircumcised', perhaps 'and show yourself to be uncircumcised'. The reading of the Habakkuk Commentary is supported by the Septuagint and other versions, and the Massoretic text has often been emended to conform to this (in the Hebrew the difference between the two readings is slight). On the other hand it is clear from line 13 that the author was familiar with the Massoretic reading; cp. the comment on iv.11. *the priest whose dishonour was greater than his glory*: it is not clear whether this 'priest' is identical with 'the wicked priest', although again it is often assumed that this is so; cp. viii.16; ix.16. The interpretation derives directly from the biblical text. *for he did not circumcise...might be quenched*: based on 'Drink then, and stagger'; the theme of drunkenness comes from the biblical text, and the word for 'and stagger' was understood as if it were 'and be uncircumcised', as in the Massoretic text. The reference to drunkenness has been used as evidence that the wicked priest was Simon, who was killed while in a drunken stupor (1 Macc. 16:11–16), and as evidence that he was Alexander Jannaeus, who died after a three-year illness contracted as a result of excessive drinking (Josephus, *Ant.* xiii.15.5(398)). *for he did not circumcise...his heart*: cp. 1QS v.5; Deut. 10:16; Jer. 4:4. *but walked...be quenched*: perhaps an allusion to Deut.

29:19, also used in 1QS II.12b–14a. *But the cup of the wrath of [Go]d*: the cup is a symbol of judgement, as in Habakkuk itself; see the comment on 4QpNah 3–4 IV.4b–6a. *will confuse him*: or 'will swallow him up'. The punishment of this 'priest' appears to lie in the future, and this suggests that he was still alive when the Habbakuk Commentary was composed. The assumption that this section refers to Alexander Jannaeus and dates from shortly before his death in 76 BC would fit in with the view (see above, p. 240) that the Commentary dates from the last decades before the time of Hyrcanus II and Aristobulus II.

XI.(17b)–XII.6a. Hab. 2:17 and interpretation; part of Hab. 2:17b is repeated and given a separate interpretation (XII.6b–10a). *will terrify you*: or 'will sweep you away'; in either case the translation presupposes a minor correction of the Hebrew. *the wicked priest – to pay him the reward with which he rewarded the poor*: the interpretation follows the thought of the biblical passage, namely that the tyrant will suffer the same fate as his victims. For 'the poor' as a term for the members of the community see the comment on 1QH II.32b–33a. *For 'Lebanon' is the council of the community*: in ancient Jewish tradition (e.g. in the Targum of Jonathan on this passage) 'Lebanon' symbolised the temple, but the community also believed that 'the council of the community' constituted the true (spiritual) temple (see 1QS VIII.4b–10a; IX.3–6). It was this understanding which made possible the equation of 'Lebanon' with 'the council of the community'. The latter term is used frequently in the Community Rule for the whole body of members. *the simple of Judah*: like 'the poor', a term for the members of the community; cp. 1QH II.9. *who observe the law*: see the comment on VII.9–14a. *God will condemn him to destruction*: the fact that a future judgement is spoken of is probably to be explained by the assumption that the reference is to the eschatological 'day of judgement', mentioned below in XII.14; XIII.2b–3a; see the comment on X.1b–5a.

XII.6b–10a. An abbreviated version of Hab. 2:17b and interpretation. The biblical text has been reworked to provide the author with the specific elements on which he wished to comment. *'The city' is Jerusalem*: the same identification is made in the Targum on this passage. *the wicked priest*: it may or may not be significant that 'wicked' was only inserted as a correction. *committed abominable deeds and made the sanctuary of God unclean*: the link between the text ('the blood of the city') and the interpretation probably lies in the first instance in the idea that the shedding of blood 'defiles the land' (Num. 35:33); the themes of bloodshed and defilement are closely linked in Ezek. 22:1–12, and in Ezek. 22:2 the prophet is told to declare to the bloody

city 'all her abominable deeds'. But there is probably also a reference
to menstrual blood, and to the idea of the uncleanness that could be
conveyed to the temple by a person who had intercourse with a woman
regarded as being still ritually unclean after menstruation; cp. Lev.
15:19–24, 31, and the accusations made in CD v.6*b*–7*a*; Ps. Sol. 8:13.
the cities of Judah, where he stole the wealth of the poor: the reference is
probably to the members of the wider Essene movement who lived
in the towns and villages of Palestine; see above, p. 15. It is not clear
whether we should think literally of theft or of excessive taxation.
Accusations of the kind made in this section (murder, defiling the
temple, robbery) were no doubt the kind of things that were said about
all the Hasmonaean high priests; they provide little hard evidence by
which to identify the wicked priest.

10*b*–14*a*. Hab. 2:18 and interpretation. *a fatling*: the Massoretic text
has 'a teacher', and this is perhaps what is intended by the scroll. But
the word is spelt differently, and its meaning is uncertain. If 'a fatling'
(i.e. an animal for sacrifice) is right, the previous word should perhaps
be understood as 'a libation', not as 'a molten image'. The last two
pieces of interpretation are both concerned with the idolatry of the
nations (not of Jews), a theme obviously indicated by Hab. 2:18–19;
these sections are probably directed specifically at the Kittim.

xii.14*b*–xiii.4. Hab. 2:19–20 and interpretation. *On the day of
judgement*: the theme of judgement was suggested by Hab. 2:20. *God
will destroy all those who serve idols and the wicked from the earth*: the
judgement affects first of all the idolaters of the nations, including no
doubt the Kittim. But by 'the wicked' are probably meant wicked
Jews and the wicked priest.

The bottom half of column xiii was left blank, and Hab.
3 was not included in the work.

The Commentary on Psalms

Fragments of two commentaries on psalms were found in Cave 4, and fragments of another psalm commentary in Cave 1, but of these it is the commentary referred to as 4QpPs^a that is the most important. Thirteen fragments of this work exist, ten of which together form the remains of four columns of text (4QpPs^a 1–10 I–IV). Only column II is relatively well preserved; little has survived of column I, and columns III and IV are seriously damaged. The material that has survived provides a commentary on Ps. 37 followed (in column IV) by the beginning of a commentary on Ps. 45; in addition fragment 13 treats Ps. 60:6–7. From this it appears that 4QpPs^a was a commentary on a selection of psalms; it should be noted that it is doubtful whether column I was actually the first column of the manuscript. The material presented here consists only of what can be read or restored with a reasonable degree of confidence. There is no break in thought, but for convenience the material is divided into two sections: I.25–II.26a, covering Ps. 37:7–17; II.26b–IV.12, covering Ps. 37:18–34. The manuscript dates from the period bridging the end of the first century BC and the beginning of the first century AD (approximately 30 BC–AD 20), but the work itself may be a little older than this.

Ps. 37 is an acrostic poem which belongs among the wisdom psalms. It consists of a series of contrasting sayings which describe the character and fate of the righteous and the wicked, and as such it provided ideal material for the commentator. Thus the psalm is interpreted with reference to the community and its opponents, sometimes more specifically with reference to the clash between the teacher of righteousness and the liar or between the teacher and the wicked priest. The content of the pieces of interpretation has a marked eschatological thrust.

Bibliography

J. M. Allegro, *Qumrân Cave 4, I (4Q158–4Q186)* (Discoveries in the Judaean Desert of Jordan, 5), Oxford, 1968, 42–50 and plates XIV–XVII (see on this J. Strugnell, 'Notes en marge du volume v des "Discoveries in the Judaean Desert of Jordan"', *Revue de Qumrân* 7 (1969/71), 211–18).

M. P. Horgan, *Pesharim: Qumran Interpretations of Biblical Books* (The Catholic Biblical Quarterly Monograph Series, 8), Washington, DC, 1979, 192–226.

D. Pardee, 'A Restudy of the Commentary on Psalm 37 from Qumran Cave 4', *Revue de Qumrân* 8 (1973), 163–94.

THE COMMUNITY AND ITS ENEMIES

^{I.25} [Be silen]t before [the LORD, and] wait patiently for him; do not be angry over the one who makes his way prosperous, over the man ²⁶ [who carries] out evil schemes.

Its [interpretation] concerns the liar who led many astray with false words, ²⁷ for they chose worthless things and did not lis[ten] to the interpreter of knowledge, so that ^{II.1} they will perish by the sword, by famine, and by pestilence.

Refrain from anger, and forsake fury. Do not ² get excited merely to do evil; for those who do evil will be cut off.

Its interpretation concerns all those who return ³ to the law, who do not refuse to turn back from their evil; for all those who rebel against ⁴ turning back from their iniquity will be cut off.

But those who wait for the LORD will possess the land.

Its interpretation: ⁵ They are the congregation of his chosen ones who do his will.

A little while, and the wicked will be no more; ⁶ (line 6 left blank) ⁷ when I look towards his place, he will not be there.

Its interpretation concerns all the wicked at the end ⁸ of forty years; they will be consumed, and no [wi]cked man will be found on the earth.

⁹ But the humble will possess the land and will delight in abundant prosperity.

Its interpretation concerns ¹⁰ the congregation of the poor who will accept the appointed time of affliction and will be saved from all the traps ¹¹ of Belial. And afterwards they will delight [in] all the [...] of the land and will grow fat on all [...] ¹² of the flesh.

¹³ The wicked plots against the righteous and grinds [his teeth] a[t him]. The LORD laughs at him, for he sees ¹⁴ that his day has come.

Its interpretation concerns those who act ruthlessly against the covenant in the house of Judah, who ¹⁵ plot to destroy those who observe the law in the council of the community. But God will not abandon them ¹⁶ into their power.

The wicked draw the sword and bend their bow to bring down the humble and poor, ¹⁷ and to slaughter the upright of way. Their sword will pierce their own heart, and their bows will be broken.

¹⁸ Its interpretation concerns the wicked of Ephraim and Manasseh who will seek to lay hands ¹⁹ on the priest and the men of his council at the time of trial which will come upon them. But God will redeem them ²⁰ from their hand, and afterwards they will be given into the hand of the ruthless ones of the nations for judgement.

²¹ (Line 21 left blank.)

²² Better is the little which the righteous has than the abundance of man[y] wicked.

[Its interpretation concerns everyone] ²³ who observes the law, who (does) not [...] ²⁴ for evil.

For the arm[s of the wicked will be broken, but] the Lo[RD supports the righteous.

²⁵ Its interpretation concerns...] ²⁶ [his] will.

1.25–II.1a. Ps. 37:7 and interpretation. *the liar who led astray many with false words*: for 'the liar' and his supporters see 1QpHab II.1*b*–2*a*, and above, pp. 23, 223. *the interpreter of knowledge*: for the expression cp. 1QH II.13*b*; the reference here is probably to the teacher of righteousness. From this passage it seems clear that the dispute with 'the liar' centred on doctrinal matters, particularly the proper interpretation of scripture. *by the sword, by famine, and by pestilence*: a recurring formula in Jeremiah (e.g. 14:12). Here it serves as a conventional description of the punishments that would overtake the wicked in the eschatological period; cp. III.3*b*–4*a*.

II.1*b*–4*a*. Ps. 37:8–9a and interpretation. *all those who return to the law*: i.e. those who join (or rejoin) the community.

4*b*–5*a*. Ps. 37:9*b* and interpretation. *the congregation of his chosen ones*: see the comment on 1QH II.13*b*–14*a*.

5*b*–9*a*. Ps. 37:10 and interpretation. (For the line-numbering, note that in the Hebrew the word for '[wi]cked' is in line 9.) *all the wicked*: literally 'all wickedness', but the following words indicate that the noun is to be understood as a collective. *at the end of forty years*: the period, based on the traditional length of time spent in the wilderness, that was expected to elapse before the end of the present age and the complete disappearance of the wicked; for the idea cp. CD xx.13*b*–15*a* and see the comment on that passage. Less plausible is the view that the 'forty years' refers to the length of the war to be fought against the nations according to 1QM 11.6–14.

9*b*–12. Ps. 37:11 and interpretation. *the congregation of the poor*: see the comment on 1QH 11.32*b*–33*a*. *who will accept the appointed time of affliction and will be saved from all the traps of Belial*: 'the appointed time of affliction' is perhaps best understood as the period preceding the end of this age, which – according to the interpretation of line 8 suggested above – was expected to last forty years. 'Accept' has the sense 'take on an obligation'. The members of the community recognise their obligation to endure the period of increasing trouble which will mark the end of this age and are in consequence delivered from the power of Belial. The passage could also be understood as 'who will take on the obligation of the appointed time of fasting', with reference to a specific period of fasting, perhaps in connection with the day of atonement (cp. CD vi.19), but this seems less likely. The word for 'affliction' and the word for 'humble' in the biblical text are from the same Hebrew root. For 'the traps of Belial' cp. CD iv.12*b*–19*a*. *And afterwards*: i.e. in the new age.

13–16*a*. Ps. 37:12–13 and interpretation. *the LORD*: the scroll actually has 'Yahweh', whereas the Massoretic text has '*^adōnāy*. In the RSV and NEB the former is rendered by 'the LORD', the latter by 'the Lord'. *those who act ruthlessly against the covenant in the house of Judah*: 'the house of Judah' is a symbolic name for the movement (cp. CD iv.11; 1QpHab viii.1), and thus 'those who act ruthlessly against the covenant' (cp. 1QpHab 11.6; 1QH 11.11*a*) are apostates. *who plot to destroy those who observe the law in the council of the community*: the apostates are accused of attacking their former brethren who remained faithful to the ideals of the community. For 'those who observe the law' see the comment on 1QpHab vii.9–14*a*.

16*b*–20. Ps. 37:14–15 and interpretation. *the wicked of Ephraim and Manasseh*: in the Commentary on Nahum 'Ephraim' and 'Manasseh' symbolise the Pharisees and the Sadducees, and it seems likely that the names have the same significance here; see the comment on 4QpNah 3–4 11.1*b*–2. *who will seek to lay hands on the priest and the men of his council*: unless this piece of interpretation (or the Commentary as a whole) goes back to an early stage in the history of the community, it is unlikely that this 'priest' is the teacher of righteousness. The use of a future tense and the reference to 'the time of trial' (see below) indicate that the passage refers to the eschatological period; it no doubt reflects disputes with the Pharisees and Sadducees in the time of the author. For 'the priest' as the title of a leader of the community cp. CD XIV.6b–7a, 'the priest who enrols the many', and for the leaders of the community see above, p. 118. *at the time of trial*: in view of the eschatological thrust of several of the previous pieces of interpretation 'the time of trial' is best understood as the period of conflict that would mark the end of the present age. For the word 'trial' see the comment on 1QS 1.17b–18a, and cp. CD XX.27a; 4QFlor 1–3 II.1. *and afterwards they will be given...for judgement*: the 'they' are the wicked of Ephraim and Manasseh; cp. the description of the eschatological punishment of 'the seekers after smooth things' in 4QpNah 3–4 II.3–6. *the ruthless ones of the nations*: an expression that recurs several times in Ezekiel, e.g. 28:7 (NEB, 'the most ruthless of nations'); cp. IV.10.

22–24a. Ps. 37:16 and interpretation. *everyone*] *who observes the law*: cp. line 15 and the comment on 1QpHab VII.9–14a.

24b–26a. Ps. 37:17 and interpretation.

MORE ABOUT THE COMMUNITY AND ITS ENEMIES

II.26 [The LORD knows the days of the perfect, and their inheritance will last for ever]; 27 they [will] n[ot] be put to shame in [the time of evil.

Its interpretation concerns...] III.1 the converts of the wilderness who will live for a thousand generations in saf[ety]; to them will belong all the inheritance 2 of Adam, and to their descendants for ever.

In the days of famine they will be sa[tisfied], but the wicked 3 will perish.

Its interpretation is [that] he will keep them alive during the famine in the appointed time of [afflict]ion, but many 4 will perish because of the famine and the pestilence, all those who do not go ou[t from there] to be [with] 5 the congregation of his chosen ones.

5A Those who love the LORD will be like the glory of the pastures.

[Its] interpretation [concerns the congregation of his chosen ones] 5 who will be heads and princes [...like] shep[herds] 6 in the midst of their flocks.

7 All of them vanish like smoke.

⟨Its⟩ interpretation concerns the princes of w[icked]ness who oppress his holy people; [8] they will perish like smoke which van[ishes in the wi]nd.

The wicked borrows and does not pay back, [9] but the righteous is a generous giver; for those who are blessed [by him will poss]ess the land, but those who are cursed [by him will be cu]t off.

[10] Its interpretation concerns the congregation of the poor [to] w[ho]m will belong the inheritance of all the [...] [11] they will possess the mountain height of Isra[el, and in] his holy [mountain] they will delight.

But [those who are cursed] by him [12] will be cut off: They are those who act ruthlessly against the co[venant, the wi]cked of Israel who will be cut off and destroy[ed] [13] for ever.

[14] For [the steps of a man] are made firm by the LOR[D], [and] he delights in his [w]ay; though he [fa]ll, he will [not] [15] go headlong, for the L[ORD supports his hand].

Its interpretation concerns the priest, the teacher of [righteousness, whom] [16] God [ch]ose to stand be[fore him, for] he appointed him to build for him a congregation [of...] [17] [and] he directed his [wa]y to the truth.

I [have been young] and now am old, but [I have] not [seen a righteous man] [18] forsaken, or his descendants begging brea[d. All the time] he lends generously, and [his] descend[ants become a blessing.

The interpretation] [19] of the passage concerns the tea[cher of righteousness... [20–6] ... [27] ...

For the LORD loves] [IV.1] jus[tice, and will not forsake his loyal servants]; they are preserved [for ev]er, but the descendants of the w[icked are cut off.

Its interpretation]: They are those who act ruthlessly against [2] [the covenant...] the law.

The righteo[us will possess the land and will dwell] upon it [for] ever.

[3] [Its interpretation...] for a thousand [generations.

The mouth of the righteous utters w]isdom, and his tongue speaks [4] [justice. The law of his God is in his heart; his steps do not slip.

Its interpretation...] the truth, who spoke ⁵ [...] told to them.

⁶ (Line 6 left blank.)

⁷ The wicked watches for the righteous and seeks [to kill him. The Lo]RD [will not abandon him into his power, or] let him be declared guilty when he is brought to trial.

⁸ Its interpretation concerns the wicked [pr]iest who w[atched for the teache]r of righteous[ness and sought to] kill him [...] and the law ⁹ which he sent to him. But God 'will not ab[andon him into his power], or [let him be declared guilty when] he is brought to trial'. But as for [him, God will] pay (him) his reward by giving him ¹⁰ into the hand of the ruthless ones of the nations to inflict [vengeance] on him.

[Wait for the L]ORD and keep to his way, and he will raise you up to possess ¹¹ the land; when the wicked are cut off, you will s[ee (it).

Its interpretation concerns...] who will see the judgement of wickedness, and with [the congregation] ¹² of his chosen ones they will rejoice in the inheritance of truth.

II.26*b*–III.2*a*. Ps. 37:18–19*a* and interpretation. *the converts of the* *wilderness*: or 'the returnees of the wilderness' (those who return to the wilderness), but the translation 'converts' is preferred here in the light of the probable meaning of the related expression 'the converts of Israel' (see the comment on CD VI.4*b*–5); in either case the reference is to the members of the community. The 'wilderness' no doubt means Qumran; for the importance of the wilderness theme see 1QS VIII.12*b*–14. *who will live for a thousand generations*: cp. CD VII.6*a*; XIX.1–2*a*; XX.22*a*. *to them will belong all the inheritance of Adam*: cp. CD III.19–20*a* and the comment on that passage; 1QS IV.23*a*.

III.2*b*–5*a*. Ps. 37:19*b*–20*a* and interpretation. *the famine in the* *appointed time of [afflict]ion*: see the comment on II.10; for famine as one of 'the birth-pangs of the new age' see Mark 13:8 and parallels. *but many will perish because of the famine and the pestilence*: cp. II.1. *all* *those who do not go ou[t from there]*: the restoration is based on the assumption that there is an allusion to Isa. 52:11, 'from there' here meaning Jerusalem, not Babylon. *the congregation of his chosen ones*: cp. II.5 and see the comment on 1QH II.13*b*–14*a*.

5A, 5*b*–6. Ps. 37:20*b* and interpretation. The line numbered 5A was orginally omitted by the copyist and subsequently inserted above line 5. The restoration of the end of line 5A is based on the assumption that the omission occurred as a result of a common scribal mistake. *Those who love the* LORD: the Massoretic text has 'The enemies of the LORD'; the commentator altered the biblical text to fit in with his interpretation. *like the glory of the pastures*: or 'like the glory of the he-lambs'. But the word in the scroll translated 'pastures' or 'he-lambs' is spelt differently from the word in the Massoretic text and is of uncertain meaning; it looks like the plural of the word for 'furnace'. It is the interpretation (line 6) that points to a meaning connected with flocks or their pastures. The Massoretic text itself is obscure and is emended by the NEB. The translation adopted here follows the RSV, but the significance of the simile in the scroll – where 'the glory of the pastures' is interpreted with reference to the leaders of the community – is quite different from that of the Massoretic text.

7–8a. Ps. 37:20c and interpretation. *the princes of w[icked]ness who oppress his holy people*: the former are probably the leaders of contemporary Jewish society (cp. CD VIII.3; XIX.15, 'the princes of Judah'), the latter are the members of the community. *van[ishes*: literally 'perishes' (not the word used in line 7).

8b–11a. Ps. 37:21–2 and interpretation. Ps. 37:22b is repeated and given a separate interpretation (lines 11b–13). *the congregation of the poor*: cp. II.10 and see the comment on 1QH II.32b–33a. *the mountain height of Isra[el, and in] his holy [mountain]*: for the restoration cp. Ezek. 20:40; the reference is to the temple mount.

11b–13. Ps. 37:22b and interpretation. *those who act ruthlessly against the co[venant*: if the same group is envisaged as in II.14, these are former members of the community; cp. 1QpHab II.6; 1QH II.11a.

14–17a. Ps. 37:23–4 and interpretation. *the priest, the teacher of [righteousness*: this passage is important because it indicates that the teacher was a priest, possibly high priest; cp. 1QpHab II.8 and see above p. 10. *he appointed him to build for him a congregation*: for the role of the teacher as the founder of the community cp. CD I.10b–12. *appointed*: the same word in the Hebrew as 'made firm' in the biblical text.

17b–(?). Ps. 37:25–6 and interpretation.

Lines 19b–27a will have contained the conclusion of the interpretation of Ps. 37:25–6 plus the quotation of Ps. 37:27 and its interpretation.

III.27b–IV.2a. Ps. 37:28 and interpretation. *they are preserved [for ev]er*: despite the damaged condition of the manuscript is seems fairly certain that the text of the scroll agrees with the Massoretic text; the latter has often been emended, e.g. by the NEB. For the words quoted the Septuagint has a double reading, 'they will be preserved for ever, but the lawless will be banished'. *those who act ruthlessly against [the covenant*: see II.14; III.12.

IV.2b–3a. Ps. 37:29 and interpretation. *for a thousand [generations*: cp. III.1.

3b–5. Ps. 37:30–1 and interpretation.

7–10a. Ps. 37:32–3 and interpretation. *the wicked [pr]iest who w[atched for the teache]r of righteous[ness and sought to] kill him*: for this attack by the wicked priest on the teacher of righteousness see the parallel passage in 1QpHab IX.9–12a. From the present passage it emerges that the attack was unsuccessful. *But as for [him, God will] pay (him) his reward by giving him into the hand of the ruthless ones of the nations*: the parallel description in 1QpHab IX.10b–11a suggests that these words are to be interpreted historically, and death at the hands of Gentiles has been thought to fit the identification of the wicked priest as Jonathan; see 1 Macc. 12:39–48; 13:23. If this is right, the use of a future tense is perhaps to be explained as due to the influence of the tenses in the immediately preceding repetition of Ps. 37:33. Alternatively these words could be interpreted of the eschatological punishment of the wicked priest at the hands of 'the ruthless ones of the nations'; cp. II.20. For the idea of a twofold judgement (at death, and at the end of this age) see the comment on 1QpHab X.1b–5a, and for 'pay (him) his reward' cp. 1QpHab XII.2b–3a.

10b–12. Ps. 37:34 and interpretation. *[the congregation] of his chosen ones*: cp. II.5 and see the comment on 1QH II.13b–14a.

Florilegium

A florilegium is a '(collection) of selected passages from the writings
of previous authors', or in other words an anthology, and inasmuch
as the work known as 4QFlorilegium provides not only a collection
of texts, but also commentary on them, the title is not entirely accurate.
In fact the work is best seen as a kind of loosely structured commentary
(*pēšer*) of the kind known from Qumran. Obvious affinities can be
seen with the commentaries, such as those on Nahum, Habakkuk and
Psalms, but it differs from these in a number of respects: it is not
concerned with a single biblical book, or even parts of a single book,
but with a selection of texts from different writings; it lacks the
consistent use of a series of stereotyped formulas to introduce the
commentary; passages from other parts of the Old Testament are
frequently used in the course of the commentary sections. This work
has also been called 'A Midrash on the Last Days'. This title is
appropriate inasmuch as the work is very much concerned with 'the
end of days' (see below), and inasmuch as the exegetical methods used
within it are comparable to those of the later rabbinic midrashim (for
the midrashim, see above, pp. 184–5). The word 'midrash' actually occurs
in the text (line 14, here translated 'explanation'), but it would be
misleading to think of 4QFlorilegium as if it were a midrash of the
type familiar from the later rabbinic literature. Within Qumran
literature 4QFlorilegium may be compared in terms of its exegetical
methods with such passages as CD VII.13*b*–VIII.1*a* (the Amos–Numbers
midrash) or with the Melchizedek document (11QMelch).

Twenty-six fragments of this work have been published, but
fragment 1 itself consists of numerous smaller pieces. Fragments 1–3
provide the remains of two columns, column I being formed by
fragments 1–2, and column II by fragments 1 and 3 – but little survives
of this; column I was not the first column of the manuscript. Only
this material is presented here (4QFlor 1–3 I–II); it covers 2 Sam.
7:10–14; Ps. 1:1; Ps. 2:1–2. Not much can be made of the other
fragments except that it is clear that some were concerned with parts
of Deut. 33. The manuscript dates from the end of the first century
BC or the beginning of the first century AD, but the work itself may
be older than this.

One of the striking features of this document is that the expression 'the end of days' occurs no less than four times within column 1 (lines 2, 12, 15, 19). The principle underlying this document (and indeed the commentaries themselves) is the belief that the biblical texts quoted were really concerned with 'the end of days', the time in which the author thought himself to be living, and the purpose of 4QFlorilegium is to explain the significance of the texts for the community to which he belonged. The texts quoted were chosen because they were taken to be relevant to the community living 'at the end of days'. The importance of this document lies in the information it provides about the community's beliefs, particularly its understanding of itself as forming the temple of the eschatological period and its messianic beliefs.

Bibliography

J. M. Allegro, *Qumrân Cave 4, I (4Q158–4Q186)* (Discoveries in the Judaean Desert of Jordan, 5), Oxford, 1968, 53–7 and plates XIX–XX (see on this J. Strugnell, 'Notes en marge du volume V des "Discoveries in the Judaean Desert of Jordan"', *Revue de Qumrân* 7 (1969/71), 220–5).

G. J. Brooke, *Exegesis at Qumran: 4QFlorilegium in its Jewish Context* (Journal for the Study of the Old Testament Supplement Series, 29), Sheffield, 1985).

A SANCTUARY OF MEN

1.1 [...].. enemy [...No] unjust man [will oppress] them [agai]n, as formerly, from the day that ² [I appointed judges] over my people Israel. This is the house which [he will build] f[or them] at the end of days, as it is written in the book ³ [of Moses: The sanctuary, O Lord, which] your hands have [es]tablished. The LORD will reign for ever and ever. This is the house into which no [one uncircumcised in heart and flesh] shall ever enter, ⁴ not the Ammonite, or the Moabite, or the bastard, or the foreigner, or the proselyte, ever, for his holy ones will be there ⁵ [...for] ever. He will continually watch over it, and foreigners will never again lay it waste as they formerly laid waste ⁶ the sanctuary of Israel because of their sin. And he has commanded that a sanctuary of men be built for him, that there they might offer before him, like the smoke of incense, ⁷ the works of the law.

And when it says of David: And I [will give] you [rest] from all your enemies. He will give them rest from a[ll] ⁸ the sons of Belial who make them stumble in order to destroy them [...], just as they came with a plan of Belial to make the s[ons] of li[ght] stumble, ⁹ and to devise evil plans against them so [that] they [might be cau]ght by Belial because of their e[vil] error.

¹⁰ The LORD has told you that he will build you a house. I will raise up your offspring after you, and I will establish his royal throne ¹¹ [for ev]er. I will be his father, and he will be my son. This is the branch of David who will appear with the interpreter of the law, who ¹² [will rule] in Zi[on at the] end of days, as it is written: I will raise up the booth of David that is fallen. This is the booth (branch) ¹³ of David that is fall[en w]ho will appear to save Israel.

¹⁴ Explanation of Happy is the man who does not walk in the counsel of the wicked. The interpretation of the passa[ge concerns] those who turn aside from the way [of the people], ¹⁵ as it is written in the book of Isaiah the prophet about the end of days: As if with a strong [hand, he turned me aside from walking in the way] ¹⁶ of this people. They are those about whom it is written in the book of Ezekiel the prophet: [They shall] ne[ver again defile themselves with all] ¹⁷ their idols. They are the sons of Zadok and the m[e]n of [their] council [...] after them [...] the community.

¹⁸ [Why] do the nations [rage] and the peoples plot [in vain? The kings of the earth take] their stand [and the r]ulers conspire together against the LORD and against ¹⁹ [his anointed. The inter]pretation of the passage [...] the chosen ones of Israel at the end of days. ᴵᴵ·¹ This will be the time of trial which will c[ome...

I.1–7a. 2 Sam. 7:10–11a and commentary.

1–2a. *enemy*: although the word for 'enemy' does not occur in any version of 2 Sam. 7:10, it seems likely that it formed part of a 'free' quotation of the verse, and that the whole of 2 Sam. 7:10–11a was included at this point, beginning at the bottom of the previous column. 'This is the house' (line 2) is best understood as referring back to 'I will appoint a place for my people Israel' at the beginning of 2 Sam. 7:10.

2b–3a. *This is the house...for ever and ever*: Exod. 15:17b–18 is quoted to support the identification of the 'place' (2 Sam. 7:10) as the temple to be built by God in the eschatological period; this temple is

subsequently identified with the community. *the house*: the play on the
meaning of 'house' that occurs in 2 Sam. 7 (see for instance verses
11–13) is found also in the present passage; lines 1–9 are concerned with
the 'house' as the temple, lines 10–13 with the prophecy about the
Davidic 'house' or dynasty.

3b–5a. Foreigners and others who might contaminate it will be
excluded from the eschatological temple formed by the members of
the community. *This is the house into which no [one uncircumcised in heart
and flesh] shall ever enter*: possible restoration based on Ezek. 44:9. *not
the Ammonite, or the Moabite, or the bastard*: based on Deut. 23:2–3,
which deals with exclusion from 'the assembly of the LORD'. By the
use of this biblical passage the temple is already being implicitly
identified as the community (for the use of 'assembly' with reference
to the community see CD VII.17; 1QSa 1.25*b*; 11.4). *or the foreigner*:
based on Ezek. 44:9, which deals with exclusion from the temple. *or
the proselyte*: in contrast CD XIV.3–6 assigns a place to proselytes.
Perhaps what is at issue here is exclusion from full membership; cp.
the limited rights assigned to those who are 'afflicted' in 1QSa 11.3*b*–11*a*.
for his holy ones will be there: cp. the similar reason given in 1QSa 11.8*b*–9*a*
and the comment on that passage. The 'holy ones' are angels (as e.g.
in CD xx.8*a*).

5b–6a. Yahweh's protection of the temple/community. *He will
continually watch over it*: or 'he will continually appear above it'. The
lack of a context as a result of the damage to the beginning of the line
makes the translation uncertain. These words perhaps belonged with
what precedes.

6b–7a. The eschatological temple to be built by God was to be
formed by the members of the community; for the idea cp. 1QS
VIII.4*b*–10*a*, and for the idea that the deeds of members took the place
of sacrifice cp. especially 1QS IX.3–6. *the works of the law*: or 'works
of thanksgiving'; the text cannot be read with complete certainty.

7b–9. 2 Sam. 7:11*b* and commentary. The biblical text is interpreted
in terms of future deliverance by God from the power of Belial. It was
believed that this deliverance would only be brought about at the end
of this age; for the defeat of the forces of Belial cp. 1QM 1.9*b*–15;
XVIII.1–3*a*, and for the dualistic background to this material cp. 1QS
III.13–IV.26. *who make them stumble in order to destroy them* [...], *just as
they came with a plan of Belial to make the s[ons] of li[ght] stumble*: attacks
by the forces of Belial had been experienced by the community in the
past and were believed to be a continuing threat. The reference to the
past may be a covert allusion to particular historical events. The

expression 'to make the sons of light stumble' occurs in 1QS III.24; in the light of the use of the verb 'stumble' in 1QpHab XI.8a it is possible that one concern at least was the threat of attack by outside bodies which might lead to doctrinal error or defection from the community. *so [that] they [might be cau]ght by Belial*: cp. CD IV.12b–19a.

10–13. 2 Sam. 7:11c–14a and commentary. The biblical text is shorter than the Massoretic text and was probably deliberately abbreviated because the three pieces omitted were irrelevant or inconvenient for the author's purposes. *This is the branch of David who will appear...[at the] end of days*: the biblical text is interpreted to refer to a messiah from the line of David, who is to be identified with 'the messiah of Israel' (1QS IX.11) and with 'the prince of the whole congregation' (CD VII.20). His task in the present passage is 'to save Israel'. For 'branch' (*ṣemaḥ*) as a messianic title cp. Jer. 23:5; 33:15; Zech. 3:8; 6:12, and the expression 'the messiah of righteousness, the branch of David' in the work known as 'The Patriarchal Blessings' or as 'The Blessings of Jacob' (4QPBless 3). *with the interpreter of the law*: probably the same as 'the messiah of Aaron' (1QS IX.11). 'The interpreter of the law' is used as a messianic title in CD VII.18, but with reference to a figure of the past in CD VI.7b–8a. It should be noted that although the present passage envisages two messiahs, the emphasis is on the Davidic messiah. *as it is written: I will raise up the booth of David that is fallen*: Amos 9:11a is quoted in support of the expectation of a Davidic messiah; this verse is also used, but for a different purpose, in CD VII.16. *This is the booth (branch) of David that is fall[en*: the author is apparently playing on the similarity between the word for 'booth' (*sukkâh*) and the word for 'bough, branch' (*sôkâh*).

14–17. Ps. 1:1a and interpretation. The biblical text is interpreted to refer to the members of the community living at 'the end of days'. *those who turn aside from the way [of the people]*: for the restoration of the text cp. CD VIII.16 = XIX.29; 1QSa I.2b–3a. *as it is written in the book of Isaiah*: Isa. 8:11 is quoted in support of the identification of 'the man who does not walk in the counsel of the wicked' (Ps. 1:1) with 'those who turn aside from the way [of the people]', namely the members of the community. *about whom it is written in the book of Ezekiel*: Ezek. 37:23a is quoted as a further description of the members. *the sons of Zadok and the m[e]n of [their] council*: probably the priests and the laity.

I.18–II.1. Ps. 2:1–2 and interpretation. The remains of the first six lines of column II have survived but too little – especially in view of the loss of much of I.19 as well – for it to be possible to reconstruct the interpretation in detail. It is clear, however, that the biblical text was interpreted to refer to the period of trial that would come upon the community 'at the end of days', and that the interpretation included (in column II) quotations from Dan. 12:10 and 11:32. *together*: or, differently understood, 'against the community'. *the chosen ones of Israel*: the members of the community, cp. CD IV.3*b*–4*a* and see the comment on 1QH II.13*b*–14*a*. *the time of trial*: cp. CD XX.27*a*; 4QpPs^a 1–10 II.19, and for the word 'trial' see the comment on 1QS 1.17*b*–18*a*.

Testimonia

The document known as 4QTestimonia, presented here as a final example of Qumran exegetical literature, consists of a single piece of leather containing one column of text; the work has been preserved almost in its entirety, with only the loss of the beginning of lines 25-9 (the one word in line 30 was written at the end of the line). The contents of this work are divided clearly into four paragraphs. The first three consist of quotations from the Pentateuch which were obviously intended as prophecies of the coming of a prophet, of a royal messiah, and (implicitly) of a priestly messiah. The fourth paragraph is a quotation from a sectarian work known as the Psalms of Joshua. This passage takes the form of an explanation of Josh. 6:26 in terms of contemporary events and refers, amongst other things, to two men, apparently brothers, who rebuilt Jerusalem, committed profanity and blasphemy, and shed much blood. The manuscript dates from the first quarter of the first century BC. The Psalms of Joshua, since they are quoted in the manuscript, must be older than this (i.e. from fairly early in the history of the community), and 4QTestimonia itself could be older.

The title given to this document, Testimonia, reflects the fact that a large part of it consists of a collection of 'testimonies' or messianic proof-texts. The same is true of another title given to it, 'A Messianic Anthology'. But neither title takes account of the quotation from the Psalms of Joshua, and it has to be said that the relationship between this quotation and the rest of the document is not entirely clear, and that the purpose of the document remains obscure. It has been pointed out that each of the messianic prophecies ends with a threat of judgement, that is, the three messianic figures are figures of judgement. It may be that part of the purpose of 4QTestimonia was to announce judgement to those who epitomised evil and were regarded as arch-enemies of the community.

The importance of this document lies in the additional light it sheds on the community's messianic beliefs. It presupposes the typical Qumran expectation of a royal and a priestly messiah, and it provides confirmation of the expectation of a prophet – a belief expressed elsewhere in the scrolls only in 1QS ix.11. Attempts have been made to exploit the quotation from the Psalms of Joshua for historical purposes, but the information that can be derived from this material is rather meagre.

Bibliography

J. M. Allegro, *Qumrân Cave 4, I* (4Q158–4Q186) (Discoveries in the Judaean Desert of Jordan, 5), Oxford, 1968, 57–60 and plate xxi (see on this J. Strugnell, 'Notes en marge du volume v des "Discoveries in the Judaean Desert of Jordan"', *Revue de Qumrân* 7 (1969/71), 225–9).

THE PROPHET AND THE MESSIAHS

[1] The LORD said to Moses, You have heard the words [2] of this people, which they have spoken to you; all that they have said is right. [3] Would that they always had such a heart to fear me and to keep all [4] my commandments, so that it might go well with them and with their children for ever. [5] I will raise up for them a prophet like you from among their brethren. I will put my words [6] into his mouth, and he will tell them all that I command him. If anyone [7] does not listen to my words which the prophet will speak in my name, I [8] will require satisfaction from him.

[9] And he uttered his oracle and said, the very word of Balaam son of Beor, the very word of the man [10] whose sight is perfect, the very word of him who hears the words of God and knows the knowledge of the Most High, who [11] sees the vision of the Almighty, in a trance, but with his eyes open: I see him, but not now; [12] I behold him, but not near: a star shall come forth out of Jacob, and a comet shall rise out of Israel; he shall smite [13] the heads of Moab, and beat down all the sons of Seth.

[14] And of Levi he said, Give to Levi your Thummim, and your Urim to your loyal servant, whom [15] you tested at Massah, with whom you quarrelled at the waters of Meribah; who said to his father [16] and his mother, 'I do not know you', who did not acknowledge his brothers, or recognise his children.[17] For he observed your word and kept your covenant. They will enlighten Jacob with your precepts, [18] (and) Israel with your law; they will offer incense before

you, and whole burnt offerings on your altar. ¹⁹ Bless his ability, O LORD, and accept the work of his hands; smite the loins of his adversaries, and let those who hate him ²⁰ rise no more.

²¹ When Joshua had finished offering praise and thanksgiving through his psalms, ²² he said: Cursed be the man who rebuilds this city; at the cost of his first-born ²³ he will found it, and at the cost of his youngest son he will set up its gates. Behold, an accursed man, a man of Belial, ²⁴ will arise to be a fowler's trap to his people and ruin to all his neighbours. He will arise ²⁵ [...that] the two of them may [b]e weapons of violence. They will rebuild ²⁶ [this city and set] up for it a wall and towers to make it a stronghold of wickedness ²⁷ [...] in Israel, and a horror in Ephraim and in Judah. ²⁸ [...and] they [will com]mit profanity in the land and great blasphemy among the sons ²⁹ [of Jacob, and will shed bloo]d like water on the ramparts of the daughter of Zion and within the boundary ³⁰ of Jerusalem.

1–8. Deut. 5:28*b*–29 and 18:18–19. These two texts are quoted in combination in the Samaritan version of Exod. 20:21 where they have the same introductory formula as in the scroll (the clear difference from Deut. 5:28*b* is more obvious in the Hebrew), and it appears that this passage has been taken, not from Deuteronomy itself, but from a proto-Samaritan text of Exod. 20:21. The thought of Deut. 18:18–19 is that God would ensure a regular succession of prophets like Moses, but the passage came to be interpreted messianically as referring to a single prophet; cp. Acts 3:22–3 (which quotes Deut. 18:15, 19); 7:37 (which likewise quotes Deut. 18:15). For the expectation of a prophet as a predecessor of the two messiahs see 1QS IX.11 and the comment on that passage. *The* LORD: the text actually has four dots (so also line 19); for this means of representing the name 'Yahweh' in the scrolls see the comment on 1QS VIII.14.

9–13. Num. 24:15–17. Verse 17 is also quoted in CD VII.18*b*–21*a*, and, as indicated in the comment there, this passage from Numbers was frequently interpreted in a messianic sense in this period. In 4QTestimonia the passage is clearly intended as a prophecy of a royal or Davidic messiah, the figure called in 1QS IX.11 'the messiah of Israel'. *in a trance*: literally 'falling down'. *the heads*: literally 'the temples (of the head)', but the ancient versions suggest that the word may mean 'the leaders'.

14–20. Deut. 33:8–11. The blessing pronounced on Levi by Moses is implicitly here a prophecy of a priestly messiah, the figure called in 1QS IX.11 'the messiah of Aaron'. The fact that this figure is apparently also called 'the interpreter of the law' (CD VII.18; 4QFlor 1–3 1.11) provides a link with the present passage, where teaching the law is one of Levi's duties (Deut. 33:10). *Give to Levi*: these words are not in the Massoretic text, but do occur in the Septuagint. This forms one of a number of links between the text of 4QTestimonia and the Septuagint version of this passage.

21–30. The fourth quotation is taken from a pseudepigraphical work known as the Psalms of Joshua (4QPssJosh, not yet published). *Cursed be the man...set up its gates*: the passage begins by quoting Josh. 6:26; the text corresponds to the Septuagint, not the Massoretic text. It is significant that the scroll, like the Septuagint, does not include 'Jericho', thus facilitating the application of the passage to Jerusalem (see lines 29–30). The quotation of Josh. 6:26 is followed by a commentary which interprets the text in terms of contemporary events. *Behold an accursed man, a man of Belial*: text uncertain; the word for 'a man' was altered, but the reading 'a man' makes good sense. *a fowler's trap*: cp. Hos. 9:8; Ps. 91:3. *[that] the two of them may [b]e weapons of violence*: 'weapons of violence' is taken from Gen. 49:5, where it refers to Simeon and Levi, and this suggests that 'the two of them' are to be understood as two brothers. It is possible, but not certain, that they are to be regarded as the sons of the 'accursed man'. *They will rebuild [this city*: the restoration is not certain, but in any case it seems likely from lines 29–30 that the passage refers to the rebuilding of Jerusalem. Considerable attention has been paid to this passage in the hope of identifying the two who rebuilt Jerusalem and thereby of shedding light on the early history of the Qumran community and the identity of the wicked priest. It is plausible to think that the two builders were the brothers Jonathan and Simon (for their building activities in Jerusalem see 1 Macc. 10:10–11; 12:35–7; 13:10, 52; 14:37), but because of the damage to the manuscript – particularly the loss of the beginning of line 25 – it is difficult to say more than this.

INDEX